Improving Intercultural Interactions

MULTICULTURAL ASPECTS OF COUNSELING SERIES

SERIES EDITOR

Paul Pedersen, Ph.D., *University of Alabama at Birmingham*

EDITORIAL BOARD

VOLUMES IN THIS SERIES

Improving Intercultural Interactions

Modules for Cross-Cultural Training Programs
Volume 2

edited by

Kenneth Cushner
Richard W. Brislin

Multicultural Aspects of Counseling Series 8

SAGE Publications
International Educational and Professional Publisher
Thousand Oaks   London   New Delhi

The editors would like to thank Sylvia Popson for her
tireless work in preparing this manuscript.

For information:

SAGE Publications, Inc.
2455 Teller Road
Thousand Oaks, California 91320
E-mail: order@sagepub.com

SAGE Publications Ltd.
6 Bonhill Street
London EC2A 4PU
United Kingdom

SAGE Publications India Pvt. Ltd.
M-32 Market
Greater Kailash I
New Delhi 110 048 India

Printed in the United States of America

Library of Congress Cataloging-in-Publication Data

Main entry under title:

Improving intercultural interactions: modules for cross-cultural
    training programs / edited by Richard W. Brislin, Tomoko Yoshida.
        p. cm. — (Multicultural aspects of counseling series; 3)
      Includes bibliographical references and index.
        ISBN 0-8039-5409-3. — ISBN 0-8039-5410-7 (pbk.)
          1. Intercultural communication. 2. Cross-cultural orientation.
        3. Multicultural education. I. Brislin, Richard W., 1945–
II. Yoshida, Tomoko. III. Series: Multicultural aspects of
counseling; v. 3.
GN345.6.I46   1994
303.48'2—dc20   93-35561

Volume 2: ISBN 0-7619-0536-7 (cloth: alk. paper). — ISBN 0-7619-0537-5
    (pbk: alk.paper)

This book is printed on acid-free paper.

97 98 99 00 01 02 03   10 9 8 7 6 5 4 3 2 1

Acquiring Editor:	Jim Nageotte
Editorial Assistant:	Kathleen Derby
Production Editor:	Sanford Robinson
Production Assistant:	Karen Wiley
Typesetter:	Yang-hee Syn Maresca/Rebecca Evans
Print Buyer:	Anna Chin

Contents

Series Editor's Introduction

Many people making effective psychological interventions would be surprised or even offended to have their intervention described as "counseling." However, as the field of counseling has responded globally to the psychological pressures of urbanization and modernization, the "functions" of counseling have been applied much more broadly even outside the professional role of counseling as it has been traditionally defined. This second volume in the **Multicultural Aspects of Counseling** series on *Improving Intercultural Interactions* continues the emphasis on practical and applied issues that define culture inclusively and broadly. Kenneth Cushner and Richard Brislin have identified issues, experiences, and strategies for psychological interventions in the fields of business, education, and society. This book is one of the many attempts to "reinvent" counseling outside its professional field, attempts that are becoming more urgently necessary.

The book is divided into 12 separate modules for examining aspects of the broad definition of culture and of counseling. Each module has a primary practical purpose and is focused on specific changes or psychological interventions. The reader is directed toward other available sources for discussions of the theoretical foundations on which these modules are based. The cross-disciplinary focus is consistent with other books in the MAC series where specific problem areas are defined across disciplines.

The Multicultural Aspects of Counseling series broadly defines culture to include ethnographic variables (nationality, ethnicity, language, religion, etc.), demographic variables (age, gender, place of residence), status variables (social, economic, educational), and affiliation variables (formal and informal) as potentially salient cultures. This inclusive definition recognizes that there are many potentially salient cultural identities for each individual and that each individual belongs to many cultures at the same time in an orthogonal configuration.

Kenneth Cushner and Richard Brislin demonstrate the implications of defining both culture and counseling broadly. The modules selected for volume one and volume two of *Improving Intercultural Interactions* have begun a process that will be continued in the future as other practical approaches to managing problems in their cultural context are implemented. These two volumes demonstrate an applied and generic approach to the management of social issues through psychological intervention. These two volumes demonstrate the direction of many future publications as the urgency of these social issues continues to increase.

These two volumes will increase the reader's awareness by challenging culturally biased assumptions; increase knowledge by presenting information about each selected problem area, method, population, or problem; and increase skills by identifying right actions based on appropriate awareness and accurate knowledge. This second volume will further stimulate the reader to consider a variety of different approaches to training across disciplines, fields, and perspectives where culture is a central factor. These volumes are intended to stimulate readers to develop their own unique approaches for training their own clients, students, and target populations.

Paul Pedersen, Ph.D.
University of Alabama at Birmingham

This book is dedicated to Hyla,
for all you have done to make everything possible and so wonderful.
And for reminding me to keep my sense of humor through it all.

Kenneth Cushner

To the members of the intercultural study group at the
University of Hawaii and the East-West Center.

Richard Brislin

1

Key Concepts in the Field of Cross-Cultural Training: An Introduction

Kenneth Cushner

Richard Brislin

Key Concepts

Intercultural education and training is a delicate and difficult endeavor that must be approached with the greatest of sensitivity. Milton Bennett (1993) points out that intercultural interaction among human populations has typically been accompanied by violence and aggression.

> Intercultural sensitivity is not natural. It is not part of our primate past, nor has it characterized most of human history. Cross-cultural contact usually has been accompanied by bloodshed, oppression, or genocide. . . . Education and training in intercultural communication is an approach to changing our "natural" behavior. With the concepts and skills developed in this field, we ask learners to transcend traditional ethnocentrism and to explore new relationships across cultural boundaries. This attempt at change must be approached with the greatest possible care. (p. 21)

In addition to the intense reactions from the world's history identified by Bennett, evidence for the unnaturalness of intercultural contact can be seen in everyday behaviors. Many people, including those who do not harbor intense prejudices, admit that interactions with culturally different others are more anxiety-provoking than interactions with very similar people. For a smaller number of people, this anxiety leads to strong preference for interactions with similar others and an active avoidance of intercultural interactions. However, such people will not fare well in today's world, where intercultural interactions are common in business dealings, schools, the workplace, places of worship, and community neighborhoods.

This book is the second in a series of collections of modules designed to assist cross-cultural trainers and educators working with a variety of audiences. Like the first volume (Brislin & Yoshida, 1994a), each module, or chapter, recognizes certain elements that are essential to good cross-cultural training. These are presented for either context-specific settings (e.g., Managing International and Intercultural Programs, Chapter 8), or have broad application across contexts (e.g., Power in the Service of Leadership, Chapter 2). The first chapter of the first volume discussed the goals and content of cross-cultural training in some detail, and these areas will only be reviewed at this time. This chapter continues the dialogue by addressing such key elements as approaches to training, building skill in cross-cultural communication and interaction, and challenges that are unique to cross-cultural training.

Goals of Training

Although cross-cultural training can never alleviate all of the problems that people will encounter in their adjustment to living and working across cultures, it can, nevertheless, have a significant effect on people's overall adjustment (Black & Mendenhall, 1990; Deshpande & Viswesvaran, 1992). Brislin and Yoshida (1994b) identify four goals that can guide the selection of program content that addresses people's awareness of culture and cultural differences and attempts to effect change in people's cognition, affect, and behavior. More specifically, training goals include (1) assisting people to overcome obstacles that could interfere with the enjoyment they experience or their sense of well-being. (2) Developing positive and respectful relationships with others in the host culture, including attention to hosts' reactions. Most readers probably know an individual who claims good relations with others but, if those people were interviewed, they would not reciprocate. Attention to a sojourner's feelings and to hosts' reactions to the sojourner's presence in their culture provides a more complete picture. (3) Assisting people to accomplish the tasks associated with their work. And, (4) helping people to effectively deal with the inevitable stress that accompanies the cross-cultural experience. Such goals should underlie all good cross-cultural training programs.

Content of Training

It is of increasing importance that trainers and teachers are purposeful and knowledgeable as they go about the work of bringing their students through four stages: (a) awareness of the issues involved, including the necessity of understanding culture and cultural differences; (b) knowledge of critical concepts useful in intercultural adjustment, including knowledge that hosts find essential for success in their own culture; (c) challenges to people's emotional states and their sense of emotional well-being; and, (d) skills related to their ability to interact effectively across cultures. At times, this fourth stage will involve a challenge that many people find quite difficult; they will be asked to modify behaviors useful and appropriate in their own culture in favor of behaviors deemed far more acceptable by hosts.

Awareness. A critical component of any training is that of raising awareness of (a) the role of culture in people's socialization; (b) how one's interactions and perceptions are affected by one's own biases and values; (c) the necessity of becoming comfortable with differences to the extent that one should not be afraid to recognize and admit that they exist; (d) the importance of recognizing that there may exist some differences to which one can not adjust (Sue et al., 1982; Pedersen, 1988); but (e) despite such differences, a person can be successful (according to the four-part criteria mentioned previously) when working in other cultures. In addition, an often-overlooked dimension of cross-cultural training is the need to raise people's awareness of the need to develop skill in cross-cultural communication and interaction. One reason why this is overlooked is trainee resistance. Many people have been successful in their own cultures because of certain skills. For example, some people in the United States have found that the time and effort they spent becoming dynamic public speakers has paid handsome dividends. They may not welcome the advice that in some cultures the ability to quietly draw out the contributions of various group members is far more important than being the center of attention during a dynamic speech.

Knowledge. Brislin and Yoshida (1994b) differentiate knowledge into four categories: immediate concerns, area-specific knowledge, culture-general knowledge, and culture-specific knowledge. *Immediate concerns* encompass such issues as obtaining travel documents, housing, shopping, information on school systems, and so forth—basic early survival knowledge that people will confront. *Area-specific knowledge* covers such topics as geography, politics, and history—general knowledge needed to engage in intelligent conversations with others. *Culture-general knowledge* refers to concepts and experiences that people are almost certain to encounter regardless of their destination. Such concepts include, but are not limited to, anxiety, ambiguity, and the grouping of specific familiar pieces of information into similar categories; these are further elaborated in Cushner and Brislin (1996). *Culture-specific knowledge* includes rules, customs, and etiquette unique to a particular culture. Good training programs will draw from this broad knowledge base.

Challenge to People's Emotions. People generally expect to confront differing customs and knowledge bases when they interact across cultures. What often surprises them is the degree to which their emotions will be engaged. Interacting across cultures, and especially living overseas, can be very stressful for many people due to such issues as isolation, disorientation, general anxiety, and so forth. Bennett (1986, and described in Brislin and Yoshida, 1994b) provides a useful model for describing six phases people go through as they enter a new culture. His model describes what happens in people's minds when they are thrust into a new and completely foreign culture where they must function according to rules that are virtually incomprehensible to outsiders. These stages include (a) denial, particularly evident in people who have had little contact with others and have difficulty entertaining the possibility that what they believe to be 'right' may not be seen so by others; (b) defense, whereby people feel threatened when they begin to recognize that their value system may not be absolute; (c) minimization, when people admit that differences may exist but believe them to be insignificant; (d) acceptance, marking entry into ethnorelativism, when people begin to accept that other cultures have values and norms that are just as respectable as their own; (e) adaptation, whereby people begin to empathize with individuals from other cultures and begin to change their behaviors when interacting with them; and (f) integration, whereby people integrate multiple sets of values into their identities and become increasingly bicultural or multicultural beings.

Skill Development. Some skills that people might develop are more culture-general, such as the ability to manage stress, tolerate ambiguity, establish realistic expectations, acquire an 'antenna' to know when a cultural difference may be playing a part in interpersonal interactions, or to develop empathy with the emotions expressed by hosts (see Chapter 12). Culture-specific skills, on the other hand, are behaviors unique to a given people or context. Examples are greetings and the exchange of business cards in Japan, answering personal questions during initial encounters with people in Greece, becoming familiar with long periods of silence in some American Indian communities, and showing one's interest in a topic through frequent interruptions and overlapping verbal exchanges in Hawaii. Adapting such skills will facilitate an individual's ability to interact more effectively with a specific group of individuals.

Approaches to Cross-Cultural Training

Most approaches to cross-cultural training can be classified on the basis of two major dimensions: the degree to which the method is experiential versus didactic, and the extent to which it is culture-general or culture-specific (Gudykunst, Guzley, & Hammer, 1996). The experiential approach rests on the assumption that culture learning is best realized when people have direct or simulated experiences from which to draw on. The didactic approach assumes that a cognitive understanding is essential before people can effectively interact with people of another culture. Such understanding can be encouraged through traditional means such as lectures, videotapes, and group discussions centered on adjustment issues such as ways of dealing with stress. Culture-general training attempts to sensitize people to the kinds of experiences they are most certain to encounter as they interact with people from other cultures. Culture-specific training rests on the assumption that information about a specific culture or about specific cross-cultural interactions is essential. At times, decisions about which of these dimensions is emphasized in a specific program are based on very specific practical concerns. Good training costs money, and decisions are often based on this fact. For example, if trainees are about to go to many different countries (e.g., a college's junior year abroad program sending 50 students to 20 different countries), a culture-general program may be most practical. If a training program is for executives who are sensitive to making mistakes in an experiential program, trainers have to keep in mind that it is these executives who are paying the bills for training. A less experiential approach focusing on trainer-centered activities such as lectures and focused discussion may be best. We realize that this may not be welcome news to many readers who strongly prefer experiential approaches, but many trainers (e.g., Goodman, 1994; several cited in Ptak, Cooper, & Brislin, 1995) point out that knowing when and how to give a good lecture in a culturally appropriate manner is an essential skill.

Experiential—Culture-General

Various approaches to training can be examined with the help of the two dimensions. Experiential culture-general strategies allow people to have experiences that are designed to mimic real-life intercultural encounters. Examples of experiential culture-general approaches include the use of simulations and self-assessments. Through such approaches, trainees are encouraged to explore how their own socialization has influenced their perceptions, attitudes, stereotypes, and subsequent behavior. In a similar manner, people having simulated cross-cultural encounters can safely 'experience' culture shock, alienation, disorientation, and so forth—some of the common responses people report when they embark on a sojourn.

Various simulations designed to capture aspects of intercultural encounters and adjustment are also part of this combination of dimensions. A general point about simulations is that trainees move from being recipients of information (e.g. , members of an audience listening to a lecture) to being active participants in a planned organization of behaviors. Culture-general simulations are designed to capture commonly encountered experiences people will confront in a variety of cross-cultural assignments. The most commonly used culture-general simulation is BAFA BAFA (Shirts, 1973), which actively engages trainees in culture learning followed by subsequent cross-cultural interaction. In BAFA BAFA, participants simulate two hypothetical cultures: Alpha culture, a male-dominated, collectivist culture; and Beta culture, a female-dominated, individualistic culture. Trainees typically spend 30 minutes learning the rules to their respective cultures before engaging in brief exchanges between the two. After everyone has had a chance to interact with the other culture, trainees attempt to describe and explain what it is that they experienced. Debriefing can explore such issues as attribution formation, anxiety, verbal and nonverbal communication, culture shock, a 'feeling of home' on return to one's 'own group,' and so forth. A minimum of 3 hours is typically required to carry out the simulation with a debriefing. Two trainers are required.

Other culture-general simulations, typically requiring less time, include Barnga (Thiagarajan & Steinwachs, 1990); Ecotonos (Nipporica Associates, 1993); and the Albatross (Gochenour, 1977). Readers will also find useful exercises in Chapter 6 and Chapter 9 of this volume.

Self-assessment instruments are another method of actively involving trainees. Often their use can be less threatening and potentially embarrassing than simulations because trainees can fill out and score the instruments without others knowing their responses. Trainees can actively assess themselves along a number of criteria that are at play in cross-cultural encounters. A variety of attitude, perception, and experience self-assessments are available that enable individuals to assess their motivations, attitudes, degree of prejudice, ethnocentrism, and uncertainty orientation. Gudykunst (1994) provides approximately 20 self-assessment instruments. Likewise, Brislin and Yoshida (1994a), and most of the chapters in this volume, begin with a self-assessment instrument.

Didactic—Culture-General

The combination of dimensions leading to the intersection of didactic and culture-general refers to training attempts aimed at presenting culture-general content using such cognitive approaches as culture-general assimilators, lectures, and films or videos. Culture assimilators are collections of critical incidents or short vignettes that relate the experiences of people from two or more cultures who face a problem resolving some task. Trainees typically read the incident and then are asked to select, from a number of alternatives, the choice that best explains the misunderstanding. The first culture-general assimilator was developed by Brislin, Cushner, Cherrie, and Yong (1986, followed by the second edition by Cushner & Brislin, 1996). The culture-general assimilator was designed to prepare individuals for the kinds of experiences they are certain to have regardless of the particular background of the individuals, their roles in the new setting, and the particular cultures that will interact.

The second edition of the culture-general assimilator (Cushner and Brislin, 1996) presents 110 critical incidents that were developed to sensitize individuals to 18 culture-general themes thought to be common across most intercultural interactions. These themes include anxiety, disconfirmed expectations, belonging, ambiguity, confrontation with one's prejudices, work or situational behavior, time and spatial orientation, communication in verbal and nonverbal modes, group versus individual orientation, rituals and superstitions, roles, status hierarchies, values, categorization, differentiation, ingroup-outgroup distinctions, learning styles, and issues surrounding people's attributions about the behavior of others. A culture-general approach to training is of special interest to many today as people are increasingly coming into contact with others from a variety of backgrounds. Chapter 3 in this volume, by Dharm P. S. Bhawuk, begins with one of the culture-general themes, group versus individual orientation, and then expands it according to four features of this complex concept. Applications are then made to intercultural interactions among leaders and subordinates when people are from different cultural backgrounds.

Lectures and discussions represent the most typical attempt to present information to trainees. Presentations through lectures by experts in the field or by individuals with experience living or working across cultures are common. The use of videotape or film may complement lectures and discussion. Two widely used film or video productions are the *Going International* (1983) and *Valuing Diversity* (1987) series produced by Copeland and Griggs. Although effective at transmitting a significant amount of information in a relatively short period of time, lectures and discussions seem to work best in combination with other approaches. Our experience has been that effective lectures and group discussions can provide trainees with the information necessary for later participation in the types of experiential exercises already discussed. In addition, lectures can demonstrate the trainers' credentials as experts and provide an effective use of time until trainees become comfortable and trusting enough with trainers to participate in active simulations and exercises.

Experiential—Culture-Specific

The typical intercultural assignment, such as an overseas business venture or a junior year abroad, involves a host of culture-specific experiences from which people typically learn a great deal about themselves, others, and other cultures. The type of approach we are calling 'experiential and culture-specific' attempts to assist trainees by exposing them to what they will later encounter: actual experiences in a specific culture. Examples include culture-specific simulations and culture-specific role plays.

Very few culture-specific simulations currently exist on the market, although many good trainers will have developed a variety of opportunities for their trainees to interact with host nationals in simulated culture-specific settings (e.g., Japanese tea ceremonies, visits to ethnic restaurants where typical behaviors considered proper in the host culture are encouraged). Gudykunst, Guzley, & Hammer (1996) describe the Markhall simulation (TRC), designed to help trainees better understand interactions between Japan and the United States and the role that culture plays in terms of work life, management styles, and interaction among workers. Although the simulation does not involve direct interaction between members of the two cultures, significant cultural differences are illustrated, such as decision-making styles, communication styles, and individualism and collectivism.

As with most role plays, culture-specific role plays attempt to help trainees learn how to interact effectively with members of a specific group. The source of role plays can be trainees themselves, the published literature, the accumulated experiences of people within an organization summarized in in-house reports, or critical incidents from the number of culture assimilators that are available (e.g., the critical incident presented later in this chapter could be the basis for role plays). Culture-specific role plays can involve people from two different cultures playing their own cultural roles (e.g., Australians playing Australians and French playing French). Role plays can also involve people trading roles and playing another's part. Outcomes can differ depending on the particular approach that is taken. When playing one's own role, trainees gain experience interacting with someone from another culture. When playing another's role, trainees gain insight into how to modify their own behavior in response to another.

Didactic—Culture-Specific

Finally, the approach combining didactic and culture-specific content and methods provides opportunities for trainees to gain information about specific cultures. Training methods include culture-specific briefings, assimilators, and readings. Culture-specific information can be provided to trainees that includes background about a country (e.g., history, economics, religion); specific attitudes, values, and behavior of the people; or specific problems that sojourners may face in a given culture. Kohls (1979) suggests that of all the content that might be covered in country-specific briefings, specific information about a country is the least important because people can generally locate this information on their own.

Culture-specific assimilators, unlike the culture-general ones discussed previously, present vignettes where trainees read a series of critical incidents that focus on potential misunderstandings between individuals from two specific cultures. The assumption behind the use of culture-specific assimilators is that, as people respond to a number of incidents and receive feedback on their responses to the questions posed at the end of the scenario, they begin to understand the other's subjective culture, or the manner in which the person from the target group would respond. A variety of culture-specific assimilators have been developed for use within the United States and abroad (see Albert, 1983; Cushner & Landis, 1996). They are admittedly difficult to find because culture-specific assimilators are designed to prepare people from one specific cultural background to interact in another, and commercial publishers have rarely been convinced that there is enough of a book-buying audience from any 'dual culture' combination to justify their expenses. Culture-specific assimilators tend to be printed in limited runs through local means (e.g., mimeographed pages or photocopies of an original) or as final reports to funding agencies. Their difficult-to-find status leads to a piece of mentoring advice for cross-cultural trainers: Nurture relationships with good reference librarians.

Culture-specific readings consist of sources that provide content designed to assist people in their interactions and adjustment to specific cultures. A variety of useful materials are available, including the *Interact* series published by Intercultural Press, *Culturegrams* available from Brigham Young University, and Alison Lanier's *Updates* (all of which are available from Intercultural Press).

Actual Programs and the Use of Critical Incidents

In the development and administration of actual programs, our experience has been that programs are rarely one of the 'pure' types represented by intersections of the two dimensions. Trainers must move in and out of the types, especially in response to trainee questions. Frameworks such as the one presented here are guides to the formulation of goals and selection of materials and are not meant to provide rigid rules for trainers. Furthermore, some methods discussed under one approach to training can be used as part of other approaches, based on trainer creativity. Critical incidents provide a good example.

Critical incidents can be culture-general or culture-specific, as discussed previously. Although often didactic, they can be part of experiential approaches when trainees role play the characters presented in the incidents. Group discussions can be very lively and heated when critical incidents are chosen to stimulate thinking about sensitive issues. For example, the following incident is from a collection designed for Americans working in China and Chinese working in the United States (currently being prepared by Mary Wang, David Williams, Richard Brislin, and La Wang). In its most direct application, it is meant to be helpful in a training session devoted to differences in communication style.

The Book Proposal

Wenhua Zhou from Shanghai recently completed his Ph.D. in government from an Ivy League university in the United States. He wrote his dissertation on developments in Chinese economics since the death of Mao Tse-tung. Wenhua had become friendly with another graduate student, Judy Miller, and often sought her advice as a "cultural informant" on puzzling American social practices. Based on a recommendation from his professors back in China, Wenhua decided to seek a book publisher for his dissertation. Wenhua knew that International University Associates in New York City, a very prestigious publisher, often accepted books on modern China. He asked Judy for advice concerning how best to approach American publishers.

Judy replied, "You're getting into an area where I, as a graduate student, am still learning the ropes because I have yet to publish a book. I think I know enough to say that you should write a proposal describing your book in about three pages, telling the publisher the contents and making predictions about what type of person or institution will buy the book. Then, you should ask one of the best-published professors to review your proposal."

Wenhua agreed to prepare a draft of such a proposal. Judy read it and then suggested that Wenhua take the proposal to Professor Brown, the author of 15 books and a frequent consultant for a number of American publishers. Even though Professor Brown had a reputation of being approachable, Wenhua was shy about approaching him, so Judy offered to do it because she had served as Brown's research assistant for a year. Judy made an appointment with Professor Brown. Brown read the proposal in Judy's presence, often thinking to himself, "This is a good first draft." He made a number of suggestions, such as expanding the material on what types of people would be interested in the book and on moving the treatment from "dissertationese" to a more readable book of widespread interest. Brown took his pen and made a swift stroke through Wenhua's final sentence, "I hope that the prestigious editors at International University Associates will consider my unworthy submission." Noticing this swift stroke, Judy said, "I thought that was a rather charming sentence." Professor Brown replied, "Well, I don't! The faster Wenhua loses it, the better." When Judy gave the draft back to Wenhua, he couldn't understand why Professor Brown didn't like the sentence.

Why did Professor Brown cross out the sentence?

1. Professor Brown is being insensitive to Wenhua's preferred style of expressing himself, which is common in China.
2. Professor Brown feels that the proposal should have been more developed prior to the request for his suggestions.
3. Professor Brown is trying to help Wenhua achieve his goal, publication by a prestigious American press.
4. Professor Brown is trying to prepare Wenhua for the letter of rejection he will probably receive (even if Wenhua accepts all of Brown's advice).
5. Professor Brown is trying to encourage Wenhua to benefit from his natural inclinations toward collectivistic thinking to which he (Wenhua) has been exposed in China.

People make their choice(s) and then read the following perspectives on the different alternative explanations.

1. This is an interesting possibility. This answer brings up the more general question, "Is it best to allow people to behave according to the guidance of their own culture, or is it best to guide them into less familiar behaviors that are more appropriate in the (to them) new culture?" Professor Brown might be very sensitive and may know exactly why Wenhua expressed himself as he did in the first draft, but he may feel that other behaviors are more appropriate, given Wenhua's goals. Please try another alternative.

2. This is an interesting possibility because it could be true if Professor Brown had been in China behaving according to Chinese norms. However, research comparing student interactions with professors has shown that American professors are much more approachable than professors in other countries. There is no evidence that Professor Brown resented the use of his time. Remember that he thought to himself, "This is a good first draft." Professor Brown probably also realized the truth of the commonly heard phrase, "Proposals, journal articles, and books are not written: they are rewritten—a large number of times." Please choose another alternative.

3. This is a good answer. Professor Brown is trying to help Wenhua achieve the goal of publication by a prestigious American publishing house. He knows that editors at the publishing house see a large number of proposals that put forth authors'

ideas in a dynamic, forceful way that call attention to the first-rate qualifications of the authors. Professor Brown knows that this is an American style and is not necessarily making a judgment about its worldwide applicability—it is simply "what works" in America. He knows that phrases about "unworthy proposals" will not be well-received by busy editors who have many dynamic proposals competing for their attention. If Wenhua decides to accept Professor Brown's suggestions, he is simply making changes to give himself a better chance of publishing in the United States.

4. There is no evidence for this. The incident mentioned that Professor Brown thought that Wenhua had written a good first draft. If Professor Brown thought that the proposal would not be accepted, there are other (more direct) ways that he could have told Wenhua about his concern. Professor Brown could also have suggested other alternatives, such as publication of the dissertation in journal article form. This is a common practice in many academic disciplines in the United States, and it is an example of "culture specific" knowledge that Professor Brown knows and would be willing to share with Wenhua and with Judy. Please choose another alternative.

5. Actually, Professor Brown is encouraging Wenhua to move beyond the collectivism of his socialization in China. In collective societies, people often develop a highly modest style because it is not their job to extol their own virtues: it is the job of their collective (uncles, bosses, former classmates) to do this. A phrase such as "my unworthy submission" is seen as properly modest. In individualistic societies, people have to learn to extol their own virtues because they have no collective to do this for them. One of us was told by a professor, "If you want a career in the United States, you'd better learn to blow your own horn because no one will blow it for you." In the United States, people must develop the important social skill of letting others know of their accomplishments and talents without being viewed as immodest or boastful. This is a difficult skill to master even for people who have spent all their lives in the United States. Please choose another alternative.

Reading all of the perspectives, trainees learn about modest vs. forthright communication styles. This incident can also be used in a culture-general program if the trainer decides that an important issue for coverage is 'whose rules are in effect.' This is a problem that all sojourners face: Should they behave according to host culture norms or would doing so be viewed as submitting to oppression? This incident, when used in a culture-general program, suggests that sojourners' goals should be thought through carefully. If host behaviors are most useful in obtaining sojourners' goals, then careful thought should be given to adopting those behaviors. Note that in this incident, Wenhua has a very clear goal: He wants an American publisher. Professor Brown knows the necessary steps to make a manuscript competitive for publishers' limited resources (see Chapter 2 by Brislin and Jane for a discussion of resources). We don't feel that issues of oppression should arise when Wenhua learns to communicate in a style that will increase the chance of obtaining his goals.

In both culture-specific and general programs, different people can role play the characters in the incident and can probably add others with relative ease (e.g., the publisher's representative). Using incidents in these different ways is what trainers actually do in their day-to-day work. We are frequently stopped at professional meetings by people who tell us they use our materials (especially Cushner & Brislin,

1996). More detailed discussions indicate that people more frequently pick and choose specific incidents from this collection of 110 than use our entire framework. They choose certain incidents based on the goals of their various programs.

Organization of the Modules

The modules in this volume of *Improving Intercultural Interactions* are presented in three major sections. Two of these sections are based on contexts in which trainers often find themselves working—the world of business and the field of education. The third section is based on more general concerns that occur in various types of intercultural experiences.

The World of Business

Building on their research on the use of power and leadership, Richard Brislin and S. Suzan Jane (Chapter 2) look at the skills necessary to participate in businessplace events that involve power. Their assumptions are that (a) power is a phenomenon that can be understood, (b) there are strategies, such as resource development, that allow people to participate in events involving power, and (c) people can accomplish their goals by understanding the role of power in the business world and by learning about resource exchange. They make applications to issues facing women, such as joining networks dominated by men, finding mentors and dealing with the challenges of sexual electricity if the mentors are men, and marshaling resources to take their swings at breaking the glass ceiling. Mentoring advice to cross-cultural trainers again enters the discussion. We have found that no matter what the title is of a given training program in the business world, people will ask about (a) applications to women, (b) power, or (c) both. This chapter on power and leadership provides a perspective on how to deal with these questions.

Dharm P. S. Bhawuk (Chapter 3) applies his research on individualism and collectivism to the development of leadership skills. He looks closely at the relationship between people's orientation toward groups and success as leaders in typically individualistic organizations. He builds on theoretical work on one of the most important concepts that allows discussion and understanding of complex cultural differences: individualism and collectivism (Triandis, 1995). All people are, at times, oriented to groups of which they are members and are at other times oriented toward their own individual goals. The relative emphasis on these two orientations is a key to understanding individualism and collectivism. In individualistic cultures, people more often consider their own goals and preferences. In collectivistic culture, people more often consider group goals. An understanding of these relative emphases assists us in understanding some common cultural dilemmas of the sort covered by Bhawuk. For example, the owners of small businesses could hire highly recommended MBA degree holders or they could hire their college-dropout nephews. Their socialization into an individualistic or collectivistic culture will influence their decision or at least the stress they will experience when making the decision. Similarly, their socialization will influence how they look at their workers. Do they treat workers as members of a family (collectivist influence) or as a collection of individuals? This will, in turn, influence specific behaviors, such as introducing unmarried workers to members of the opposite sex or viewing such a behavior as unwise and inappropriate.

Jan Fried and Izumi Matsumoto (Chapter 4) look closely at an especially interesting issue in the workplace: how do people react to being diverse individuals day after day, month after month, and year after year? There are training programs that are meant to orient people to their first weeks of work, but issues surrounding the issue of continued diversity are less frequently found. Jan Fried draws from her extensive experience working with the deaf, and Izumi Matsumoto draws from her experience preparing people from various ethnic groups in Hawaii to work with each other and with Japanese visitors.

Interest in this topic began with an anecdote. One of the editors (R. B.) was asked to a working luncheon to review guidelines put out by an agency wanting training materials that would be disseminated on videotape. Jan Fried went over the names of people who would be coming: Mary, Tomoko (note: Japanese names ending in "o" are almost always female), Susan, Rosilita, Yolanda, and Charmaine. R. B. said, "I'm going to be uncomfortable—I'll be the only male there." Jan responded, "Now you know how we feel all the time at work meetings." This feeling of being 'the diverse person all the time' was always part of the preparation of this module.

One of the exercises began with an actual dilemma. In our experience, exercises that capture elements of problems that people actually have faced are often effective because trainers can say, "People have actually dealt with this." The office in which Jan Fried and Izumi Matsumoto works has a sign language program and several of the instructors are deaf. At the office Christmas party, the main activity was singing Christmas carols and reformulating old lyrics into modern prose (e.g., updating "don we now our gay apparel.") One of the deaf instructors, who is not the type to complain frequently, mentioned that she did not feel part of this office party. How might the party have been changed to make her feel more included?

Roya Ayman (Chapter 5) applies her research on gender in organizational hierarchy. Used here, the term *glass ceiling* refers to two issues. In one instance, the glass ceiling refers to a barrier whereby those who are behind it see what they are missing. At the same time, this barrier is elusive and invisible, thus causing its elimination to be more challenging. Such is the issue, confronted regularly by many women and people of color, that is explored in the module on *Leadership and the Glass Ceiling*. In this module, the reader is presented with a number of practical exercises that engage participants in examining their own stereotypes about gender, culture, and leadership. Finally, an exercise that challenges individuals to consider themselves and their organization's responsiveness to the elimination of the glass ceiling is presented.

Education

As presented earlier in this chapter, cross-cultural trainers are constantly faced with making decisions concerning the best approach to training. They often develop the ability to mix approaches, lecturing at times, leading group discussions at other times, and introducing exercises involving active participation by trainees at still other times. College professors sometimes see good trainers in action and ask about how best to incorporate active exercises into their classroom teaching.

Richard Brislin (Chapter 6), again based on his extensive years of experience and research, presents guidelines and suggestions for teachers who wish to integrate active exercises into the college classroom. He takes the point of view of professors who may be members of departments where powerful others take a dim view of exercises and view classroom teaching and lecturing as virtually synonymous. His key recommendation is that professors should think through the material they want to cover. If they have been covering certain topics successfully in lectures, there may be little reason to change their approach for this given set of material. But if they leave their classes with the feeling, "I think that students understand some of the material, but I wish there was some activity or demonstration that would communicate the material more effectively and give them a better grasp of it," then the development of an activity may be a good use of time and resources. The effective communication of course material should drive the decision to use exercises, rather than some other reason, such as to "give the students something different to do."

The next two chapters have applications to the field of education and to other segments of society in which intercultural interactions have become a part. Mary Wang (Chapter 7) presents materials that are useful in aiding people's readjustment to their home society. Although applicable to the student returning from an educational experience (Mary Wang's own background is in education), this material is just as relevant to the returning businessperson, diplomat, technical assistance adviser, or missionary. The starting point for discussions of reentry is an interesting observation that has been made by many people. The culture shock stemming from reentry into one's own culture is often more intense than the initial culture shock stemming from one's adjustment to the host country. There are several reasons for this. One is that people are sometimes aware that they will experience an initial culture shock when living in another country, but are unprepared for any difficulties on reentry. "What could be easier than returning to my own country that I know so well?" is a common reply on receiving an invitation to a reentry training program. As Mary Wang points out, many things have changed back home: the job market, friends, family members, sometimes the physical environment people remember, coworkers, issues that individuals consider a part of everyday conversation (part of the "Oprah" approach), and so forth. In addition, sojourners themselves have changed in ways they cannot yet articulate. They may have become more open-minded, leading to less patience with old friends who still use racial epithets. They may have adopted new eating habits, leading to problems choosing restaurants when going out with old friends.

Another reason for reverse culture shock is that people do not take advantage of opportunities to prepare themselves for their return. Organizations that offer reentry workshops often report disappointingly low attendance figures. Returnees often have many things to do: pack boxes, finish up work, say good-bye to host country friends, buy presents for home-country friends, update their resumes for their upcoming job search, and so forth. A reentry workshop does not always compete well with these demands on returnees' time. A glance at Mary Wang's chapter will communicate her passion for the subject, and we concur with her views concerning the importance of reentry programs. We have to note, however, that marketing these programs is often a "tough sell."

While educational institutions increasingly develop international exchange opportunities for students, the business community is increasingly bringing together people from two or more cultures to engage in such things as future planning and growth. Based on their experiences, (Kenneth Cushner organizing travel programs for educators and directing study abroad programs and Charles Nieman preparing military and university personnel for a variety of sojourns), the authors of the module on *Managing International and Intercultural Programs* (Chapter 8) present an outline that international program directors and organizers will find useful. The chapter centers around a set of guidelines that program administrators can use as they go about planning and executing a variety of relatively long-term international or intercultural programs. Key to the presentation is the attention that must be paid to a variety of places in the program, from predeparture to postreturn. The authors carefully point out the many pitfalls and opportunities that are ever-present in such programs.

Concerns in Various Types of Intercultural Experiences

Certain issues exist in cross-cultural training regardless of the specific context or audience. These issues can form the basis of a training program or can be the issues sophisticated trainers are prepared to cover if they arise during question-and-answer sessions during any training program.

Questions surrounding ethics in cross-cultural training are central to the chapter by Paul Pedersen (Chapter 9). Concerned that ethical principles generated in one cultural context may not be universally applied to other substantially different contexts without modification, Pedersen carefully presents four alternative perspectives or orientations from which one can respond. Carefully making the distinction between "fundamental" ethical principles, which are not negotiable, and "discretionary" aspects, which must be modified and adapted to various settings, Pedersen elaborates on the four alternative perspectives of consequentialist, nonconsequentialist, absolutist, and relativist. Readers are then presented with a number of realistic dilemmas from which they are asked to delineate appropriate responses from each of the four perspectives.

Ann-Marie Horvath (Chapter 10) explores the concept of ethnicity, particularly in terms of how it affects people's interactions across groups. She makes several important points concerning ethnicity and ethnocultural identity and examines them with compelling self-assessment devices and exercises. Horvath makes the important distinction between *ethnicity,* definitions of which almost always start with a shared heritage from a certain part of the world, and *ethnocultural identity.* The latter term includes people's self-defined feelings of the importance placed on ethnic group membership, their knowledge concerning this group, and their participation in activities associated with it. At times, people can casually claim membership in an ethnic group but place little importance on membership and participate in few activities associated with the group. For some of these people, ethnic identity is simply not an important part of their lives. Other aspects of their identity, such as their profession, role as mother or father, active church member, or volunteer in community activities may be far more important. If this type of identity does not lead to a rejection of or discrimination toward others who do value their ethnocultural heritage, then mutual respect for differing feelings of importance is to be called on. At times, ethnic group concerns arise when we examine the categories that others use. Some people do not place importance on their ethnicity, but others who observe markers such as skin color and accent may place such people into a category. They may become upset when the categorized people don't engage in the types of behaviors expected. One of

Ann-Marie Horvath's exercises deals with this concept. People are asked to form groups and to identify the traits and qualities of group members. Part of the discussion following this exercise often deals with the goals people have when forming or joining groups. Some people, for instance, mention that "I could have gravitated toward a certain bunch of people who seemed to be forming a group based on a certain criterion, but I made a point of moving toward another because I wanted to expand myself and didn't want to get stuck in that group." Groups serve different purposes, can be fluid rather than static, and can celebrate diversity rather than a shared heritage, and this basic message is part of this module on ethnicity.

"With increased urbanization and modernization globally, the traditional sources of help for mediating personal conflict through the village or family have been displaced by professional mediators, helpers, and counselors." So begins Chapter 11, by Theodore Singelis and Paul Pedersen, on conflict and mediation across cultures. Singelis and Pedersen make the point that any culture is made up of a set of complex guidelines for behaviors and the interpretation of events, and that individuals bring their own unique interpretations and understandings to bear on situations. They go on to point out how complex culture is and to explore the multiple cultures that influence each individual.

Understanding culture's influence on people's assumptions is one of the first steps in increasing one's competence in intercultural mediation. Singelis and Pedersen help the reader develop intercultural competence, paying particular attention to the distinction between Eastern and Western polarities. The module then provides a series of critical incidents that vividly present conflicts that can be analyzed according to a variety of perspectives.

Colleen Mullavey-O'Byrne (Chapter 12) presents a module that encourages understanding and empathy for the points of view presented by others. The ability to be empathetic is considered vital for people in the helping professions, such as social work, health care delivery, and human resource development. Furthermore, empathy is extraordinarily helpful in other professions, such as teaching and international business, and in areas such as conflict resolution. As covered in the chapter by Singelis and Pedersen, an important skill for mediators is to identify the underlying bases of conflicts. At times these are nearly invisible because they are covered by layers of factors stemming from individual differences in personalities, perceived slights in the history of relationships among people, cultural differences, and current competitions for scarce resources. If mediators have empathetic skills, they will be better able to "put themselves in the shoes" of various people and to identify possible underlying causes of conflict.

There is an important connection between a theme covered in all the modules—understanding differences—and the development of empathy. People have first to understand the reasons for observed differences if they are then to attach their empathetic skills to their understanding of cultural differences. For example, both of us have been in interactions such as the following. The scene is the office of an American college professor, and the visitor is a newly arrived graduate student from a highly collectivistic culture outside North America.

Professor: [*with a friendly demeanor, smiling*] Welcome. How was your trip?

Student: It was O.K. I still feel jet-lagged, but I am ready to start my studies.

Professor: Have you found housing yet?

Student: No, I'm staying with a friend. I should find my own place soon because my friend's place is real small.

Professor: The student activities center keeps a list of apartments and rooms to rent. A lot of students get leads there.

Student: Thanks, I think I passed that building coming to this office. I'll give it a try.

Professor: If you haven't met a lot of the other graduate students, there is an informal get-together tomorrow at noon. I recommend that you attend.

What problems could possibly stem from this conversation? People who read Dharm P. S. Bhawuk's chapter may have insights. The professor has given out signals, from the student's perspective, that she or he wants a special relationship with the student. The student may later expect help in the form of setting up a thesis committee, assistance in obtaining grants, and other personal advice (note the advice about housing and informal get-togethers in the conversation). From the professor's viewpoint, there is no special relationship being promised. The professor is behaving in a neutral way from his or her cultural perspective and has behaved in similar ways with many other students. The point related to Colleen Mullavey-O'Byrne's chapter is that understanding this cultural difference is central to the application of one's empathetic skills. The professor needs to know that 'neutral' behavior according to one cultural viewpoint is 'very friendly and demonstrative of special interest' in another. Ideally, the student will also learn of this difference and will learn the important cultural feature that individualists develop a friendly demeanor to allow them to interact with others who are not members of a permanent collective. Without mutual empathy, however, it is unlikely that the two people will be able to understand each other's reactions, realize the amount of emotion attached to these differing reactions, explain their perspectives to each other, and formulate a compromise concerning the professor-student interaction.

References

Albert, R. (1983). The intercultural sensitizer or culture assimilator. In D. Landis & R. W. Brislin (Eds.), *Handbook of intercultural training, Vol. 2* (pp. 186-217). Elmsford, NY: Pergamon.

Bennett, M. (1986). Models of cross-cultural training: Conceptualizing cross-cultural training as education. *International Journal of Intercultural Relations, 10,* 117-134.

Bennett, M. (1993). Toward ethnorelativism: A developmental model of intercultural sensitivity. In R. M. Paige (Ed.), *Education for the intercultural experience* (pp. 21-71). Yarmouth, ME: Intercultural Press.

Black, J., & Mendenhall, M. (1990). Cross-cultural training effectiveness: A review and a theoretical framework for future research. *Academy of Management Review, 15,* 113-136.

Brislin, R., Cushner, K., Cherrie, C., & Yong, M. (1986). *Intercultural interactions: A practical guide.* Newbury Park, CA: Sage.

Brislin, R., & Yoshida, T. (1994a). *Improving intercultural interactions: Modules for cross-cultural training programs.* Thousand Oaks, CA: Sage.

Brislin, R., & Yoshida, T. (1994b). *Intercultural communication training: An introduction.* Thousand Oaks, CA: Sage.

Copeland, L., & Griggs, L. (Producers). (1983). *Going international* [Film and videotape]. (Available from Copeland Griggs Productions, 302 23rd Avenue, San Francisco, CA 94121).

Copeland, L., & Griggs, L. (Producers) (1987). *Valuing diversity* [Videotape]. (Available from Copeland Griggs Productions, 302 23rd Avenue, San Francisco, CA 94121).

Cushner, K., & Brislin, R. (1996). *Intercultural interactions: A practical guide.* (2nd ed.). Thousand Oaks, CA: Sage.

Cushner, K., & Landis, D. (1996). The intercultural sensitizer. In D. Landis & R. S. Bhagat, (Eds.), *Handbook of intercultural training, 2e* (pp. 185-202). Thousand Oaks, CA: Sage.

Deshpande, S., & Viswesvaran, C. (1992). Is cross-cultural training of expatriate managers effective: A meta-analysis. *International Journal of Intercultural Relations, 16,* 295-310.

Gochenour, T. (1977). The albatross. In D. Batchelder & E. Warner (Eds.), *Beyond experience* (pp. 125-129). Brattleboro, VT: Experiment in International Living.

Goodman, N. (1994). Cross-cultural training for the global executive. In R. Brislin & T. Yoshida (Eds.), *Improving intercultural interactions: Modules for cross-cultural training programs* (pp. 34-54). Thousand Oaks, CA: Sage.

Gudykunst, W. B. (1994). *Bridging differences; Effective intergroup communication* (2nd ed.). Thousand Oaks, CA: Sage.

Gudykunst, W. B., Guzley, R. M., & Hammer, M. R. (1996). Designing intercultural training. In D. Landis & R. Bhagat (Eds.), *Handbook of intercultural training, 2e* (pp. 61-80). Thousand Oaks, CA: Sage.

Kohls, R. (1979). Conceptual model for area studies. In D. Hoopes & P. Ventura (Eds.), *Intercultural sourcebook* (pp. 172-178). Washington, DC: Society for Intercultural Education, Training and Research.

Nipporica Associates (1993). *Econotos.* Yarmouth, ME: Intercultural Press.

Pedersen, P. (1988). *A handbook for developing multicultural awareness.* Alexandria, VA: American Association for Counseling and Development.

Ptak, C., Cooper, J., & Brislin, R. (1995). Cross-cultural training programs: Advice and insights from experienced trainers. *International Journal of Intercultural Relations, 19*(3), 425-453.

Shirts, G. (1973). *BAFA BAFA: A cross-culture simulation.* Del Mar, CA: Simile II.

Sue, D. W., Bernier, J. E., Durran, A., Feinberg, L., Pedersen, P., Smith C. J., & Vasquez-Nuttall, E. (1982). Cross-cultural counseling competencies. *The Counseling Psychologist, 19*(2), 45-52.

Thiagarajan, S., & Steinwachs, B. (1990). *Barnga.* Yarmouth, ME: Intercultural Press.

Training Resources Group, *Markhall simulation.* (Available from Training Resources Group, 1021 Prince Street, Alexandria, VA 22314).

Triandis, H. (1995). *Individualism and collectivism.* Boulder, CO: Westview.

PART I

The World of Business

2

Power in the Service of Leadership

Richard Brislin
S. Suzan Jane

Imagine the following reactions that we or others have experienced from participants when offering cross-cultural training programs.

1. A trainer is contracted to carry out a program that deals with diversity in the workplace. Given the area of the country in which the program is to be offered, all communications about the program have emphasized that the content will deal with workplace interactions among African Americans and Anglo-Americans, with special attention to boss-subordinate relationships. The trainer, a 50-year-old woman of European descent, begins the training program with a statement of goals. After 15 minutes, she is interrupted by an African American: "You talk about cultural sensitivity, but who is being sensitive to what? It seems to me that African Americans have to be sensitive to people with power, and that means you want sensitivity to a Euro-American viewpoint." Another African American says, "You're right, but whites have things we can use, so let's learn to deal with them effectively."

2. Another trainer, an Anglo-American man, is asked to give a workshop on understanding intercultural communication for business dealings among Americans and Chinese. Specifically, the Americans are software specialists living in California, and the training is to prepare them to work with managers from a computer manufacturing company in Beijing. At the beginning of the second day of the 3-day program, an American woman asks, "When are you going to deal with the problems facing women and the glass ceiling?"

3. A third trainer is asked to work with oil company executives in Texas who insist that they are committed to affirmative action policies. Indeed, employment records for the last 3 years indicate that more Hispanics, African Americans, and Native

Americans have been hired than would be expected from statistics showing the percentage of these ethnic groups in Texas. However, not as many members of these culturally diverse groups have been selected for advanced training programs that would lead toward middle-management positions. The executives cannot find evidence of intentional bias but suspect that one factor might be the everyday social interactions among current executives and potential "up and comers."

What do these three scenarios have in common? One is that they involve people who are considered when the term "diversity in the workplace" is raised. A second commonality is that they involve leadership: boss-subordinate relations, movement through the glass ceiling, and the move to middle-management positions. A third commonality is that they elicit several pieces of tacit knowledge or "gray-haired wisdom" that expert trainers know and sometimes can pass on to less-experienced colleagues (e.g., Ptak, Cooper, & Brislin, 1995). One piece of wisdom is that, "No matter what the advertisement, if a program deals with diversity, then someone will want coverage of women's issues." Another piece of tacit knowledge is that, "Trainers will be challenged by members of various culturally diverse groups concerning issues of power." These three common features lead to a fourth, which can be stated in the form of direct advice that can be given to all cross-cultural trainers: "Always be prepared to make program changes if trainees clearly want material and active learning opportunities related to women's issues, power, or some combination of issues surrounding women and their concerns about power."

The purpose of this module is to present concepts and training materials that we have offered in workshops on power. Our aim is to present enough information so that people can offer a workshop on understanding power in the service of leadership and at the same time can take into account the needs and concerns of women. Furthermore, some basic points about cultural differences in the relation between power and leadership are discussed. Alternatively, we feel that trainers can adopt parts of this module when faced with the challenge of making changes in their programs (dealing with any issue related to cultural diversity) when faced with trainee demands for coverage of power, women's issues, or both. To begin, participants can complete a self-assessment instrument that assesses their familiarity with various aspects of power.

Contents

Self-Assessment: Understanding Power
For the Accomplishment of One's Goals

The items on this self-assessment measure consist of short descriptions of strategies and tactics that people use to acquire or to use power. How familiar are you with these strategies and tactics? Please answer according to the following scale.

5	4	3	2	1
very familiar	familiar	not sure	unfamiliar	very unfamiliar

In filling out the scales, please keep in mind that *familiarity* and *frequency* are not necessarily the same. A person can be very familiar with the effects of putting their hands on a hot stove, even though they may have done this only once many years ago! Many of the items refer to *projects*. This is a shorthand phrase that refers to important plans and proposals that people would like to see implemented in the organizations where they work.

_____ 1. People who receive favors being very careful about finding opportunities to return those favors.

_____ 2. People developing a resource that they can share with others in exchange for the resources that these others possess.

_____ 3. After identifying power holders, asking the questions, "What are the goals of these power holders? What are they interested in doing?" Then, linking your ideas to the goals and preferences of these power holders.

_____ 4. When presenting one's ideas to power holders, being ready to answer the question, "How will this benefit me?" Furthermore, being ready to answer this question even if it is not asked explicitly.

_____ 5. Holding many behind-the-scenes meetings with people who might help with, or be affected by, one's projects. Then, when there is a public meeting about one's project, people know a great deal about it and are ready to respond favorably.

_____ 6. Developing a network of influential people within one's community who can help in various ways with one's projects. Many of these people will be outside one's organization and will have a wide variety of skills (e.g., some politicians, journalists, academics, lawyers, physicians).

_____ 7. Realizing that power is a part of life (as is one's family, one's friends, one's need for food and water) that has to be taken into account in negotiations surrounding important decisions.

_____ 8. Interacting effectively with people who stress the authority inherent in their position of power rather than their expertise.

_____ 9. Trying to formulate win-win outcomes in negotiations about important matters, that is, trying to make all concerned feel they will benefit if one's recommended outcomes are accepted.

_____ 10. Cultivating long-term relationships. Getting to know others very well, so that people are very comfortable with each other, before proposing that these others help with one's projects.

_____ 11. Going to various events in one's community (e.g., lectures for the general public at a university, fund-raisers for the symphony orchestra, receptions for political candidates) to meet people who later might help in various ways on one's projects.

_____ 12. Before meeting with power holders, reading as much as possible (and asking questions of others) about the past accomplishments of the power holders.

_____ 13. Joining volunteer groups in one's community that clearly do good (e.g., blood bank, support group for symphony orchestra, youth sports) for the purpose of meeting influential people.

_____ 14. When considering a large project, starting with a small piece of the project (or starting with a small step) that will almost surely be accomplished.

_____ 15. Being careful to develop and to maintain cordial relations with people in one's organization who have responsibilities for the flow of paper (e.g., budget forms, travel reimbursement forms).

Although the purpose of this exercise is simply to encourage participants to think about power in their lives and in their organizations, we realize that many people want to score the test. If this is the case, people can give themselves one to five points, according to the scale. After adding up points, trainers can point out that anyone scoring 50 or more has been exposed to a wide variety of strategies and tactics that effective power holders use in various social settings. If people scored lower than 50, they might want to consider becoming more "skillful" concerning how successful people use power to achieve their goals.

Power: Resources, Strategies, and Tactics

Whenever "power" is discussed, different people approach the topic from many perspectives. Discussions can center on politics; on analyses of "haves and have-nots" in a society; on social structures that maintain a status quo consisting of the traditional power elite; on the skills that power holders possess; on the revolution necessary to force change; on the power of institutions such as businesses, the press, and government; and other issues. Power is more likely to be attributed to men than to women or more positively to men than to women. To be a woman and be powerful is a contradiction of her sociocultural gender role.

Recognizing these varied approaches, we have chosen the "power skills" viewpoint; that is, we will focus on the skills that powerful people possess that less powerful people do not. One reason for this is that training programs have long emphasized the acquisition of skills, and consequently there are well-established guidelines to help trainers introduce new skills. These skills are especially advantageous to women who aim at breaking through the glass ceiling. A second reason is that, beyond encouraging open discussion of many issues surrounding power, such as "haves and have-nots" and the difficulties of dismantling or opening up the traditional power elite, there is little that can be done in a training program. People enjoy talking at such sessions but little change arises from talk alone. A third reason (and this one is especially relevant to readers who disagree with our second), is that people who have these relevant skills are necessary if changes are to be made in the status quo and if traditional power structures are to be challenged. Put another way, dismantling the status quo demands people who (a) want change and who (b) have the skills necessary for power acquisition and maintenance or (c) are aware of the inside track to follow toward dismantling the vested power structure. These skills include nurturing resources desired by others, exchanging these resources with other people, working effectively with traditional power holders, such as the media, developing effective strategies to communicate one's message to potential allies, defusing the efforts of opponents, and so forth.

Needs and Concerns of Women in the Service of Leadership

Whenever the term *power* is discussed in relation to women, many emotions are evoked. Some of these emotions are negative or counter to the perspective associated with the male model of power. Powerful women are at times perceived as manipulative, foreign, unfeminine, and pushy. Women have not had as many years' experience in the exercise of power and are at times not comfortable with using power (Cantor & Bernay, 1992), or not comfortable with the associations implied about those who use power. For these reasons—some of them involving double standards—special attention needs to be paid to women and the use of power.

What are the skills that women need to possess that less-powerful people do not have, and what female-specific concerns come to light? Because women are in positions of unequal power distribution and are seeking career advancement or satisfaction, the following issues may be helpful to consider (see also Chapter 5).

First, women need to have a "thick skin"; they will undoubtedly face great challenges and resistance to their acquisition of power and prestige. Some of the harshest criticisms will come from other women. Another issue that women need to pay attention to is their personal and professional life balance. Whether we like it or not, if you are a married professional woman with children, when a child is hurt or ill, you are more likely to be called and asked or expected to attend to the needs of the child. This additional life burden, as rewarding as it is, demands great amounts of energy from women. Not only do women need to focus on their personal lives, but also on the lives of their children and the needs of their home and spouse. Even within most progressive marriages, women hold the majority of responsibility around the home. If women are to seek power and be successful, having a healthy balance in their lives is a key to this success.

At the same time, these responsibilities may be looked down on and viewed as nonprofessional and detrimental to career advancement. For example, taking time off to attend to an ill child or to take children to baseball games may appear to disrupt the demands of long hours of professional development. In this instance, women face a double standard. Therefore, women need to pay attention to how they handle these commitments yet project a committed, professional persona that will serve to build power and respect. Carrying a laptop computer and making notes, or editing proposals while attending functions with family demands, will help keep the woman productive and viewed as professional. Personal knowledge and insight into one's abilities will also yield positive outcomes if women assess their abilities and set realistic professional goals. Do not bite off more than you can chew. Better to succeed on small projects than to fail on large ones.

A third key to women's success in leadership and power lies in their search for mentors. The mentor relationship can be the single most important aspect to a women's career development (Jane, 1995). Along with a mentor relationship come subtle issues that need attention. First, because professional women are still in the "pipeline," there are few female role models to serve as mentors to younger aspiring women. Therefore, much of the time women are resigned to facilitating a professional relationship with a male mentor. Although this can be a rewarding and extremely beneficial experience, the male/female chemistry will need to be cautiously maneuvered around. Women will need to be very careful in their mentor selection and monitor the relationship at all times to maintain it at a professional, supportive, and educational level. Women may seek the advice of a seasoned female supervisor who can suggest which men would be better mentors and which men should be avoided. Of course, such knowledge is delicate and will only be shared with women who are discreet and trusted. Being aware of sexual chemistry is the first big step; learning how to defuse its potential and accompanying obstacles leads women into the exercise of power and enhances their opportunity for advancement. The issue of defusing sexual attention is a delicate yet very important issue and will be discussed in greater detail on page 28.

On page 36, general examples of mentor advice are listed. For women, creativity is a key to making the most of mentor advice and relationships. An example of this creativity is balancing home and professional commitments. Although it may not be practical to bring your child to the office, if you can set up a modem at home, you can correspond via e-mail while spending time with your children. Telenetting and laptop computers are important tools for professional women with home responsibilities.

Women should seek additional important information from their mentors by asking the right questions. Such questions can include advice on the actual workload and hours necessary to succeed, so a woman can structure and balance her professional goals and home responsibilities without getting overwhelmed and trying to do all and be all. Women also need to ask about resources that would assist their work, such as facility use; after-hours access, possibly from a remote location; travel allowances; reimbursements; professional development; corporate benefits; and networking opportunities. Mentoring advice in such areas can be extremely beneficial to up-and-coming women, who can be left out of the "loop" much of the time.

Language plays a special role in business and power. Men use sports metaphors to explain their successes or failures; for example, "He dropped the ball," "This is our quarterback," and "The negotiations went into overtime but the final score put the home boys into the league." These metaphors allude to a game that few women have ever played. Whether intentional or unconscious, the use of such metaphors excludes women from the dialogue of business.

Language is also gender-sensitive. A woman faints, a man passes out; men are forceful but women are feisty (Tannen, 1990). These subtle differentiations have an effect on gender and perceptions. This can be positive or negative, depending on the context. Being aware of the subtleties language plays in everyday interactions is useful.

Finally, the last issue women need to pay close attention to is their sophistication about asking questions of knowledgeable people—learning who is reliable, honest, trusted, and powerful. Learning these skills is more than half the battle.

Many of the concepts presented in this module were developed during a research project designed to discover the resources, strategies, and tactics of successful power holders (Brislin, 1991; 1994). In this project, 102 power holders (e.g., business executives, diplomats, university presidents, elected politicians, newspaper editors) were asked questions such as the following.

1. Imagine two groups of people. All are well educated, work hard, have good ideas, and are physically attractive. But members of one group accomplish their projects—they get a lot done. Members of the other group do not. What is the difference between the two groups?

2. What do you know about the successful use of power that you did not know when you first started your career?

3. If you were the mentor to an individual, what would you say when this person asked about the use of power in the service of leadership?

Answers to these questions centered on the understanding and successful use of power. Some of the respondents' insights can be summarized through discussions of power-related resources, the strategies of successful power holders, and key tactics in the use and maintenance of power (the most detailed presentation can be found in Brislin, 1991). Since the publication of this book, additional work has been carried out on issues surrounding women and power (Jane, 1995), and some of this work has been integrated into this module. Similarly, some basic points from work done by colleagues concerned with cultural differences in the use of power (Schwartz, 1994; Triandis, 1994) have been included.

The Development and Use of Resources

In both the self-assessment inventory and the previous discussion of the questions answered by power holders, references were made to "getting things done." In the self-assessment inventory, projects that people wanted to see accomplished were discussed. In the questions asked of power holders, project accomplishment and "getting a lot done" were discussed. In analyzing who is good at project accomplishment, power holders agreed that successful people use resources well.

A resource is something that is useful in accomplishing people's goals. The clearest resource is money—people find it extremely useful when they have plenty of money to hire specialists who can take responsibility for various aspects of a project. Discussions of money also bring up another aspect of resources. When people have a resource that is scarce, they themselves have power because they can share the resource with some and withhold it from others. When they share, they can expect the favor to be returned (Cialdini, 1988).

A major recommendation for people who want to use power effectively is to develop and use resources wisely. In broad terms, there are seven types of resources that people have, develop, and exchange (Foa, 1971).

1. People with *money* can gain access to power with steps such as contributing to the campaigns of political candidates, financially supporting charitable causes favored by power holders, investing in business ventures proposed by powerful people, and so forth. Those who contribute generously to the campaigns of political candidates will be invited to fund-raisers and seated at tables with prestigious and powerful people. They can then learn about good opportunities for future investments by simply listening to the conversations of these powerful people.

2. *Status* is a resource because most people enjoy the company of those who have prestige. The clearest examples are well-known entertainers who are courted by politicians, leaders of charitable organizations, university officials who need commence-

ment speakers, and so forth. At times, people can use status from one arena in society to influence other arenas. If a person has written a best-selling book, he or she is thought by many to have worthwhile opinions on topics far beyond the content of the book. If a person is a well-known movie actor, for some reasons their opinions about brands of coffee are sought by advertisers. Many people who achieve some status do not use it: Honor students, college athletes, and the subjects of recent media coverage often do not take advantage of their temporary notoriety. For example, we know coaches of college athletic teams who are surprised that their well-known players do not take advantage of their status and take steps such as meeting potential future employers during charity events. Women often brush off the "limelight." For example, if a woman secures a substantial research grant or job promotion, she may be likely to comment that she was "just lucky" or "in the right place at the right time," instead of acknowledging her skills and status. Women may be more likely not to recognize and attribute their hard work and standing in the community or institution to their advancement or to use this to further their status.

3. *Love* and *sex*, and related aspects such as *physical attractiveness*, constitute another family of resources. In many cultures, it is considered improper if not illegal to exchange sex for a resource such as money. The romantic ideal is that love and sex offered by one person are exchanged for these same resources with a desired other. However, only naive people would argue that love and sex are never exchanged for other resources. People who are very physically attractive have long exchanged this resource and have entered into marriages and liaisons with wealthy individuals who can provide status and security. Furthermore, fair or not, physically attractive people often are given opportunities denied to the less attractive, such as fast-track positions where they are asked to represent a company at professional conferences and trade shows. Attractive women often have a burden not experienced as frequently by attractive men. How can they fend off sexual overtures from the powerful without alienating themselves from networks controlled by the powerful?

Managing the resources of *love* and *sex* must include experience at fending off sexual overtures from powerful people without suffering alienation from their networks. When such occasions arise, not only is the woman caught off-guard and unprepared much of the time, but the man is put in a precarious situation, as is the institution. Allegations of harassment can ruin a man's career, and corporations can be held responsible for large settlements. Therefore, the stakes are high if and when such situations occur. How a woman handles the issue can make all the difference in power distributions and working relationships.

Women can lead the relationship by using subtle cues to head off any such attention—simple things, such as wearing a ring on the left hand, having fresh flowers arranged in one's office, or having photos of friends and family displayed can suggest a mood of personal fulfillment. Often these subtle cues are enough to thwart such attention, but not all the time. If subtle cues are unnoticed or ignored and sexual overtures are made, women need to prepare a supportive, firm, professional response. She may wish to role play this response with a male or female friend until it rolls out naturally and confidently. Simply ignoring such overtures and redirecting the conversation back on task or asking for professional clarification from the power holder may be enough. Such tactics will put the power holder in the spotlight as he prepares the necessary information, and this may suffice to reestablish the professional relationship in a clear manner. Unfortunately, there will be occasions where continued address will be demanded—when the power holder clearly does not "get it." In such situations, a firm reiteration of the nature of the professional relationship will need to be stressed. This may be uncomfortable and is best when well rehearsed and natural, not defensive.

4. When people do not have a great deal of money, *information* is the resource that is often developed. The question to ask is, "What information do power holders need but may not have themselves? Can I become the holder of this information?" Examples of answers to the first question include the use of personal computers, laws regarding the uses and abuses of power, accounting, how best to "work" the political system, how best to work with the media, and insider knowledge about investment possibilities. In general, people in many cultures attend college and obtain advanced degrees so that they will have an area of expertise that others will find useful. The usefulness will, ideally, lead to job offers. In some cultures, bureaucracies are so complex and inert that individuals who know the names of people who can cut through red tape have highly valued information. If these cultures are collectivist, the names of people are often those of cousins, people who attended school with the resource holder, and long-time family friends.

The category called *information* also includes knowledge held by mentors, who may or may not pass this resource on to newcomers to an organization. Mentoring advice often takes the form of "You learned in college about this, but the way it works in the real world is . . . ." For example, Ptak, Cooper, and Brislin (1995) collected mentoring advice from experienced cross-cultural trainers and obtained the information captured in the three anecdotes at the beginning of this module. A female-specific example could be the knowledge that laws protect women against discrimination in wages and advancement, but that reality presents a different picture, one that is subtle yet discriminatory. Women need to be aware of and keep a keen lookout for subtle forms of discrimination. Mentoring advice often recognizes human frailties and consequently is not shared with people who cannot be discreet. For example, advice might be given about the cues that suggest when it is a good time to communicate with a certain power holder and when it is time to avoid contact; which volunteer organizations might be joined to meet important people and which constitute a poor investment of time; which people are "all smoke and no fire" or "all hat and no cattle"; and which bureaucrats should be courted because they can make people's life miserable if organizational policies are flouted.

Information also includes knowledge of strategies and tactics for the use of power. There are methods of preparing oneself so that one's organization receives good media coverage. There are ways of organizing one's efforts toward goal accomplishment so that people increase the chances of gaining the reputation of winners (Weick, 1984). There are ways of distracting the opposition to one's projects so that the chances of goal accomplishment are increased (Brislin, 1991; Smith, 1988). If people know these strategies and tactics, they have an advantage over people who do not.

5. *Services* refer to activities that individuals can offer to some people but can withhold from others. Only legislators can introduce bills. Do they introduce them only to those who contribute to their political campaigns or do they introduce bills for any worthy cause in which they believe? Entertainers often become quite powerful figures in their communities because they can donate their services to certain fund-raising groups and can withhold them from others. Secretaries can control their services by doing excellent work for people they like and merely adequate work for

people who shout at them. When they have influence over the flow of money, such as the timing of travel advances and reimbursements, the wise advice from powerful mentors that "secretaries should be treated well" becomes clear. In some organizations, people who control the distribution of parking permits become power holders whose wrath is carefully avoided.

6. *Goods* can be exchanged for access to powerful people. For example, retailers can sell goods at wholesale prices to power holders and have the reasonable expectation that this constitutes a favor to be returned. Especially in times of economic recession, jobs are a scarce good that can be offered to some and withheld from others. In some cities, political machines have been built on the practice of offering jobs (e.g., policemen, firemen, sanitation workers) in exchange for votes and after-hours campaign work from the recipients.

7. The *time* and *energy* that people can expend on certain projects and withhold from others is another resource that can be nurtured by people without the easy access to power that money allows. The intelligent use of time and energy often distinguishes people moving toward power from people who find themselves unable to implement their projects. Which are the committees one should join, and which are a waste of time? Which community activities will allow people to meet powerful others, and which will not? I have been asked to give a gratis lecture for a professional organization—is this a good use of my time? People able to answer these questions have an advantage over people who are not.

The following scenario may capture the wisdom of thinking through the use of one's time and energy. A person is out of work. In addition to looking for a job, he or she volunteers to work on a political campaign. Consider the benefits. Rather than a blank space on one's resume corresponding to a recent period of time, the entry "Worked on the senatorial campaign of _____ _____" can be listed. People who might know of job openings will be met. Networking skills can be practiced; meeting others quickly, putting them at ease, becoming memorable, and so forth. The candidate may even place a few phone calls as part of the person's job search.

Note to the Trainer, and a Possible Short Exercise

At this point, trainees have been exposed to a number of points and many will be uncomfortable. Some will not be comfortable with the idea that they have to worry about power in their quest to implement their projects. They have not yet accepted that understanding power is necessary for leadership, and they will view discussions of power acquisition as distasteful and sleazy. Other trainees will be unfamiliar with the need to return favors. They may be happy to receive favors from power holders but may be unready to consider returning the favors. Still others will be uncomfortable when asked to look on certain relationships as networks of people who look for opportunities to exchange resources. They will view such behavior as "using people."

These are very emotional issues because they address a basic aspect of the human experience: relationships with others. There is no way that, in a 1- or 2-day workshop, people uncomfortable with power will become smooth power holders. We have found, however, that the following short exercise encourages people to begin thinking about the relation between resource exchange, favors, and networks.

People are asked, "Think of people you know well, who are close to you and with whom you share the ups and downs of important events in your life. Your emotions become part of their emotional life and vice-versa. How many people can you list?" (Most people can think of fewer than 20 people). "Now, think of people who you are comfortable calling by their first names and with whom you interact cordially." (Most people can imagine at least 100 people). "What is a good term for the first list?" (Typical answers are close friends, intimate friends, and family members). "What is a good term for the second list?" (Typical answers are acquaintances or casual friends). "Is *network members* an acceptable term for the second list?" (Given this sequence of questions, most trainees will accept this term for the moment).

"Considering this second list, can you think of a benefit you have received from interactions with one or more of these people?" (Most trainees can, and typical examples have been a job lead, name of a potential customer, previously unknown opportunity for professional development, name of a person with specialized services, etc.). "Did you return the favor? Have you ever cut down the amount of contact with someone from the second list? Was one reason because you gave them your resources, but over time there was no attempt by them to return favors?" (Many people answer "yes.").

Critical Incidents

At this point, trainees should be ready to consider problems involving power in two critical incidents.

Fund-Raising Activities

Jack Sato was a personnel specialist within his state's Department of Education. He was also active in various community activities and worked as a volunteer at one of the large hospitals in his state. He found himself enjoying the work at the hospital more than his salaried job at the Department of Education. After a few years, recognizing Jack's ability to write, one of the hospital administrators asked him to join the fund-raising committee associated with the hospital's volunteer support group. This administrator hinted that people who were successful in this volunteer activity often made themselves known to health care professionals in the city. There had been a few cases in the past where young professionals who were successful at volunteer activities competed well for jobs in health care administration.

Jack noted that the hospital for which he did volunteer work did not have a kidney dialysis unit. Patients needing dialysis had to travel to another hospital, often at great expense and inconvenience. He proposed to the hospital administration that he lead a fund-raising drive for a dialysis machine, and his proposal was accepted. He began his fund-raising with a reception for other hospital volunteers who would, he hoped, become involved. Next door to the room in which his reception was being held, a television crew from the highest-rated local news show was doing a story on a patient who had survived a shark attack. The TV crew wrapped up its story more quickly than it had planned, and its leader noted that there was an eager-looking group of people at a reception in the adjoining room. Asking about it, the leader was told that it was the first fund-raising meeting for the purchase of a kidney dialysis machine. This leader was interested because his uncle had died of a kidney disease.

The TV crew leader asked who was in charge. Jack was pointed out, and the leader asked him for an interview. Jack agreed, and the TV crew set up around him. The interviewer asked about the fund-raiser. Jack said, "Our city can be in the forefront of modern medicine if there is more than one hospital with a dialysis unit." By the time this interview was completed, the TV crew was running slightly behind schedule and its members left the hospital. Jack watched the TV news the next three evenings, but there was no TV airtime given to his interview. Realizing that Jack was interviewed for TV but that it had not been broadcast, potential volunteers for his fund-raiser became less enthusiastic.

Did Jack do anything wrong? What he might have done differently?

Advice and Analysis

The purpose of this story is to introduce several aspects related to project implementation. There are others besides the following, but two important issues are working with the media and communicating the image of a winner. People who are sophisticated about power know how to make the work of print and television reporters easy. They have learned to communicate their message in easy-to-understand, emotionally involving statements; in sound bites that are easy to edit into a TV story; and (where possible) through interesting visuals that can be integrated into TV reports. For example, Jack should have been prepared for the possibility of media coverage. He was lucky that the TV crew stopped by, but luck favors the well-prepared. Rather than the dull generalization about "forefront of knowledge," Jack should have personalized the message by referring to one or two specific children who would be helped if a machine was available. He might also have obtained the necessary permissions to include a needy and attractive child in the TV report. This inclusion might have been on a previously prepared, broadcast-quality tape that the TV station could edit into its coverage. If Jack had taken these steps, he would have clearly communicated to those around him that he is sophisticated, "a winner," and consequently he would have attracted attention from people who want to attach themselves to winners.

Formerly on a Swim Team

Beth Whitman recently turned 23 years old and found herself on the job market. She had received her bachelor's degree in business administration but found herself looking for a job during poor economic times in her state and in the nation as a whole. In a book of advice for job searchers, she read that people might make a list of individuals they know who have responsible positions in their communities. Then these people might be contacted for informal interviews about possibilities in the job market.

In making this list, Beth considered her experiences on a swim team during her junior and senior years of high school. She was a good swimmer and had traveled to many meets around the state, often winning ribbons and trophies. As part of these meets, she often met the parents of her competitors. Even though there was not time for extensive interactions, a swimmer's parents typically would exchange greetings with their daughter's competitors and would certainly know who the best competitors were.

Beth remembered swimming against Jane Haley. Jane Haley's mother was a vice president in a prominent construction firm in their city. Beth called Mrs. Haley to make an appointment. Mrs. Haley responded, "Oh, yes! You used to swim against my daughter! Those were exciting times! How can I help you?" Beth then asked for an appointment to have a general discussion about the job market. Mrs. Haley scheduled this appointment and in it gave Beth some very good leads regarding specific jobs. After this appointment, Mrs. Haley did not hear from Beth for about 2 months. Then Beth called to say that she had been able to secure an interview for one of the jobs that Mrs. Haley had suggested as a possibility. Beth then asked for a letter of recommendation. Mrs. Haley was less enthusiastic in her response than she had been to the original request for the general discussion about the job market.

What are possible reasons for Mrs. Haley's lack of enthusiasm?

Advice and Analysis

Up to the point where Beth had the first meeting with Mrs. Haley, she was engaging in appropriate behavior: listing people who might remember her, asking them questions for which they have answers, and so forth. As often happens, Mrs. Haley found the meeting enjoyable and was probably flattered that she was remembered. However, Beth was inattentive to returning favors and so the second request could easily be interpreted as "using" Mrs. Haley rather than benefiting from her kindness. What form might the returned favor have taken? Certainly a thank-you note with information about how Mrs. Haley's recommendations were pursued was essential. A possible addition is that Beth might have asked Mrs. Haley about her favorite charity and arranged to carry out some volunteer work.

Structured Exercise I: Resources, Networks, and Exchanges

After an introduction to key concepts related to power, the following exercise (which takes approximately $2\frac{1}{2}$ hours) gives trainees firsthand experience with a number of important concepts (from Brislin, 1991). These include identification of projects, identification of resources, resource development, and the exchange of resources in project implementation. This exercise has been carried out with graduate students in colleges of business and with young professionals during weekend training programs. This is admittedly a complex exercise, and our examples and guidelines regarding possible stumbling blocks are based on our recent experiences with it.

Step 1. Participants identify a project that they would like to implement in the near future. As much as possible, this should be a "real" project in which they have an interest and that they actually would like to implement. It should have a budget of approximately $250,000 U.S. Recent participants have identified projects such as starting a grocery chain specializing in Asian foods, developing a method of administering medicine to babies based on patches placed on the skin, developing a program to prepare teachers to take jobs in inner-city schools, expanding a family hobby into a small business, preparing former athletes for careers in communication or public relations, and producing a series of television shows on the contributions of less well-known ethnic groups.

Step 2. Participants list resources they have that might be helpful in the development of their project and in the projects of others. These should be participants' actual resources; one goal of this step is to encourage people to think through the various ways they can benefit themselves and others. People's lists are often stimulated by presentations such as those summarized earlier in this module, and recently participants have listed the following resources: lived in another country for several years; experience working for a newspaper or a television station; experience with public speaking; enjoys writing; knows a lot of people because of community volunteer work; worked through college as an orderly in a hospital, so knows something about the business of medicine; was an athlete who attracted a great deal of publicity, so is a person known to many; speaks and writes a language in addition to English.

Step 3. Participants are asked to imagine that they have an additional resource, and to carry out the rest of this role-play exercise with this resource. The purposes of this step are to encourage participants to think of resource development as a career-long process and to expose participants to a wider variety of resources than those identified in step two. Participants draw a card on which the trainer has printed one of the following additional resources:

> You are a good administrator of complex projects. You can see how the many pieces of complex projects fit together.
>
> You have extraordinary social skills. You are charming and gracious. People have a difficult time becoming upset with you.
>
> You have written a bestseller (topic of your choice) and consequently are viewed as both a public figure and as an expert.
>
> You can talk and negotiate with opposing factions and be trusted by both.
>
> You have a large network in your community.
>
> You are an extremely effective public speaker and can address crowds of any size.
>
> You are a great salesperson. You can sell objects and ideas to people almost without regard for what they are.
>
> You write very well in a wide variety of styles (e.g., persuasive, diplomatic, scientific, popular appeal).
>
> You have $1,000,000 to invest or to give to worthwhile causes.
>
> You have tax expertise and can set up organizations that can take advantage of all tax laws.
>
> You have very good contacts among newspaper and television reporters.

You have a very good sense of politics—you know who has power and who will be in favor of various projects and who will be against them.

You have very good previous job experience in the production of consumer goods.

Some of these resources can be put on several cards and given to several people. For example (and especially when the exercise is organized for businesspeople), we have several cards presenting these resources: a million dollars to invest, tax expertise, excellence in sales, and production of consumer goods.

Step 4. Participants interact with others for the purpose of project development. They can be given instructions such as the following:

You want to interact with others, exchanging resources so that contributions are received for your project and contributions are offered to assist others. For the exercise, you will have:

A. $5,000 from your own savings;

B. your actual resources, based on the list you prepared in step two;

C. the additional resource on the card that was presented to you;

D. a list of the resources others have (from step three) so that you can look for these as you develop your project;

E. your name tag—please wear this because it will make interactions with other easier.

In this role play, please imagine that you are at a gathering where influential people meet. Depending on your community, this could be the support group for the local opera, a political fund-raiser, a reception for a visiting dignitary, and so forth. Interact cordially with others. While talking with people, tell them (perhaps indirectly at first) about your project and resources if you think that they might be able to do business with you. They may reciprocate by telling you about their resources. Then, combine the resources so that your project is assisted, and the projects of others also take steps toward implementation. Remember, there should be a balance between what is given and what is received. If you only receive resources from others, you will eventually become known as a "leech" or as a "taker" who does not return favors. If you only give resources to others, you may become known as a "sucker" who is overextended and never develops your own project. Regarding the "rules" of this exercise, you can make your own rules as long as they are legal and consistent with ethical business practice.

Participants then interact, exchanging resources and developing projects for about an hour. Because people are wearing name tags and know that they are participating in a role play, almost none have had trouble starting the exercise. If trainers suspect that people are not comfortable starting a conversation with someone else, the first two conversations can be assigned. After that, we have never encountered problems and have only suggested, "Be sure to talk to different people, perhaps including someone else and coordinating a three- or four-way conversation." For the final hour, participants report how their projects developed and what they learned about the process of networking and resource exchange. For example, the person who wants to start a company that produces medicine in patches for children may find people with money to invest, people with writing skills to work on advertising, people with sales and manufacturing experience, tax experts, and a public person (e.g., the best-selling author) who might be a spokesperson. A person interested in a social cause, such as preparing young teachers for jobs in inner-city schools, may find wealthy people willing to donate tax-deductible money, people with media contacts to help publicize the project, public speakers to address various audiences about the importance of the program, and people with political sensitivities who might know how to approach the legislature for public funds.

Participants also discuss what they learn. Some report that they are shy but realize that they must become more comfortable interacting with others at social gatherings and exchanging information about current projects. One said that she had little trouble talking with others and offering her resources but that she would have to become more assertive about suggesting how others might make contributions to her projects. One reported, "I vaguely knew what networking was, but now I have a clearer idea and I realize that there are resources out there that can be tapped." Women and members of minority groups sometimes complain that the rules seem to favor Anglo males. "Networking, with its emphasis on quick interactions and resource exchange, seems to favor males," some women report. "I have to decide if I want to participate or perhaps form a women's resource exchange group like the ones that seem to be popping up in large cities." Minority group members observe that the Anglo males have shared interests and communication styles that make it comfortable for them to meet quickly and to interact quickly. People from other cultural backgrounds have to consider developing the interests and skills that will permit frequent interactions with Anglos (this is one of the issues raised in the third anecdote from the beginning of this module, p. 21). There are alternatives: Anglos can work on becoming more sensitive to communication problems faced by culturally diverse people (a theme of the module by Fried and Matsumoto in Chapter 4, or people from diverse groups can develop support networks among those who share their cultural background, possibly including others who have clearly shown interest and sensitivity.

Structured Exercise II: Mentoring Experience

After there has been some brief introduction to mentoring, the following exercise (which takes approximately 1 hour) gives trainees direct experience in mentoring and being mentored.

For women, one of the greatest tools for the use of power and career advancement is the enlistment of a mentor. Mentoring advice is not readily experienced by women through socialization or during career development. Therefore, it is vital that women actively seek opportunities to develop this attribute.

Step 1. Trainees identify a work-related issue that causes them distress or confusion. This should be a real issue. Past participants have identified issues such as, How do I know who really makes the decisions or has power? How do I handle a male colleague who interrupts me and talks over me at meetings? How do I know how much money to ask for when interviewing for my first professional position? How do I balance my time as a wife, mother, and professional? How do I fend off sexual overtures without cutting myself off from this person's network?

Step 2. Trainees list two or three of their resources that might be helpful to others seeking mentoring advice. These should be real attributes or experiences. Past participants have identified resources such as experience as a personnel interviewer with a major corporation, having worked in a highly bureaucratic institution, having filed suit and won a court case against gender discrimination, and having been a president of a corporation or an elected official.

Step 3. The resources are listed on a board or overhead along with the person's name. The participants are divided into two groups; one will be mentors and the others will seek mentoring advice. Participants can choose their mentor and discuss their issue with the other participant for 15 minutes. After the initial session has been completed, the participants switch positions.

Step 4. After each participant has served as a mentor and been mentored, there is a debriefing session and a discussion for the remaining half hour. Participants can discuss what they learned and how it felt to find and give advice. Some may report that they felt their issue was trivial or would not happen to others, and found out that it was a common occurrence. Some may declare that they knew little about mentoring but now see its necessity for career development. Some participants may find a mentor whom they will remain in contact with long after the training session. *The goal of the exercise is to familiarize women with the mentoring process and to give them experience in mentoring.*

Critical Incident

Susan Gray was an African American project manager for a consulting company. She had worked 15 years with the company and had received the company's highest national award for performance excellence and her project management skills. Her company's profits were highly dependent on such project management skills. Her company won a multimillion-dollar, high-profile contract that opened up new perspectives for it. Susan was delighted with the opportunity and felt she was the most qualified to manage the contract, as did most people to whom she spoke. Susan pursued the project and was available, but the project was assigned to someone else with much less experience. When Susan questioned the directive, she was told she did not get the project because she was "too laid back" for such a high-profile project.

The damage to Susan's confidence and to her sense of participation as a full member of the corporate team was shaken. Susan wondered if racism or sexism were the reasons behind her not being assigned the project. When Susan pressed corporate executives harder for the reasoning behind the decision, she was told that she lacked "political skill."

Susan filed a gender and race discrimination action against her employer.

Discussion Questions

1. Why do you think Susan would be passed over for this project?
2. Is Susan overreacting?
3. What are the real damages of this issue to Susan's career and the careers of other women within the corporation?
4. What could Susan have done differently, and why?
5. If Susan were a white male, would your answers for any of the above questions be different, and why?

Advice and Analysis

This incident was written with gender and race bias, and the subtle nature such issues can take, in mind. Political skill or political savvy are common rationales for "glass-ceiling" incidents. This is a classic case: Women and minorities are frequently derailed just as they are about to make a move that would make them truly visible and powerful. Women and minorities are often denied opportunities to gain credential-building experiences. In addition, the American public feels much more comfortable if the woman is seen as a "behind-the-scenes" influence on power and not out front, in public, actually achieving the objective (Cantor & Bernay, 1992).

The derailing that occurs has a direct, devastating effect. Susan was removed from the "pipeline" and lost credibility as a role model. When other women or minorities within the corporation witness their role models treated unjustly, or see that equal opportunity is only given lip service, a profound negative effect is felt.

If Susan was perceived as lacking political skills, it could be argued that she had not developed or maintained her networks in ways that could be beneficial to her and to the business. Is Susan attending public functions and meeting people? Is she lubricating relationships by returning favors? How could Susan better develop her political sophistication so that the next time an opportunity such as this comes around, she will be considered a more powerful candidate?

Field Exercises

People are asked to list their interests, with special attention to activities they enjoy during their free time. With the help of trainers, participants then choose a group whose meetings they will attend. The newspapers in many cities list volunteer organizations that desire more members, and these lists will often provide the name of a group. Then, participants attend a few meetings and later report who they met, what resources they learned about, and so forth.

As another possibility, participants use the list of skills they developed as part of the networking and resource exchange exercise (pp. 33-37). Then they ask themselves, "Which of these would I like to improve and which were not listed because I don't have them?" Trainers can then give advice, when asked. We have, for example, worked with people who want to develop their public-speaking skills, and we suggest that they join an organization such as Toastmasters. Many colleges have evening courses that allow people to work on their writing skills. Some of these same colleges have noncredit courses dealing with skills such as "meeting others gracefully" and "the art of conversation."

Concluding Remarks

The purpose of this module was to present concepts and training materials that we felt would be useful in the development and training of individuals in workplace diversity, leadership, boss-subordinate relations, and movement through the glass ceiling by way of tacit knowledge, examples, exercises, and theory. Our focus emerged from a "power-skills" viewpoint that presents many of the skills that powerful people possess and less powerful people do not. Through various examples, we presented training concepts that, when practiced to a degree of comfort, will assist individuals in power acquisition and professional development in diverse situations. In addition, our focus on women's issues provided examples for defusing the efforts of male colleagues who use sex or sexually offensive gestures as a power tactic. Several other women's concerns were addressed about resource management and development. The short exercises should encourage thinking and behaviors that will lead to power exchanges, networking, and avoiding pitfalls.

"Excellence . . . is not an act, but a habit," said Aristotle. Power in the service of leadership is habitual attention to behaviors and skill development over one's career. This module has set up the building blocks or groundwork for assisting participants in understanding the concepts and uses of power. Although understanding these theories and working through the structured exercises will not guarantee immediate results, the format gives participants firsthand experience with a number of important concepts that can be taken outside the training session and repeated until they become habitual.

References

Brislin, R. (1991). *The art of getting things done: A practical guide to the use of power.* New York: Praeger.

Brislin, R. (1994). Power: Strategies and tactics. In R. Corsini (Ed.), *Encyclopedia of psychology, 3* (pp. 105-109). New York: John Wiley.

Cantor, D. & Bernay, T. (1992). *Women in power.* New York: Houghton Mifflin.

Cialdini, R. (1988) *Influence: Science and practice* (2nd ed.). Glenview, IL: Scott Foresman.

Foa, U. (1971). Interpersonal and economic resources. *Science, 171,* 345-351.

Jane, S. S. (1995, January). Women and power: Strategies and tactics. In *Proceedings of the 4th annual East-West Centerwide Conference.* Honolulu: East-West Center.

Ptak, C., Cooper, J., & Brislin, R. (1995). Cross-cultural training programs: Advice and insights from experienced trainers. *International Journal of Intercultural Relations, 19*(3), 425-453.

Schwartz, S. (1994). Beyond individualism/collectivism: New cultural dimensions of values. In U. Kim, H. Triandis, C. Kagitcibasi, S. Choi, & G. Yoon (Eds.), *Individualism and collectivism: Theory, method, and applications* (pp. 85-119). Thousands Oaks, CA: Sage.

Smith, H. (1988). *The power game: How Washington works.* New York: Random House.

Tannen, D. (1990). *You just don't understand: Women and men in conversation.* New York: William Morrow.

Triandis, H. (1994). Cross-cultural industrial and organizational psychology. In H. Triandis, M. Dunnette, & L. Hough (Eds.), *Handbook of industrial and organizational psychology, 4* (pp. 103-172). Palo Alto, CA: Consulting Psychology.

Weick, K. (1984). Small wins: Redefining the scale of social problems. *American Psychologist, 39,* 40-49.

3

Leadership Through Relationship Management

Using the Theory of Individualism and Collectivism

Dharm P. S. Bhawuk

Because such a general regards his men as infants, they will march with him in the deepest valleys. He treats them as his own beloved sons and they will die with him.

Sun Tzu, *The Art of War*

The cross-cultural literature provides a unique perspective in understanding relationships in the workplace. This chapter presents an emerging theory of relationships and proposes a new approach to leadership through relationship management, called Value Added Relationship Management, a productive way to manage one's interpersonal relationship in the workplace. This is particularly important in the context of the global economy, where the workplace is becoming increasingly diverse.

Contents

40

Self-Assessment Exercise

Please rate the degree to which you agree or disagree with each of the following statements using a 6-point scale.

6	5	4	3	2	1
very strongly agree	strongly agree	agree	disagree	strongly disagree	very strongly disagree

_____ 1. I think my relationships with others are more important than my own accomplishments.

_____ 2. I do not like to be under any obligation from the people I know.

_____ 3. I have a large network of friends whom I can count on.

_____ 4. If I rode with a friend regularly on his way to work, I would insist on paying him for the gas.

_____ 5. I have many obligations to many people.

_____ 6. If someone takes me out to lunch, I will buy him a lunch of equal value within weeks.

_____ 7. I like my good friends to become my family friends.

_____ 8. I do not owe anybody a favor.

_____ 9. If I have to, I go out of my way to maintain my relationships.

_____ 10. If I receive a favor, I try to return something of equal value.

Add up the total of the odd items (1, 3, 5, 7, and 9) and then the even items to create two scores ranging from 5 to 30. The score on the odd items indicates people's inclination to be relational, whereas the score on the even items indicates people's inclination to be rational. Please continue with the next assessment for now.

In the following scenarios, two alternatives are provided. Please choose the one that describes you the best.

1. Someone took you out for a dinner. What is your likely response?

   A. Buy him or her a dinner in a similar restaurant soon.

   B. Bring a souvenir for him or her sometime not so soon.

2. Someone helped your close one (spouse, son, daughter, brother, sister, etc.) find a job. You will

   A. invite him or her for a special dinner to say "thank you."

   B. be indebted to him or her for life and help him or her in whatever way you can in the future.

3. You are going to a foreign country for a 6-week trip. You will

   A. find necessary information from official sources.

   B. find out the addresses of people your friends know in that country.

4. A friend who lives an 8-hour driving distance from you has suffered a major setback in life. You will

   A. send him or her an appropriate card.

   B. personally visit him or her.

5. A friend's friend is in your city on a business trip. You will

   A. exchange pleasantries with him on the telephone.

   B. invite him or her for dinner at your home.

6. You recommended your subordinate for an advanced training program in which he was accepted. Your subordinate should

   A. simply keep doing the good work.

   B. feel obliged to you.

7. You are going on a business trip to another city where one of your close friends lives. You will

   A. not stay with him or her.

   B. stay with him or her.

8. You are visiting a city in which you have a close friend. You

   A. may not even talk to him on the telephone.

   B. will at least talk to him on the telephone.

The more *A*'s you have, the more inclined you are to be rational; the more *B*'s you have, the more inclined you are to be relational. The objective of these assessments was to provide you with some insight into your own inclination to use one of these strategies more frequently than the other in your interpersonal relationships. Please study the following two cases and the explanation provided to get a more complete understanding of the rational and relational approach to relationship management.

Case Studies: Critical Incidents

The Unfair Director

Lee was a Ph.D. student from Korea at the Institute of Labor and Industrial Relations, University of Minnesota. He was very happy with life in general; he had a wonderful adviser, an assistantship (financial support) that was not bad, friends who were warm and hospitable, and his wife and children had found friends at the university's family housing complex. He often wondered what more he could ask for!

In his third semester, the director of the institute asked him to become a teaching assistant because the American student who was assigned the job (a 20-hour-a-week contract) had declined the offer. Taking up the teaching responsibility would definitely slow down his research activities, which were most important for his career, and he would be paid for only 15 hours a week. However, his adviser encouraged him to help the institute in the time of need, and he agreed to be a teaching assistant without any additional financial incentive (clearly, he was being paid less than what his colleague had been offered!). For the following two semesters, after his first semester as a teaching assistant, he was again offered a teaching assistantship. He ultimately ended up making more money because he was offered a 20-hour-a-week contract instead of the earlier 15-hour-a-week deal.

At the end of his fifth semester, Lee received a letter from the director informing him that he would be a teaching assistant the following semester (his sixth), and that because he was promised financial support for only six semesters at the time of his admission, he would be given only a 10-hour-a-week research assistantship during his seventh semester. Lee was surprised because he was aware that the institute had recently passed a new policy according to which he could get full financial support (a minimum 15-hour-a-week assistantship) for eight semesters. Other elements of the policy were already being implemented, and he saw no reason for not exercising this provision of the policy. Besides, he had helped the institute when it needed him.

Lee spoke to his adviser, who suggested that he petition to the director for full financial support (a 15-hour-a-week research assistantship) considering that he had made satisfactory progress toward his degree. He suggested that Lee also mention in his petition how he had helped the institution in its time of need. Lee wrote the petition and spoke personally to the director. His adviser also wrote a letter of recommendation supporting his case. A few weeks later, Lee received a letter from the director stating that his request had been turned down in view of the old policy, according to which Lee was entitled to a financial support for only 3 years. The letter made a special note of the fact that Lee had been promised financial support for 6 semesters at the time of admission. Lee was confused about what he should do.

How would you advise Lee?

1. It may be an error of omission and Lee should go and speak to the director again.
2. Lee was wrong in assuming that the new policy would apply to him.
3. Lee is clearly being discriminated against and he should complain about it to the chancellor of the university.
4. The director does not think Lee did anybody a favor by accepting to teach the course, because he had been paid for the job.

Rationales for the Alternative Explanations

1. This is a plausible explanation. Administrators do things that are unintended, and this may very well be the case here. However, there is a better response. Please try again.

2. Because many aspects of the new policies apply to Lee, he was not really wrong in assuming that the new policy would apply to him. Please try again.

3. There is no evidence that another student in Lee's position was given a 15-hour-a-week assistantship in the seventh semester. Hence, a case of discrimination cannot be made. Please try again.

4. Lee is a collectivist and thinks that by agreeing to teach the course when the institute needed him, he developed a communal relationship, whereas the director, who is likely to be an individualist, thinks that it was an exchange relationship because Lee was paid for the job he did. Thus, the director does not feel any obligation toward Lee. This is an example of a conflict arising from differences in people's inclinations to be exchange-oriented versus relationship-oriented. Collectivists view

relationships as communal in nature, whereas individualists view them as exchange-based. Communal relationships are characterized by unequal exchange and long-term duration, whereas exchange relationships are characterized by equal exchange and short-term durations. Communal relationships reflect the relational attitude, whereas exchange relationships reflect the rational attitude. This is the best response.

Get to the Point

Alfred, an American businessman, was visiting a supplier in Brazil. He was very pleased with the courtesy extended to him—his host came to receive him at the airport, drove him to his hotel, took him out to dinner in the evening after allowing him sufficient time to wash and change his clothes, and showed him around the city after dinner. He looked forward to his business meeting the next day.

Mr. Lorenzo sent his chauffeur to pick Alfred up from his hotel. He had asked three of his senior managers to the meeting, and Alfred was introduced to everyone. Coffee and pastries were served and the managers were generally being nice to him, asking him about his trip, what he liked about Brazil, what his hobby was, and so forth. As time passed and the managers showed no sign of talking business, Alfred started to worry. He gently suggested that he had many things to discuss with Mr. Lorenzo and his colleagues. Mr. Lorenzo said that there was no rush to get into the drudgery of business talk, and that they needed to understand each other and that business would take care of itself.

After about 40 minutes, Alfred started looking at his wristwatch and brought up the business issues to be discussed. Mr. Lorenzo and his colleagues steered him away from business talk and led him into discussing golf. One of them proposed that they should take Alfred to the golf course after lunch because it was a pleasant, sunny day. Alfred was quite confused about his hosts' lack of desire to discuss business and was not certain that he would be able to get a contract signed in the next 24 hours.

How would you advise Alfred?

1. Mr. Lorenzo and his colleagues have not done their homework and are buying time to develop the proposal that they want to discuss with him.
2. Mr. Lorenzo is playing the pressure tactic. He will not allow enough time for Alfred to think through his proposal, and will thus obtain a favorable agreement from him.
3. Mr. Lorenzo is a shrewd businessman and is trying to divert Alfred's attention to nontask details to take advantage of him.
4. Mr. Lorenzo is genuinely trying to develop a relationship of trust with Alfred so that he can reach an agreement quickly when it comes to the negotiation.

Rationales for Alternative Explanations

1. Mr. Lorenzo could have rescheduled the meeting with Alfred if he needed more time to prepare for the meeting. He could have also saved some time by sending his

chauffeur or a junior colleague to receive Alfred at the airport when he had arrived. This does not seem like a plausible reason. Please try again.

2. If Mr. Lorenzo wanted to use pressure tactics, he would get into the negotiation sooner to find out what Alfred had to offer. One does not use pressure tactics without knowing what the opponent wants in a negotiation situation. Please choose again.

3. One could take advantage of the other party by getting him or her intoxicated, but it is hard to imagine that a businessperson will lose sight of business goals by drinking coffee and talking about golf. There is a more pressing issue involved here. Please choose again.

4. Negotiation involves four stages: socializing and rapport building, information exchange, persuasion, and arriving at an agreement. In collectivist cultures, the thrust is on the first stage of negotiation process, that is, developing trust through socializing and getting to know each other better. Business cannot be done without knowing a person's needs and preferences and establishing a relationship of trust. This is a result of an interdependent concept of self and collectivists' early socialization process into the extended family and kinship. Collectivists deal with only those they know or trust. They try to integrate those they do not know into their primary network of family, relations, and friends. This is also related to the collectivists' tendency to be relational (valuing a relationship even when it is unprofitable to do so) rather than rational (choosing relationships that serve one's immediate interests). Hence, while interacting with a foreigner, collectivists strive to develop a trust relationship before sharing any business information.

In individualist cultures, especially in the United States, people usually spend very little time on socializing and rapport building (briefly talking about golf, weather, or family), and like to get on with information sharing. The main thrust is on persuasion, convincing the other party of one's point of view—the third leg of the negotiation process. This is the result of their drive to be independent and desire to influence others. Persuasion is thought of as a competitive task: Those who can convince the other party and achieve their goal are successful. In the United States, businesspeople are interested in the arguments and logic that people present rather than in the people themselves. Also, as mentioned previously, individualists make a rational choice about which relationships to cultivate and hence would not like to spend a lot of time with someone with whom they cannot do business (why play golf with someone if one cannot get a contract from him or her, and how can one get a contract if one does not know his or her arguments or logic?). Therefore, they may signal that they would like to return to business issues by simply looking at their wristwatch, thinking, "Cut the nonsense and come to the point." However, a collectivist would become apprehensive to see impatience and would try to find out more about the person by asking nontask-related questions to decide if the other person can be trusted. Thus, this is another example of how the rational versus relational approach to relationships can affect business in the international arena or in a diverse workplace where people from many ethnic background are present. This is the best response.

Skill Concepts: A Theory of Relationship

Reviewing both theoretical and empirical studies, Triandis (1995) proposed that the cultural syndromes of individualism and collectivism have four universal defining attributes: independent versus interdependent definitions of the self (Markus & Kitayama, 1991), goals independent from those of the in-groups versus goals compatible with those of the in-groups (Triandis, 1990; Schwartz, 1990), emphasis on attitude versus norms (Bontempo & Rivero, 1992), and emphasis on rationality versus relatedness (Clark & Mills, 1979; Kim, 1994). The fourth defining attribute deals with how people in different cultures manage relationships and could be called a universal theory of relationships.

Clark and Mills (1979) discussed the difference between exchange and communal relationships. In an exchange relationship, people give something (e.g., a gift or a service) to another person with the expectation that the other person will return a gift or service of equal value in the near future. The characteristics of this type of relationship is "equal value" and "short time frame." People keep a mental record of exchange of benefits and try to maintain a balanced account, in an accounting sense. In a communal relationship, people do not keep an account of the exchanges taking place between them; one person may give a gift of much higher value than the other person and the two people may still maintain their relationship. In other words, in communal relationships it is the relationship that is valued and not the exchanges that go on between people. Mills and Clark (1982) suggest that in this type of relationship, people feel an "equality of affect" (i.e., when one feels up the other also feels up, and when one feels down the other also feels down). This is similar to the sense of common fate (e.g., parents working hard for the success of their children, who in turn will help them in their old age) found among collectivists that Triandis, McCusker, and Hui (1990) described.

According to Triandis (1995), individualists pick and choose their relationships based on the exchange principle. Relationships are characterized by short-term duration, equal exchange, and rationality (i.e., if a relationship is not cost-effective, it is promptly dropped). People continually move from one social organization to another, change work organizations, get divorced, and so forth in pursuit of their individual happiness or satisfaction. Affluence, high degree of mobility, and an independent concept of self facilitates the exchange principle. This characterization is similar to what Fiske (1992) has identified as a fundamental *socialite,* that is, market pricing. A lunch is worth x dollars, a ride to the workplace is worth y dollars, a birthday gift is worth z dollars, and so forth. Most of the activities have a market price, and therefore it is possible to achieve equality in exchange. Thus, the social and cultural milieu promotes the exchange principle in an individualistic culture.

Contrary to this, collectivists are relational (Triandis, 1995), and relationships are characterized by long-term duration (our grandfathers were friends, so we are friends), unequal exchange (you help me in harvesting, I will help you during your daughter's wedding; or to use an example in the more familiar Western context, you provided me a ride, I will buy you a lunch), and nonrationality (i.e., even if a relationship is not cost-effective, it is maintained). In collectivist cultures, people are born in communities where they have close ties with each other, mobility (geographic or organizational) is low, divorce is avoided even if marriages are not working out, and people do what they are expected to do, that is, people carry a lot of what Hsu (1971) has called "social baggage." Collectivists' preference for kinship types of relationships is what researchers (Clark & Mills, 1979) have described as communal relationships in which people seek equality of affect rather than exchange. This is similar to what Fiske (1992) has identified as communal sharing, another fundamental socialite. A more detailed analysis of the four defining attributes of individualism and collectivism and their implications for management practices can be found elsewhere (Triandis & Bhawuk, in press).

The question is, on the continuum of exchange and communality, where do business relationships fall? Are business relationships rational or relational? There are two reasons for business relationships to appear short-term in orientation and based on an exchange principle. First, the United States is an individualistic culture (Bellah, Madsen, Sullivan, Swindler, & Tipton, 1985; Hofstede, 1980; Hsu, 1971; Triandis et al., 1986; Triandis et al., 1990), and rationality, market exchange, and short-term orientation characterize this cultural syndrome. Second, the dominant organizational paradigm views organizations and the activities therein as rational. In other words, both the macro- (i.e., national) and the micro- (i.e., organizational) cultures apparently value rationality, short-term orientation, and equality of exchange in relationships.

However, it is not possible to have an exchange relationship between a superior and a subordinate because there is more than "you pay for my time" involved in a workplace. This is especially the case for the managerial cadre, because managers are evaluated for the results they produce rather than the time and effort they put in on the job. A promotion cannot be earned by delivering a quantifiable amount of service, simply because it is not possible to establish a perfect exchange between the two. Similarly, a transfer to a different location or the opportunity to participate in an advanced management program cannot be quantified. There are numerous other organizational behaviors that fall in the nonquantifiable region, making an exchange relationship between managers and subordinates extremely difficult, if not altogether impossible.

Organizational relationships are also not typically short-term ones. In the United States, people do move from one organization to another, but it is not a success strategy to move too soon. Therefore, managers do spend at least 5 to 7 years in an organization and develop networks and cliques. Furthermore, some organizational cultures are very supportive of long-term employee-organization attachments, and value long tenure. J. C. Penney, for example, places a premium on its employees, attempting at all costs to avoid layoffs. As a result, the average tenure of managers at J. C. Penney is 30 years. If relationships are not short-term (typical short-term relationships would include one in a grocery store, with a car dealer, or a waitress in a restaurant, and so forth), then the exchange type of relationship does not work or is not effective. In fact, a case could be made that the lack of long-term perspective between managers is indeed the cause of many problems in superior-subordinate dyads in present U. S. organizations.

Relationship Between Superior and Subordinate

Baird and Kram (1983) described superior-subordinate relationships as "exchange relationships," in which the nature of exchange depends on the phases of the managers' career, those phases being establishment, advancement, maintenance, and withdrawal. Their heuristic of "career dynamics" is reasonably deterministic, and subordinates are not left with much choice but to pray for a good "fit" with regard to their superiors' career phase (i.e., if the subordinate is in the establishment phase, the boss should be in the advancement or maintenance phase; if the subordinate is in the advancement phase, the boss should be in the maintenance phase; etc.).

Baird and Kram (1983) exhort subordinates to "understand the constraints" on the superior. This is a critical aspect of a superior-subordinate relationship that is compounded by increased span of control, or the presence of many subordinates reporting to a superior and the inherent competition among subordinates for resources. Subordinates are better off developing a long-term relationship with their boss based on unequal exchange.

Leach and Murray (1979) analyzed the superior-subordinate relationship and suggested that it is a "contract." They contended that people change jobs in search of a better fit with their superiors. They viewed the career contract as an implicit, dynamic relationship and suggested that the subordinate moves on when the contract is broken. They alluded to the value of a long-term relationship in suggesting that the superior must be a relationship-oriented person, a person who is willing to sponsor his or her subordinate, and a perfect mentor or role model for the subordinate. However, they, too, tended to describe the superior-subordinate relationship as contractual, short-term in nature, and exchange-based.

Graen's Theory of Leadership

Graen and colleagues (Graen, 1969; Graen, 1976; Graen, Novak, & Sommerkamp, 1982; Graen & Schiemann, 1978; Graen & Uhl-Bien, 1991; Graen & Wakabayashi, 1994) present a theory of leadership by examining the superior-subordinate dyads in organizations in a number of longitudinal studies. They found that managers are able to influence their subordinates to produce beyond formal organizational expectations by developing "mature leader relationships," which are characterized by extracontractual behavior, mutual trust, respect, liking, and superordinate goals. On the other hand, those managers who do not develop mature leader relationships often indulge in formal, contractual, and mostly downward (unidirectional) influence processes. Mature leader relationships, evidently, are developed over a long term and resemble the communal relationship, whereas "immature" leader relationships are short-term and focus on exchange relationships. The communal relationship is to be preferred over the exchange relationship in the workplace because it has organizationally beneficial long-term consequences. First, the exchange relationship may satisfy short-range needs and lend temporary satisfaction, but the communal relationship will instill a long-term, sustained sense of commitment. Second, whereas the exchange relationship may obtain the desired behaviors from subordinates through contingency-driven behavioral compliance (i.e., external control), the communal relationship promotes an internalization of values and goals by the subordinate, thus resulting in desirable behaviors being exhibited through self-control.

Graen and Wakabayashi (1994) found in their studies of Japanese transplants in the U. S. that there are a number of problems faced by both Japanese and American managers due to the differences in their leadership styles. For example, Japanese managers are shocked by American managers' underdeveloped sense of obligation to their coworkers and company. Japanese managers were surprised to find the absenteeism rate to be identical among both American managers and workers during a deer hunting season; they expected the managers to be more committed to the work than the workers. This lack of commitment is attributed to the individualists' exchange-relationship perspective of the job.

Another interesting difference Graen and Wakabayashi (1994) found involves American managers' difficulty dealing with the absence of punishment for insubordination in the Japanese transplants. According to the Japanese philosophy, the managers and workers invest in their mutual relationships and build mutual obligations over a number of years, usually a lifetime, of work contact. This mutual obligation completely rules out the possibility of insubordination. In effect, if workers are resisting a manager's decision, the manager may have committed a mistake and is better off discussing the problem with the workers than imposing disciplinary sanctions. Again, the difference lies in the Japanese, and in general the collectivist, approach to relationship building, versus the American, or in general the individualistic, approach to short-term exchange relationships in the workplace.

Graen and Uhl-Bien (1991) present other striking similarities between the rational-relational approach to relationship building and leadership making. For example, mature leadership is characterized by an in-kind type of reciprocity, an indefinite time span of reciprocity, and high leader-member exchange, whereas early leadership dyads focus on "cash and carry" reciprocity, an immediate time span of reciprocity, and low leader-member exchange. Therefore, it is clear that a relational approach to leadership is likely to be more effective than a rational one.

There is evidence that some effective managers do look at business relationships as long-term and relational. Consider the recent case of the advertising agency Ogilvy & Mather's acquisition of the IBM account. The strategy adopted is characterized by an orientation toward long-term relationships that is exemplified in statements such as "It would be a shame, just because they switch jobs, not to keep in touch with them," or "If some who are clients left their jobs tomorrow and went to some company that had no advertising potential, that doesn't mean I would not stay in touch" (Bird, 1994, p. 7). Managers could, it can be argued, be following the relational or the communal approach to relationship building. The success of the relational approach, it was argued in this case, is due to the nature of the advertising business (e.g., "Advertising is a relationship business" and "Winning the trust of client executives is necessary . . . because advertising is hardly a science, and investing in a new campaign is always somewhat risky for clients," Bird, 1994, p. 7). The relational approach, it is proposed here, may be useful in the workplace in general, and executives need to pay special attention to this.

At the CEO level, Herb Kelleher of Southwest Airlines appears to follow the relational approach to leadership. La Barre (1996) reported that Kelleher even remembers the names of his 20,000 employees, though he may forget where he parked his car. He treats every worker at Southwest as part of a family, and workers describe him as a humanitarian who can be honest about financial matters without being harsh or negative (Quick, 1992). He visits his sick employees, even the ones at the very bottom of the company (Jaffe, 1991). His relational leadership approach crystallizes in the statement, "You have to be with your employees through all their difficulties, that you have to be interested in them personally" (Labich, 1994).

Most researchers, with the exception of Graen and colleagues, have assumed work relationships to be contractual, rational, and characterized by exchange, thereby neglecting the relational approach to leadership. In the context of an increasingly diverse workforce, the relational leadership style has important implications. First, many ethnic minorities, such as Asian Americans and Hispanics, are collectivist

(Bhawuk & Triandis, 1996) and, in general, prefer communal relationships over exchange relationships. Therefore, managers should be sensitive to these different approaches to relationship management. Second, there is some evidence that women are more relational than men (Triandis et al., 1995) and that women's leadership styles are relational rather than hierarchical and authoritarian (Helgesen, 1990). Therefore, it is important for managers to be sensitive to different styles of relationship management. In any case, it will not be wise for managers to use the rational, market-exchange approach to relationship management at all times. Therefore, a new approach to leadership, Value Added Relationship Management, fundamentally relational in nature and consistent with the leadership theory advanced by Graen and colleagues, is proposed.

Value Added Relationship Management

Value Added Relationship Management (VARM) is an approach to consciously managing one's organizational relationships. VARM is a philosophical position, a state of mind, or an attitude that successful managers and public leaders show toward their relationship with people; it is a skill that can be acquired or cultivated. The characteristics of VARM are described in the following pages.

Long-Term Perspective

VARM requires a long-term perspective; one must understand that relationships are built over years and nothing can be achieved in a day or two. For example, a supervisor observes subordinates over an extended period of time before making any global judgment about them. In the university setting, a professor evaluates research assistants (PhD students) over an extended period of time to judge their abilities, and their work relationship is founded on this extended evaluation.

Short-term relationships are managed by evaluating what one gains from versus what one has to contribute to the relationship. Taking a long-term perspective allows one to look at a relationship as an investment that is likely to bear fruit, but only over a long time. When there is an implicit assumption that the relationship may not bring any immediate gain to a person, it cannot be termed insincere. Thus, the long-term view of a relationship makes it ethical to indulge in managing relationships that could otherwise be considered questionable. Also, because managers spend almost 50% of their time on networking and politicking (Luthans, Hodgetts, & Rosenkrantz, 1988), if they follow a long-term approach they are likely to get more return on investment in their networks than otherwise.

An aspect of the long-term approach is building trust. Often there is a possibility of misunderstanding, and one's behavior may be erroneously considered insincere. But if the approach is to build a relationship over the years, people can always clarify and, if necessary, apologize for their behavior if a superior considers that behavior to be insincere. There is always some slack or flexibility in relationships, and most lasting long-term relationships go through ups and downs.

Practical Tips:

1. Identify which relationships are short-term and which are long-term.
2. Focus on the long-term relationships by investing time and resources in them.

3. Because long-term relationships demand a lot of time and attention, do not have too many of them.
4. Keep old relationships warm and current by occasional communications. For example, a twice-a-year communication between people who are not working closely is an acceptable level of communication to keep the relationship going in the long run.

The Bank Account Approach

A relationship should be looked on as a bank account. What people can draw from their bank account is limited to what they have deposited. Similarly, one can ask for favors from superiors or friends only to the extent one has obligated them. In the same way that people cannot write a check for an amount that is more than the available balance in the account, they cannot request a person to do things for them too often without standing the risk of facing refusal. The simple principle of managing one's bank account is that one should keep depositing to the account so that one can write a check when needed.

This approach sounds very rational or exchange-oriented. However, that is not the intent. When two people are in a communal relationship, the exchanges that take place between them are neither of equal value nor taking place over a short period of time, but on the whole (i.e., in a global perspective of the relationship) both of them must feel that the relationship has not been exploitative or characterized by extremely uneven exchange. Even among collectivists, the prototypical relational people, relationships get strained from overuse. For example, a son may find his parents' demands unreasonable on his financial resources; a daughter-in-law may find her in-laws' expectations of her (e.g., to do all the household chores and also to work 10 hours at the workplace) physically and emotionally excruciating; a father may find his adult children's social company disrespectable and thus objectionable; a high-ranking official may find relatives asking for too many favors, making it difficult to function effectively in the workplace; and so forth. These are examples of overdrawing from the relationship account, which often leads to strained and damaged relationships accompanied by psychological stress.

Graen and colleagues (Graen & Scandura, 1987; Graen & Wakabayashi, 1994) use the term *psychological account* to describe the investments and withdrawals made by leaders and followers in each other. They proposed that the account is a socioemotional relationship and the transaction is measured in psychological, not material, units. Their description of the relationship account closely characterizes the communal relationship discussed earlier. The question is: How can one deposit in a relationship account or invest in a relationship?

Usually, in a work relationship, superiors have more resources under their control than subordinates. The way a subordinate can add value to the relationship is by being dependable. Every organization goes through crises, and that is the time when a superior needs the help of a subordinate the most. Subordinates should look at these situations as opportunities to invest in their relationship. Their investment may require working extra hours, doing tasks not included in their job description, doing things at odd hours, and so forth.

Another way to add value is to find out what the superior's other needs or interests are and try to be of help. This may appear to be insincere but it is more like adding lubrication to a bearing to make it run smoothly. Subordinates could bring an appropriate souvenir from a trip to a foreign country (a bottle of wine is a souvenir; a Rolex watch is not). Subordinates could also share information that they have access to that may help their superior in some way. In the university setting, if students come across an interesting paper during their library research that they know is in their professor's area of interest, it does not hurt them to make a copy for their professor; it shows that the students care. The key issues here are perspective, interpretation, and attribution. In a short-term exchange relationship, such efforts could be construed as manipulative. However, in a long-term communal relationship where the focus is not on "me" or "you," but on "us," these efforts are viewed as benefiting "us" (i.e., the relationship).

The idea is to use one's resourcefulness to make the relationship rich. Because superiors have more organizational resources at their command, subordinates face the challenge of finding out both formal and informal, and professional and personal, avenues to add value to the relationship. Taking stock from time to time helps one discover how much one has taken from a relationship and how much one has added to the relationship, thus avoiding overdrawing. Too much of a short-term, "me" versus "you" approach can "bankrupt" relationships.

Practical Tips:

1. Take a moment to think about how you have added value to your relationships.
2. If you have received much from a relationship, it is time to start giving.
3. A refusal may be an early symptom of a "bounced check." Evaluate the relationship.

Beyond the Organizational Role

VARM requires subordinates to look for ways to contribute beyond their organizational roles, and in large organizations this can increase their value and indispensability. Volunteers are always needed to organize social events, and this provides an opportunity to interact informally with many people. For example, I helped the publicity department start *Aakash Bhairab,* the house journal for Royal Nepal Airlines, and served as its managing editor in addition to my organizational role as training manager. This allowed me to network with managers of all departments and with the CEO, which on many occasions facilitated my function as training manager. In general, any assignment for which one does not receive direct remuneration provides opportunities to enrich one's network, which can eventually be used to invest in one's relationship with a supervisor.

Informal situations provide other avenues to go beyond one's organizational roles. In a formal situation, one cannot share one's hidden talents with a superior, but in an informal situation, one can. Informal interaction also allows one to discover superiors' interests and hobbies. One cannot get close to a superior by playing tennis if the superior loves to play golf. There is nothing wrong in cultivating new interests or hobbies, if one can. But if one cannot, the information still can be used effectively. For example, to start a business discussion with informal talk is customary, and one can talk about what interests a superior, say, the forthcoming big golf event. Such efforts are perhaps more symbolic than substantive because they demonstrate caring and concern for the relationship.

Others (Jennings, 1971) have also recommended developing skills and expertise that are crucial to one's superior's success as a "route to the executive suite." Managers should develop other skills that are not directly related to their work or organizational roles but that facilitate their interaction with their superiors to add value to the manager-subordinate relationship. There are instances of superior-subordinate "teams" that move in tandem up the organizational hierarchy to successful careers (for example, Gerstner and Kohnstamm moved from American Express to IBM).

Practical Tips:

1. Look for opportunities beyond your prescribed organizational role to add value to your relationships.
2. Use informal situations to nurture your relationships rather than to extend your "superficial" network.

Predisposition to Relationship Management

There exists an asymmetry in power and resources between a manager and a subordinate. Subordinates have to manage superiors and hence they must take the initiative in cultivating the relationship. Therefore, to effectively add value to a manager-subordinate relationship, a positive attitude or a predisposition to relationship management is required. An attitude of "I don't care what he or she likes" is a definite hindrance to VARM. This is consistent with Brislin's (1991) suggestion that interest in managing power is a precondition to success in organizations. I believe it is this callousness on the part of efficient subordinates that allows the less efficient ones to succeed in gaining the grace of the superiors.

Practical Tips:

1. Are you inclined to say "I don't care"? If yes, you need to change your attitude to be able to develop long-term relationships.
2. Do you think that work and work alone should be your focus? If yes, you need to be more sensitive to the relational concepts of tasks.
3. Do you think that the politicians are ruining your organization? If yes, you need to focus a bit more on the functional aspects of politics in organization (See Brislin, 1991; Brislin, 1994).

Rationalizing "Insult"

This is one of the "hard-to-practice" strategies but a definite characteristic of VARM. There always is an occasion when a peer gets that coveted trip, training, or promotion and one is inclined to lose composure. However, the subordinate is better off accepting the situation and working at the relationship with the superior with a positive attitude. Even a put-down by a superior has to be taken as a bitter pill, a suggestion for improvement.

If one feels insulted because of a superior's behavior, it is important to clear it up rather than to simply consider the relationship to be over, or worse, to let the incident fester inside until such resentment builds that it destroys the relationship. The subordinate has more to lose and, therefore, must rationalize "insult." Mastery of relationship management requires a continuous rationalization of negative feedback, put-downs, and criticism offered by the superior, beyond what would normally be expected as good citizenship behavior. In other words, subordinates need to develop emotional muscle to handle their supervisors' negative behaviors. The following brief incident illustrates these notions.

> The CEO of a government-owned company in Nepal apparently did not like one of his subordinates. To punish this subordinate, he assigned him to the morning shift and denied him office transportation on some pretext, causing the poor fellow to leave home at four in the morning to start his work at six.
>
> This fellow took the transfer in his stride. He did it for months without ever complaining, and when the CEO asked him how he was finding his new assignment, the subordinate gracefully thanked him and expressed his joy at enjoying his morning walk. He told the CEO that his health had improved in just a few months, and that much to his own surprise, he loved being a morning person. The CEO was as peeved as the subordinate was cheerful.
>
> The subordinate was immediately transferred to the late night shift. This allowed the subordinate to use the day for many things he always wanted but had never found the time to do. He was cheerful as ever when reporting his feelings about his job to the CEO. This earned him a transfer to a difficult location outside the city, and finally to a city away from home.
>
> The subordinate was not discouraged and stuck it out. He never complained about these arbitrary transfers. He always expressed his gratitude to the CEO and his desire to carry out any assignment that the CEO thought fit for him.
>
> Finally, the CEO gave in. He even took a liking to this subordinate and brought him into his own office as a special assistant. The glaring arbitrariness of the CEO's behavior may appear appalling and characteristic of the developing world. However, when we come to think of it, we find that such arbitrariness is not uncommon in the United States either (the firing of Lee Iacocca by Ford is a well-known example of such arbitrariness).
>
> The moral of this incident, and a tip for practice, is, *Rationalize "insult."* In the long run, it will pay off.

In Conclusion

VARM provides a way to build a relational or communal work relationship. In following this approach, people invest in a relationship over a long period of time rather than looking for quick gain, and take care that they do not overuse the relationship. The strategies needed to adopt VARM are to think about the long term, exploit the relationship sparingly but constructively, look for roles beyond one's organizational roles, develop a predisposition to relationship management, and develop emotional muscle to rationalize the supervisor's negative behaviors.

Leadership is an interpersonal influence process and peoples' useful networks are made up of others with whom they have significant interdependent relationships (Graen, 1990). Research on social relationships shows that relationships can be categorized as exchange or communal. There is evidence in the literature that individualists are more inclined to have exchange relationships, whereas collectivists prefer communal relationships. Based on the theory of individualism and collectivism, diagnostic tests, cases, and strategies for developing relational leadership skills were presented. The value added relationship management approach will provide, it is hoped, a middle path for both individualists and collectivists.

References

Baird, L., & Kram, K. (1983). Career dynamics: Managing the superior/subordinate relationship. *Organizational Dynamics, 11,* 46-64.

Bellah, R. N., Madsen, R., Sullivan, W. M., Swindler, A., & Tipton, S. M. (1985). *Habits of the heart: Individualism and commitment in American life.* Berkeley: University of California Press.

Bhawuk, D. P. S., & Triandis, H. C. (1996). Diversity in work place: Emerging corporate strategies. In G. R. Ferris & M. R. Buckley (Eds.), *Human resource management: Perspectives, context, functions, and outcomes* (3rd ed.) (pp. 84-96). Englewood Cliffs, NJ: Prentice-Hall.

Bird, L. (1994, May 26). Lazarus's IBM coup was all about relationships: A longtime bond formed by executive drew IBM to Ogilvy. *The Wall Street Journal,* pp. B1, B7.

Bontempo, R., & Rivero, J. C. (1992). *Cultural variation in cognition: The role of self-concept in the attitude behavior link.* Paper presented at the meetings of the American Management Association, Las Vegas, Nevada.

Brislin, R. W. (1991). *The art of getting things done: A practical guide to the use of power.* New York: Praeger.

Brislin, R. W. (1994). Working cooperatively with people from different cultures. In R. W. Brislin & T. Yoshida (Eds.), *Improving intercultural interaction: Modules for cross-cultural training programs* (pp. 17-33). Thousand Oaks, CA: Sage.

Clark, M. S., & Mills, J. (1979). Interpersonal attraction in exchange and communal relationships. *Journal of Personality and Social Psychology, 37,* 12-24.

Fiske, A. P. (1992). The four elementary forms of sociality: Framework for a unified theory of social relations. *Psychological Review, 99,* 689-723.

Graen, G. B. (1969). Instrumentality theory of work motivation: Some experimental results and suggested modifications. *Journal of Applied Psychology, 53,* 1-25.

Graen, G. B. (1976). Role making processes within complex organizations. In M. M. Dunnette, (Ed.), *Handbook of industrial and organizational psychology* (pp. 1201-1245). Chicago: Rand McNally.

Graen, G. B. (1990). Designing productive leadership systems to improve both work motivation and organizational effectiveness. In E. Fleishman (Ed.), *International work motivation* (pp. 200-233). Hillsdale, NJ: Lawrence Erlbaum.

Graen, G. B., Novak, M., & Sommerkamp, P. (1982). The effects of leader-member exchange and job design on productivity and satisfaction: Testing a dual attachment model. *Organizational Behavior and Human Performance, 30,* 109-131.

Graen, G. B., & Scandura, T. (1987). Toward a psychology of dyadic organizing. In B. Staw & L. L. Cumming (Eds.), *Research in organizational behavior, Vol. 9* (pp. 175-208). Greenwich, CT: JAI.

Graen, G. B., & Schiemann, W. (1978). Leader-member agreement: A vertical dyad linkage approach. *Journal of Applied Psychology, 63,* 206-212.

Graen, G. B., & Uhl-Bien, M. (1991). The transformation of professionals into self-managing and partially self-designing contributors: Toward a theory of leadership making. *Journal of Management Systems, 3*(3), 33-48.

Graen, G. B., & Wakabayashi, M. (1994). Cross-cultural leadership making: Bridging American and Japanese diversity for team advantage. In H. C. Triandis, M. D. Dunnette, & L. M. Hough (Eds.), *Handbook of industrial and organizational psychology, Vol. 4* (2nd ed.) (pp. 769-827). Palo Alto, CA: Consulting Psychologists Press.

Griffith, S. B. (1963). *Sun Tzu: The art of war.* New York: Oxford University Press.

Helgesen, S. (1990). *The female advantage: Women's ways of leadership.* New York: Doubleday.

Hofstede, G. (1980). *Culture's consequence.* Beverly Hills, CA: Sage.

Hsu, F. L. K. (1971). *The challenge of the American dream: The Chinese in the United States.* Belmont, CA: Wadsworth.

Jaffe, C. A. (October, 1991). Moving fast by standing still. *Nation's Business,* pp. 57-59.

Jennings, E. E. (1971). *Routes to the executive suite.* New York: Macmillan.

Kim, U. (1994). Individualism and collectivism: Conceptual clarification and elaboration. In U. Kim, H. C. Triandis, C. Kagitcibasi, S. Choi, & G. Yoon (Eds.), *Individualism and collectivism: Theory, method, and applications* (pp. 19-40). Thousand Oaks, CA: Sage.

LaBarre, P. (February 5, 1996). Lighten up! *Industry Week,* pp. 53-54.

Labich, K. (1994, May 2). Is Herb Kelleher America's best CEO? *Fortune,* pp. 45-52.

Leach, J. J., & Murray, W. A. (1979, October). The career contract: Quid pro quo between you and your boss. *Management Review,* pp. 20-28, 51-52.

Luthans, F., Hodgetts, R. M., & Rosenkrantz, S. A. (1988). *Real managers.* Cambridge, MA: Bollinger.

Markus, H. R., & Kitayama, S. (1991). Culture and the self: Implications for cognition, emotion, and motivation. *Psychological Review, 98,* 224-253.

Mills, J., & Clark, M. S. (1982). Exchange and communal relationships. In L. Wheeler (Ed.), *Review of personality and social psychology, Vol. 3* (pp. 121-144). Beverly Hills, CA: Sage.

Quick, J. C. (1992). Crafting an organizational culture: Herb's hand at Southwest Airlines. *Organizational Dynamics, 21,* 45-57.

Schwartz, S. H. (1990). Individualism-collectivism: Critique and proposed refinements. *Journal of Cross-Cultural Psychology, 21,* 139-157.

Triandis, H. C. (1990). Cross-cultural studies of individualism and collectivism. In J. Berman (Ed.), *Nebraska symposium on motivation, 1989* (pp. 41-133). Lincoln: University of Nebraska Press.

Triandis, H. C. (1995). *Individualism and collectivism.* Boulder, CO: Westview.

Triandis, H. C., & Bhawuk, D. P. S. (in press). Culture theory and the meaning of relatedness. In P. C. Earley & M. Erez (Eds.), *New perspectives on international industrial/organizational psychology.* New York, NY: Jossey-Bass.

Triandis, H. C., Bontempo, R., Betancourt, H., Bond, M., Leung, K., Brenes, A., Georgas, J., Hui, C. H., Marin, G., Setiadi, B., Sinha, J. B. P., Verma, J., Spangenberg, J., Touzard, H., & de Montomollin, G. (1986). The measurement of etic aspects of individualism and collectivism across cultures. *Australian Journal of Psychology, 38,* 257-267.

Triandis, H. C., Chan, D., Bhawuk, D. P. S., Iwao, S., & Sinha, J. B. P. (1995). Multi-method probes of allocentrism and idiocentrism. *International Journal of Psychology, 30*(4), 461-480.

Triandis, H. C., McCusker, C., & Hui, C. H. (1990). Multimethod probes of individualism and collectivism. *Journal of Personality and Social Psychology, 59,* 1006-1020.

4

Everyday Work Experiences
of People Designated as Diverse

A FOCUS ON STRATEGIES

Jan Fried

Izumi Matsumoto

> The Taoists claimed that the comedy of life could be made more interesting if everyone would preserve the unities. To keep the proportion of things and give place to others without losing one's own position was the secret of success in the mundane drama. We must know the whole play in order to properly act our parts; the conception of totality must never be lost in that of the individual.
>
> Kakuzo Okakura, *The Book of Tea*

In today's global economy, the workplace is going through a shift in traditional thinking while experiencing an increasingly diverse workforce. At the same time, people are faced with the task of integrating new technologies and needing to be more productive. What do diverse individuals face in the workplace today when they are diverse day in and day out? This module expands the definition of *the minority* or *the diverse* and focuses on the acquisition and use of effective strategies. Participants in the training are given the opportunity to expand their view of "being different," rethink training approaches, learn alternative coping strategies, and apply them in a work setting to examine their relative effectiveness.

The authors would like to thank Dr. Richard Brislin, Ms. Ann-Marie Horvath, and Ms. Noriko Kumoi, who were invaluable contributors to this module.

Contents

Self-Assessment Exercises:
Feeling Different: Advantages and Disadvantages

Respond to the following statements using the following scale. If the statement is contingent on a certain situation or exception, please note that condition. (For example: More diverse opinions and ideas can enhance the end result of a project if there is a time limit.)

5	4	3	2	1	D
strongly agree	agree	not sure	disagree	strongly disagree	it depends

_____ 1. More diverse opinions and ideas can enhance the end result of a project.

_____ 2. Everyone has felt different from other employees at one time or another.

_____ 3. There are times when being different is an advantage.

_____ 4. It is helpful to know specific information about other cultural groups to get a job done.

_____ 5. Working in a group means the members have everything in common.

_____ 6. The way things are done is determined by who holds power in the workplace.

_____ 7. Successful people in the workplace are those who use their diversity to their advantage.

_____ 8. Successful people in the workplace are those who follow the "mainstream."

_____ 9. Technology such as e-mail and the Internet can enhance the diverse individual's work.

_____ 10. To get along better, everyone's culture and rituals should be acknowledged by the company.

Debriefing Suggestions for Facilitators

The self-assessment exercise encourages participants to start thinking about relevant issues for the training that follows. The exercise includes workplace issues such as the dynamics of power holders, restraints to getting things done, the changing workplace and new technology, and the expanded definition of what is "diverse." Responses will depend on the background of the participants, perhaps with more responding "it depends" from those specific cross-cultural or work experiences. The debriefing sessions should include discussion of the preceding issues and draw out specific scenarios and strategies.

Critical Elements at Work: Potentially Prickly Situations

Context can never be ignored when defining strategies. The following is a collection of critical elements that can be used in assessing a job-related situation; the focus is on what brings people together and what separates them. Culture determines the values put on various behaviors at work (Hofstede, 1980) and the first step is to become aware of one's working environment. In cross-cultural training, awareness of the critical elements of a situation will allow the individual to gain more knowledge and then effectively use new strategies.

Importance/Mechanism of Power

This translates into the large hierarchy of an organization, its hidden structures, channels of communication, and its importance. This element is at the top of the list because awareness and effective behaviors using power can directly lead to successful strategies (Brislin, 1991). A small power distance culture (Hofstede, 1986) will downplay differences in status, whereas a large power distance culture will have more criteria with regard to receiving power and perceived distance in status. There is an assumption that those seen as having power decide how things are done. In addition to the obvious power structure, there are underlying structures and channels of which one must be aware. Secretaries often display their power by connecting us to the person we want to speak with in the office, taking our messages, and even making them a priority. They have the ultimate power to reserve a room for the meeting we want. Age, gender, and ethnic differences, connections and relations (e.g., being a member of a prominent family), and length of time at the organization all create a web of power structures that can affect this element.

Concepts of Time

Whether one has to be at a meeting on time or can arrive 10 minutes early or late is determined by culture. This unwritten rule can change depending on the kind of meeting, priority over another element (e.g., it is acceptable to be late if there was traffic), and the role of the individual to the group. These concepts can also affect the way people view the definition of certain time durations, such as whether 2 months is seen as a short term or long term. We must also include the time factor that determines its importance to events. A Japanese business manual states that to be most effective, it is best to call a business around 10 a.m., after the rush of urgent work in the morning and before lunch. In Hawaii, for example, arranging a meeting on a Friday after 4 p.m. is unwise unless it is a social meeting. Edward T. Hall and William Foote Whyte (1973) offer five dimensions of time as potential differences in a workplace: appointment time, discussion time, acquaintance time, visiting time, and time schedules.

Dress and Demeanor

How one looks and carries oneself is the most visually apparent of the elements. Some organizations have written guidelines on appropriate dress in the workplace. Others have unofficial criteria. Using Hofstede's "Four Dimensions Model of Cultural Differences" (Hofstede, 1986), cultures that fall into the strong uncertainty avoidance category will have more structured rules than those in the weak uncertainty avoidance category. Therefore, concepts of time, dress, and demeanor, and their degree of importance, will be greater for strong uncertainty avoidance cultures, requiring more awareness of these elements. In contrast, with the latest trends of technology, such as the Internet and an increased telecommuting workforce where one does not necessarily have face-to face-contact, the weight of these elements might be less important. This said, "the way we look" is still a large part of how others gain insights about us. With trends toward decentralization and a focus on teams and matrix organizations, there is an advantage in looking like a team player. In addition, how a person's image is perceived is often translated into values. An Asian woman may look young and as a consequence may not be given respect as a leader. Those who dress like students might not be taken seriously in the world of business.

Consequences and Rewards

This relates to the weight placed on doing or not doing something. When one does not get something done on time, what happens? Does it affect the group? Are rewards given as a recognition of the group's work or the individual's? What is the expectation when receiving such rewards? When we observe consequences within a working organization, we must bear in mind the short-term successes and the long-term effects. If recognition of an individual's accomplishments was made in a public forum, some workplace cultures might expect the awardee to reciprocate in kind to those coworkers who supported that successful project, to ensure future cooperation.

Language and Specific Jargon

There is much power in knowing the language, the tools to communicate. In the state of Hawaii, the ability to speak Japanese and English can be an advantage in the workplace, often superseding actual experience in a particular field. When one does not speak the language, knowing how to effectively use an interpreter becomes imperative. In addition to knowing the primary language, other factors, such as understanding specific jargon, vocal intonation, emotions, the role of physical contact, accents, and the use of silence, are also determining and important elements in the workplace. For example, no matter what a worker's competencies are at a given task, if his or her speech is perceived as being difficult to understand because of a strong accent, acceptance and progress on the job can be hampered.

Communication Styles and Channels

Sometimes written communication is more effective than verbal communication. At other times, leaving a message on someone's voice mail can be most effective. Knowing when to use which and with whom is valuable information. Using or not using humor can also be critical when conveying a message.

Technical and Mechanical Ability, Including Computer Literacy

Being able to make copies, send a fax, or design impressive bar graphs for reports using the computer are important aspects of today's workplace. These skills not only show workers to be "doers" but connect them to outside resources through e-mail, the Internet, faxes, and phones. Technology can also be the great equalizer (Pati and Bailey, 1995) for people with and without disabilities, where face-to-face interactions lose their relevance.

Work Ethic

How much the organization "owns" the individual varies from one organization to another. Japanese workers are often expected to work 6 or 7 days a week and well into the night until a project is completed. What we consider private time in the United States is expected to be sacrificed when going out with important colleagues. In Japan, it is common for businesses to send employees on company trips or long-term assignments without their spouses and families.

Food and Its Assigned Values

In many cultures, eating at the workplace is a crucial affair. We hear stories in which a negotiation fell through because an American businessman declined to eat something that was offered at a dinner function. Especially in a collective society (Hofstede, 1980), there is importance in eating the same things together. Sharing recipes and positive comments about a dish means approval and mutual respect. With individualistic societies (Hofstede, 1980), what one eats expresses one's view on health, the environment, and one's taste.

Education, Experience, Skills

One's kind and quantity of education, experience, and specialized skills affects the way things get done.

Culture-Specific Elements

Elements that are significant in some cultures will add many more items to this list. These elements might include how people with disabilities are regarded (e.g., there are not sufficient ramps and allowances made to overcome physical barriers for wheelchairs), gender restrictions (e.g., female workers are not allowed into certain work areas or to participate in certain job functions), gift giving, information on family, marital status, who is married to whom, whether the marriage is intercultural or interfaith, which part of town one is from, from what high school or university one graduated, if one commutes by train or car, and more.

Critical Elements to Strategies: Awareness of Successful Behaviors

Identifying the critical elements in a workplace is the first step in turning the situation to one's advantage. Because workplace culture can vary tremendously, the preceding critical elements can serve as a loose checklist leading to further examination. The ultimate strategy is to build a bridge over the cultural gap between the majority and the diverse individual. In addition, we must not forget that most often the goal in the workplace is for the employees, as a team, to perform together to attain a common goal of success. One does not have to agree or disagree about another's religious belief or sexual orientation to get a task done, but one does need to develop strategies that allow ideas and behaviors to be accepted in the process of working together. In fact, it may be more beneficial for organizations to foster a work environment that encourages their employees to become congenial coworkers rather than bosom buddies (Brislin, personal communication, 1996). Regardless, for diverse individuals, a workplace that is naturally different from their own culture can be stressful to work at on a daily basis.

Building Bridges as a Strategy

Kakuzo Okakura is the author of a magnificent book called *The Book of Tea*. Written in 1906, this book is widely regarded as significant in introducing the world of Japanese life and thought to the West. Okakura writes that he was successful in documenting the intricacies of this art with much eloquence because he was not a tea master. His strength was in knowing the languages, behavior, contacts, and supporters of both Japan (the East) and the West. He is seen as the pioneer in the cross-cultural bridge-building effort between East and West.

By observing successful diverse individuals such as Kakuzo Okakura, we see commonalities in their strategies, such as (a) understanding "how things work" for others, (b) broadening our knowledge of ourselves by revealing some of our own unconscious ideas and actions (Hall & Whyte, 1973), and (c) connecting the two to get the task done. Soon we find ourselves defining what is meant by *success*. For Kakuzo, living with the Western influences of the Meiji period, his founding a government art school and serving as curator of the Imperial Museum of Fine Arts while still in his 20s made him a success. To most of us, success means getting the work accomplished and ultimately, earning promotion or recognition. People of different cultures will define success in a variety of ways that will draw out more process-oriented strategies for this "success."

Case Study: Critical Incident and Debriefing Notes

What to Do?: The Company Christmas Party

_____

Last year's company Christmas party committee came up with the following agenda and group activities:

- Opening blessing/prayer
- Catered luncheon buffet
- Holiday Christmas carol quiz (Christmas song titles purposely obfuscated, e.g., "My sole desire for the Yuletide season is receipt of a pair of central incisors"; the original title of this carol is "All I want for Christmas is my two front teeth")

- "Eh, what dis song?" (Identifying Christmas carols translated into Hawaiian Pidgin. An example of this is, "Shuddap, you day goody-goody flyin' buggahs goin' jam!," which translates to, "Hark!, the herald angels sing")
- Chinese trivia game (An English phrase, e.g., "a very bashful man," would be matched with the pseudo-Chinese transliteration, "Sum shai gai")
- Gift exchange with a twist ("grab bag" gifts are passed to the right whenever the narrator/leader utters the word "right" during a story; "It was the woman's right to make a right turn, right away.")

Even though all the employees turned out for the party with the best intentions, not everyone in the company enjoyed the festivities. Some openly complained to management about feeling excluded, whereas others aired their feelings to each other. Your planning committee is charged with organizing this year's Christmas party, bearing in mind that your organization has an extremely diverse workforce, including people who are gay, straight, Jewish, Buddhist, Christian, deaf, recent arrivals from other states and countries (e.g., Vietnam and Malaysia), Caucasian, Japanese, Hawaiian, Chinese, Filipino, African American, and of mixed heritage.

You are to address these questions during your planning session:

- What kind of party activities will your group host?
- What is the company's role in party-planning, and what does it need to be mindful of?
- What could the "complainers" do to get ready for this year's bash? (suggestions and strategies)
- What do they and the other partygoers need to mindful of?

Debriefing Notes

Taken from an actual situation, this critical incident points to several issues that are at the heart of this chapter. With your participants, it may be beneficial to further discuss how diversity can be handled at the job site, "getting over it" or coping skills used by diverse individuals, different strategies companies can use in the face of potentially volatile cultural conflicts, and if and how everyone's celebrations can be observed or honored.

Skill Concepts: Challenges for the "Diverse" Individual, Where Diversity Takes a Wrong Turn, and Bosom Buddies Versus Congenial Coworkers

Some Challenges for the "Diverse" Individual in the Workplace

In light of the discussion generated from the critical incident, it is relevant to point out other challenges those who see themselves or are seen as different face on a regular basis at work. Several of these challenges may never be openly discussed with coworkers or management for fear of retaliation or misunderstanding, whereas others are aired immediately. The following list can either be added to or completely generated by the participants in your group, depending on their sophistication and experience with this issue.

- Reconciling that the corporate culture may be at odds with one's own culture (e.g., companies that value overt theatrical presentation styles)
- Working successfully when being the "only one" of a group. Often being chosen to be the "spokesperson" for that group
- The burden of being seen as a unique individual versus being seen as the representative and standard-bearer for one's culture or identity group
- Maintaining group loyalty while trying to adapt and succeed
- Understanding the difficulty in finding positive images at work
- Constantly being faced with being the one who needs to be flexible
- Compromising too much
- Dealing with hurt and guilt
- Losing oneself in and overidentifying with the majority culture. Becoming like the "other"
- Having access to resources (including the "rules to the game") and developing them. Finding appropriate mentors to aid in this process
- Dealing with "compassion fatigue" (Taylor, 1991). Coworkers' "well of guilt" may be running dry and they may be tired of being bullied into feeling kind, good, and sensitive to each other
- Being considered the "enemy" because change or diversity training is mandated from the top, apparently on your account
- Feeling as though one needs to develop a thick skin to survive in the workplace

Where Diversity Training Takes a Wrong Turn

Although most companies and their human resources officers often have the best intentions for training programs when faced with an increasingly diverse workforce, they typically fall prey to a variety of pitfalls. Little attention is given to these issues when training is developed, but it is becoming more apparent that they must be given as much consideration as the content of the training. Training must be useful, timely, and focused on how the company can continue to operate within an atmosphere of cooperation and mutual respect. Much can be said to support the notion that a more productive workplace is one where employees are "congenial coworkers" instead of being coerced into being "bosom buddies." Those exploring this module may decide to discuss several of the following items in large or small working groups, while adding their own observations.

1. *The emphasis is on the white male employee as the culprit who is in need of sensitizing.* This group becomes an easy target for blame and guilt-driven training. Any demographic change will affect everyone and therefore everyone will benefit from diversity-awareness training.

2. *Diversity-awareness programs are often guilt-driven (Karp & Sutton, 1993).* The danger of focusing too much on past injustices and inequities is that the entire experience turns into a competition involving whose group has been oppressed the most at the hands of those being trained. No one individual is personally culpable for a group's suffering. Most beneficial is to acknowledge each group's struggle with oppression and then move on to other aspects of the training that emphasize the present state of affairs, an organizational commitment to change, respect for individual

and collective differences, and the role that each employee plays in accepting responsibility toward these ends.

3. *The more training, the merrier.* The immediate remedy for change in the workplace is typically seen as quickly developing a plethora of sensitivity workshops. The rationale behind this is that once employees have enough information, positive attitudinal change will automatically occur and coworkers will be more aware of each other.

4. *The trainers are often organization "outsiders"—usually women or ethnic minorities.* Rigid adherence to this approach tends to ignore the group that is being trained. Even though it is important to have minority (and thus diverse) input, the crucial question to ask is, can the trainers relate either personally or through the training program to the people being trained and vice versa? Perhaps it may be more effective to have two-person teams, one trainer representing the minority viewpoint while the other reflects the participant group (Karp & Sutton, 1993).

5. *The training usually endorses specific values that are seen as the only ones to be adopted.* Most diversity programs directly or indirectly espouse a particular formulaic philosophy of correct and incorrect values, attitudes, and behaviors (Karp & Sutton, 1993). Anything that does not fit this prescribed manner is taken as aberrant and unacceptable. This approach does not do much to promote the healthy and constructive exchange of differing perspectives while acknowledging the group's diversity. The last thing diversity programs want to do is promote stereotypes and easy answers to a complex situation.

6. *Nothing else is dealt with except attitude adjustment.* Diversity training has the greatest effect when those who work together are trained together and the training is incorporated into all aspects of corporate interaction. Training that focuses on positive behavioral changes to rectify real and immediate challenges is more effective in the long run. When the emphasis is on performance, then there is no pressure to satisfy the needs of every identity group; it is no longer an issue of rectifying social injustices.

7. *How something is said is more important than what is said or intended.* Politically correct jargon can be overdone, overshadowing the real issue at hand. Correcting offensive language should only play a minor part in the overall training content. Perhaps the intention behind what is said needs to be examined, in addition to how it is perceived. This can easily be accomplished with a modicum of humor and an emphasis on understanding why a particular lexical choice is insulting.

8. *Training is "top down."* Often an organization is forced into diversity training and accommodating their employees' diversity by federal and state laws such as affirmative action and the Americans with Disabilities Act. Many people do not understand the full thrust or history of these laws, which only serves to compound feelings of coercion. If the desire to improve relations does not come from within, training can be met with considerable hostility. The challenge lies in defining the work situation at hand, integrating technology, developing supportive leadership, and establishing strategic partnerships in and outside the company (Pati & Bailey, 1995).

9. *Promising more than the company can deliver.* Situations may arise among the employees that require large-scale change and a radical shift in how work gets accomplished. To appease employee discontent or circumvent a potential crisis, an organization's management may be tempted to recommend a flurry of reforms long before they are fiscally able or have the necessary resources in place to guarantee

their success. Meaningful change occurs in stages and requires complete cooperation between, and input from, employees and management.

Bosom Buddies Versus Congenial Coworkers: Finding and Defining Strategies—Guidelines for Effective Diversity Training

As diversity training continues to surge into the forefront of topics presented to a corporation's employees and is seen as a "bottom-line" concern, several issues must be taken into consideration. The long-term effect of any training program needs to be carefully weighed and the desired outcomes strategically planned. Likewise, administrators and managers must be convinced that strong diversity-awareness programming is good business. A congenial workplace makes for more productive employees and more satisfied customers.

1. *Do not start training hastily, simply to jump on the diversity bandwagon.* Clearly define your company's goals and employees' needs. Systematic and sustainable changes must coincide with a carefully managed training program. Thoroughly examine your company's motivations for initiating this kind of training; is it strictly for the customer's sake or is it from a genuine desire to improve workplace interactions?

2. *Position diversity education and training in such a way that it becomes an organizational way of life, not a one-shot program.* Stand-alone programs can lack compatibility with the company's core education and do not do much to change the matter at hand. If change in employees' performance is the goal, then training must be supported by everyone. Several programs may be integrated to present a stronger, more consistent and effective training package.

3. *Differentiate between general awareness education and skills building/ training (Perkins Delatte & Baytos, 1993).* Incorporate both into your training by focusing on changing attitudes, creating a framework for understanding, and developing usable skills for the workplace. All are needed for long-lasting outcomes. Employees need to see that everyone profits when diversity works. Be aware that mandatory training can breed resistance.

4. *Conduct a thorough needs analysis, just as you would with any other training program or organizational development initiative.* Training can be costly when entered into without the appropriate preparation. What concerns does each cultural and ethnic group have? Take advantage of focus groups. Your corporation's demographics, needs, and objectives are likely to differ radically from another's.

5. *Position training as part of an overall strategy for managing diversity, not as an end in itself.* Training is not the only strategy for ridding a company of the status quo (Perkins Delatte & Baytos, 1993). Human resource practices must also be examined, bringing changes to the corporate culture. To this end, comprehensive managerial support for this as a critical business issue is paramount.

6. *Include diverse input into the design process to increase relevance.* Training is likely to be ineffective if designed by only one homogeneous group. Diverse opinions can often develop the most successful diversity programming. Do the proposed objectives and exercises really tackle the issues most germane to your organization? Does the training take into consideration your employees' communication and learning styles? Be careful to avoid "tokenism" when selecting training development committees.

7. *Use a mix of internal and external resources to enhance efficiency and credibility.* Many corporations are tempted to hire only consultants from outside the company. These trainers are often seen as possessing more expertise and credibility than those coming from within the company (Perkins Delatte & Baytos, 1993). If your internal resources are limited or insular, then it is beneficial to augment the training with external resources. The benefit of using both is that insiders are familiar with the company's makeup and may be more cost-effective, whereas outsiders can often provide a refreshing and yet-unexplored perspective.

8. *Test your program thoroughly before implementation to reduce risk and generate enthusiasm.* Developing a program that will promote change in people's attitudes without unduly upsetting or insulting them can be a very delicate process. Therefore, it is crucial that any new training be given one, if not a few, pilot runs before it is presented to the company at large. A variety of individuals with diverse backgrounds and who are given ample feedback time can be invited to participate in these pilot tests. A well-honed training module will lead to one that is well received by all individuals in the company. As a way of reaching corporate goals and dealing with a heterogeneous workforce, many organizations choose training. Diverse individuals, on the other hand, often opt for something more immediate and less formalized—coping strategies. These strategies are either ones workers have developed individually from necessity and have tailored to their specific workplace, or are strategies that they have observed others successfully using or that were passed along by others who found themselves in similar situations.

Coping Strategies—Yours

The challenge faced by the diverse individual is finding appropriate strategies for dealing with an organization's status quo and perhaps stagnant policies. Each strategy may have its own relative degree of success, depending on whether the individual chooses to make the adjustments internally or externally. The following are several options that can be discussed or implemented by employees during and after training.

1. *Know your rights.* Become familiar with the Americans with Disabilities Act, affirmative action policies, and any other relevant legislation.

2. *Know the personality types of your coworkers.* Be aware of others' communication styles and how they interact with each other during times of stress and relaxation. The more you know about the majority culture, the more strategies you can develop.

3. *Find a mentor or cultural informant.* This can happen formally and informally. Pay attention to casual "office talk." Seek advice about the "rules of the game" and complex corporate bureaucracies from those who are in the know, hold power, or have gone through similar experiences.

4. *Maintain a sense of humor.* Sometimes the situation may not be as grim or insurmountable as it seems.

5. *Continue to demonstrate your value to the company.* Take the initiative whenever possible and appropriate.

6. *Become proactive versus reactive.* Be flexible, objective, and willing to examine differing perspectives. Reach out and discuss your needs and concerns when appropriate. Whining and constantly complaining without offering reasonable solutions is often ignored. Separate yourself from groups and positions that are viewed negatively.

7. *Change your attitude and/or behavior.* This may simply take the form of clarifying your actions and the underlying reasons for your behavior.

8. *Be patient, "get over it," and rise above it.* Allow time for change to occur. Some requests are more reasonable and easily accommodated than others. Taking a moderate position is often more successful over time.

9. *Suffer in silence.* One can decide to do nothing about discriminatory policies and exclusive company practices, particularly if one is feeling consistently stonewalled. There may be several benefits to choosing this tactic, if individuals feel silence and inaction will behoove them in the long run.

10. *Look for a new job.* When all else fails, this may be the best and only option.

Coping Strategies—Theirs

There are changes that the organization can make to enhance productivity and personal interactions that are cost-effective, reasonable, and inclusive.

1. *Draft scenarios (case studies) from actual incidents that will promote discussion and show rational approaches for getting along.* Be proactive versus reactive.

2. *Establish working teams and partnerships that have clearly defined goals and tasks.*

3. *Get legal and executive backing for a plan.*

4. *Encourage mentorships between employees.*

5. *Work with a diverse group to establish "working together" job etiquette (Baridon & Eyler, 1994) that respects each other's rights.*

6. *Let the employees make the choice rather than have the decisions imposed on them.* Let employees deal with the consequences of *their* decisions.

7. *Listen to your employees; they will guide you to effective accommodations.*

8. *Be willing to entertain alternative solutions (e.g., "telecommuting," or job or schedule restructuring).*

9. *Focus on workers' aptitudes rather than their perceived limitations.*

10. *Remain flexible and resist pigeonholing employees.*

11. *Form strategic alliances with community groups for feedback and methods to address physical barriers and special needs.* Accommodations need not be burdensome or all-consuming; they can be considered and implemented case by case.

12. *Change your attitude and/or behavior.* This may simply take the form of clarifying your actions and the underlying reasons for your behavior.

13. *Become proactive versus reactive.* Be flexible, objective, and willing to examine differing perspectives. Reach out and voluntarily discuss your needs and concerns when appropriate. Whining and constantly complaining without offering reasonable solutions is often ignored. Separate yourself from groups and positions that are negatively viewed.

Skill Applications

The following is an exercise adapted from one developed by Mauney (1995). The overall purpose of the exercise is to establish a superordinate goal that all participants must achieve within imposed limitations and that supersedes the individual's own goals. The activity's secondary purpose is to encourage participants to uncover effective strategies, given the scope of the exercise, that can later be applied to real work situations. Two pertinent questions to bear in mind while conducting this activity and to be asked later during debriefing are: do preconceived notions about another's culture interfere with or enhance the task at hand? and, what are the most effective ways to complete the task in light of diversity? Part I presents the directions given to the participants, complete with the building materials list. Part II presents the "cultural" information the participants know about themselves and have supposedly learned about their coworkers during the 2-day workshop, as described in the following directions for the exercise. Part III contains considerations for facilitators and suggestions for the postactivity discussion.

I. Building Bridges

To improve its productivity and to become more sensitive to its increasingly diverse workforce, your company presented a 2-day workshop, "Cross-cultural Awareness & Diversity in the Workplace," for all employees. You attended and learned much about your colleagues' cultures.

This workshop came at a good time because your "diverse" work team has just been given the task of designing and building a bridge.

Your team's goal: To make a structurally sound and aesthetically pleasing bridge that can support a toy vehicle.

Materials List (suggested)

Styrofoam cups

Modeling clay (yellow, red, white, blue, purple, orange, green, pink)

Balloons (assorted colors)

Straws (assorted colors)

Wooden chopsticks

Plastic dinosaurs or other toys

Aluminum foil

Ribbon (assorted colors)

Metallic garland (gold and red)

Tissue paper (assorted colors)

Colored pens and crayons

Shredded paper/tinsel

Cotton puff balls

Wafer cookies

Sandwich cookies

Cheese puffs

Empty toilet-paper or paper-towel cardboard rolls

Birthday candles

Pipe cleaners (assorted colors)

How Materials Are Secured

- One to two people are designated as Materials Distributors
- All requests must be written on yellow paper and submitted by one person to the Materials Distributor
- No more than one request at a time
- You can submit a total of 12 items per written request
- Your team is limited to four separate written requests for materials
- The bridge must be 2 feet long, strong, and beautiful
- You must find a way to get the job done within the time allotted and despite your differing opinions
- Everyone in your group must participate
- Resources are limited

No oral communication is allowed once the design has been completed.

Group Incentives

If your team's design appropriately meets the design standards and criteria, it will be chosen by the company for immediate implementation. Accordingly, your design team will merit a group photo and commemorative plaque on the company's Wall of Achievement.

Individual Incentives

If your design element is included, you will be awarded an additional 2 days' vacation with pay and a letter of commendation in your personnel file. Good luck!

II. Instructions

This information should be given to the participants prior to their working group and bridge-building assignments. They have recently learned about their coworkers' various cultural identities. It is important that they have ample time to assimilate their newly acquired knowledge with members of their same cultural/color group. There are several strategies for randomly assigning people to their respective cultural and working groups. Dividing the months of the year into four units and dividing the participants according to their birth-month is a particularly successful strategy. Ideally, you should have at least 4 but not more than 10 people per working group.

Each person will receive a description of their color, cultural preferences, and the information learned about others. Once the participants have been given their cultural information, they will identify their color identity by pinning a swatch of corresponding colored paper to their clothing. Allow for at least an hour and a half to complete the activity and postactivity discussion. As the facilitator, you can set the time limits for each part of the activity according to the size and needs of your group.

You are a *Blue* person who wants shiny and bright decorative features on the bridge that will look fabulous during the day and evening. You do not favor organic building materials but will tolerate them if necessary.

You learned that people who are

Green are used to getting their way in most situations and are very efficient decision-makers. Although hard workers, people from this culture are often seen as clannish.

Purple are procedure-oriented and reluctant to make their personal opinions known to the group. They are gregarious and quite creative.

Orange tend to get easily sidetracked and end up talking about other things. They feel strongly about the color orange and prefer that hue over all others. They are quite friendly yet can appear a bit constrained.

You are a *Green* person who wants a wide, several-lane bridge to accommodate large vehicles and heavy traffic. Strength is more important than beauty. You never work with scissors because you prefer to work unencumbered by any implements.
You learned that people who are

Blue are interested in consensus. They will work to make their opinions known so the group can be informed and truly come to a complete agreement.

Purple are procedure-oriented and prefer not to make their personal opinions known to the group. They are gregarious and hard workers.

Orange tend to get easily sidetracked and end up talking about other things. They feel strongly about the color orange and prefer that hue over all others. They are quite friendly.

You are a *Purple* person who wants a bridge supported by arches that uses various types of textures and building materials. You are willing to consider innovative materials, particularly organic components, to get the job done. You only use purple paper or pens to communicate with others.
You have learned that people who are

Green are used to getting their way in most situations and are very efficient decision makers. People from their culture are often seen as clannish.

Orange tend to get easily sidetracked and end up talking about other things. They feel strongly about the color orange and prefer that hue over all others. They are quite friendly.

Blue are interested in consensus. They will work to make their opinions known so the group can be informed and truly come to a complete agreement.

You are an *Orange* person who wants a colorful bridge design with liberal doses of orange and a minimal amount of materials. You feel food is only for eating and using it for other purposes is disrespectful.
You have learned that people who are

Purple are procedure-oriented and prefer not to make their personal opinions known to the group. They are gregarious and hard workers.

Green are used to getting their way in most situations and are very efficient decision makers. People from their culture are often seen as clannish.

Blue are interested in consensus. They will work to make their opinions known so the group can be informed and truly come to a complete agreement.

III. Debriefing Notes

Although quite enjoyable and interactive for its participants, an exercise of this nature is also extremely thought-provoking. Therefore, it is important that a thorough debriefing follow the activity. This activity was designed to encourage the players to examine the efficacy of diversity-awareness training practices, negotiation and communication strategies people employ when working in a group on a specific task, and the effect individual and collective differences have on the process. Following are questions we have found to be particularly salient when conducting debriefing discussions about the Building Bridges exercise. These questions are intended as guides and should in no way should limit the discussion or other questions you or the group may pose.

About the Activity . . .

- How were your and your team members' needs negotiated?
- How well did your group handle the directions forbidding oral communication?
- How did communication occur?
- What strategies did you use or observe to get the job done?
- How helpful was the cultural information given to you about the others in your group?
- Did you feel at all constrained by it?
- How accurate was this information?
- How did you feel when you were with others who shared your color versus those who did not? Was there a difference?

. . . and its Outcomes:

- How did your strategies change over the course of the exercise?
- How was work negotiated?
- What motivated you to get your needs met—consequences, compromise, and cultural awareness?
- Did your group find it necessary to have a leader?
- Did your group change the rules in any way to meet your goals? If so, how? What were the consequences?

About Diversity Training and Preparation in General:

- Does traditional diversity training work or do we need to look at team-building strategies, focusing on what brings us together rather than what separates us?
- Are individual differences often overlooked in favor of stereotypes during diversity training?
- Does the "diverse" individual stand a chance? What can the "diverse" individual do to be successful?

Alternative Exercises

Crossing borders as a sojourner is not the only situation in which a person may feel different. Any number of circumstances separate us from others. If it becomes apparent that your group is having difficulty understanding that each of us, at one time or another, will be seen as the "diverse" individual, you may want to introduce any of the following introductory exercises.

"Have you ever felt diverse?" Present these questions to the group: "Have you ever felt you were different from the others at work?"; "Think about a situation when there was no one like you and explain that situation—how did you feel and why?"

Stand up/sit down. Participants are asked to stand or sit if they can identify with certain statements. Some of the characteristics you can mention are: "Do you wear glasses (or contacts)?"; "Do you smoke?"; "Do you have light (or dark) hair?"; "Are you a vegetarian?"; "Are you left-handed?"; and so forth.

Obvious and less obvious characteristics. Have the group generate a list of obvious and less obvious characteristics that would make someone feel different from others.

Develop other case studies and critical incidents.

Show excerpts from popular television shows and commercial videotapes that address this issue. Some of our favorites include *Babe, Mr. Baseball, My Stepmother Was an Alien, Working Girl, White Man's Burden* and selected *Murphy Brown* episodes.

References

Baridon, A. & Eyler, D. (1994). *Working together: The new rules and realities for managing men and women at work.* New York: McGraw-Hill.

Brislin, R. (1991). *The art of getting things done: A practical guide to the use of power.* New York: Praeger.

Hall, E. T. & Whyte, W. F. (1973). Intercultural communication. In C. David Mortensen, (Ed.), *Basic readings in communications theory* (pp. 295-313). New York: Harper & Row.

Hofstede, G. (1980). *Culture consequences: International differences in work related values.* Beverly Hills, CA: Sage.

Hofstede, G. (1986). Cultural differences in teaching and learning. *International Journal of Intercultural Relations, 10,* 301-320.

Karp, H. B. & Sutton, N. (1993). Where diversity training goes wrong. *Training, 30*(7), 30-34.

Mauney, C. (1995). *Problems of communication in the administration of international organizations: A bridge exercise.* Emporia, KS: Emporia State University.

Perkins Delatte, A., & Baytos, L. (1993). 8 guidelines for successful diversity training. *Training, 30*(1), 55-60.

Okakura, K. (1906). *The book of tea.* Tokyo, Japan: Kodansha International.

Pati, G. & Bailey, E. (1995). Empowering people with disabilities: Strategy and human resource issues in implementing the ADA. *Organizational Dynamics, 23*(3), 52-69.

Taylor, J. (1991, June 3). Don't blame me! The new culture of victimization. *New York.*

5

Leadership and the Glass Ceiling

Roya Ayman

The happiness of mankind will be realized when women and men coordinate and advance equally, for each is the complement and helpmeet of the other.

Abdu'l-Baha (1922, p. 182)

Many societies around the world have a history of depriving women of the right to advance, to be active and contributing members of their communities. This deprivation has not been unique to women; in the United States, for instance, people of color have also been excluded from many opportunities (Morrison & Von Glinow, 1990). These limitations seem to be based on prejudices that create barriers for success. In the last 25 years, especially in the United States, with the passing of the Equal Employment Opportunity Act and the presence of affirmative action, an aggressive move has been made toward empowering women and minorities to progress and to become leaders. Although these recent laws and policies have opened doors for women and people of color, there still remains an invisible barrier that is referred to as the *glass ceiling*. To break through this glass ceiling, many factors must be considered and acted on (Morrison & Von Glinow, 1990).

This chapter focuses on a training program that has as its objective to make individuals aware of their stereotypical expectations and the effect these expectations may have on their judgment and actions. Although the main focus of the discussion will be on women, most of these processes are also experienced by people of color in the United States. As a result of such a program, awareness of the complexity of stereotyping and the presence of barriers that impede success is established. Finally, a checklist of recommendations to rectify these situations is presented.

This training program is activity-driven and based on experiential learning. In most traditional training programs on this topic, attitude assessments are used as the primary awareness tool. However, such techniques may be affected by social desirability and political correctness. The use of experiential activities followed by debriefing, as presented in this module, should help participants understand their beliefs and reactions with more ease. Without any background being given, the participants are asked to participate in a variety of exercises. The order of the activities in this module capitalizes on the participants' naiveté as it progressively heightens their awareness.

Contents

Self-Awareness of Mental Maps

The following activity is an adaptation of the research paradigm that was used by Virginia Schein (1973) and later further developed by others. Through her research, Schein provided repeated evidence that regardless of gender and position (manager or student), people have a similar mental map or schema of men and their role as managers. People's schema for women differs from their schema of men and of managers (Schein, Mueller, & Jacobson, 1989). This technique has also been used to analyze the differences of mental maps for white and blacks and for managers in the United States (Runkle & Ayman, 1996). Others have also used variations of this technique, demonstrating differences between mental maps of Americans, Japanese, and managers (O'Connell, Lord, & O'Connell, 1990). For training purposes, the exact experimental technique cannot be used. Therefore, the following is a modification of the original.

Activity

Provide each participant with a sheet of paper, prefolded once in half and then folded again in half. On top of one of the quadrants the participants are instructed to write the word *man,* and to write all the attributes they can think of that describe men. They are then instructed to turn to the back of the quadrant, write the word *woman* at the top, and to write all the attributes they can think of that describe women. As the last step, the participants are asked to open the first fold, and write the word *manager* on top of the half page. Finally, they are instructed to write all the attributes they can think of that describe managers. The attributes listed should be whatever comes immediately to their minds without thinking for too long.

Debriefing

The format of the debriefing can vary based on the size of the group and the time available. The discussion can be directed to all participants or to small groups. If small group discussions are used, each group, after a specified time, should have someone to report a summary of their discussion.

The following are questions that can guide the discussions:

1. How similar were each person's descriptions of *man, woman,* and *manager?*
   A. How many found overlap between attributes for *man* and *manager?*
   B. How many found a lack of overlap between attributes of *man* and *woman?*
   C. How many found a lack of overlap between attributes of *manager* and *woman?*
2. What could be the reason for the similarity and differences of the descriptions? (If the participants are diverse, the following questions can also be informative.)
3. What role does the gender of the respondent play in the similarity and difference of the responses?
4. What other experiences or backgrounds influence the similarity and difference of the responses?
5. What effect did the respondents' gender or ethnicity have on the content of the descriptors?

The following paragraphs provide a summary of some of the literature related to the preceding activity. For individuals who have worked in fields where women and people of color have worked for a long time in decision-making roles (e.g., elementary school), fewer discrepancies of expectations may be present compared to those working in traditionally white, male-dominated work environments (e.g., engineering and financial institutions). This reduced discrepancy for those who have had female or ethnically diverse bosses is evidence to support the effect EEO and affirmative action has had on breaking the initial barriers to success for women and people of color. The presence of such guidelines has gradually opened doors of opportunity in traditionally closed work settings to women and people of color. Over time, people's exposure to diverse managers can deter the strong European American, masculine image that has been dominating our mental image of a manager.

In training sessions, due to the lack of control, the results may not be as neat as they typically are in the experimental setting. In the experimental context, each person either describes the man, the woman, or the manager. This activity typically brings to the attention of the participants that they operate with sets of assumptions and expectations that stereotype women to be different from men and managers. In addition to Schein's work, which was referred to earlier, the research of Heilman et al. (1989) suggested that although people differentiate between women and managers, the distinction between an effective male or female manager seems not to be as significant. This is not surprising, because research on stereotyping and prejudice formation has demonstrated that more often prejudicial stereotypes are manifested in either unclear or adverse conditions.

Research has also demonstrated that people hold different mental maps for leaders in different types of organizations, such as the military and in political contexts (Foti et al., 1982). Therefore, depending on a person's experience in one setting or another, their mental map for a leader may be influenced by the setting's normative features.

Similarly, if individuals are cued to describe a leader in a given setting, even a naive respondent can be influenced. For example, people most often will describe a military leader differently than a political leader. However, overall it seems that people do have a general mental map of "a manager" or "a boss."

Awareness of the Effect of Stereotypes on Making Judgments

Activity

Participants observe two skits or two short (4 minutes each) video segments from the videotape, *The Watched and the Watcher* (see Batdorf, 1991). The scripts of these two segments are based on nonverbal movements that are either indicative of women or men, presented by an actor who once appears in a woman's outfit (with a skirt and feminine top) and once in a man's three-piece suit. The behaviors are scripted identically for both conditions. The participants are asked to note the behaviors that make them uncomfortable or embarrassed during their observation of the two segments. After each segment, participants are asked to take time to complete their notes. Sometimes, if the participants include a good representation of men and women, it adds to the debriefing discussion if, for the second skit, women are asked to observe the men as they are watching the skit.

Debriefing

The following questions can be used to lead the discussion:

1. How would you rate the person you saw in each segment on acceptability and appropriateness?
2. Which behaviors in each segment made you feel as if you wanted to giggle or look the other way?
3. How did the men feel, being watched by women?
4. What observation do the women have about watching the men?

This discussion should lead to participants understanding that judgments about others are governed by the expectations and beliefs one holds. For example, in urban U.S. culture, women are expected not to sit with their legs apart. Therefore, a woman who sits this way is behaving contrary to her role and may be judged in a negative manner. Another example can be that, in the United States, a man is not expected to have refined, delicate hand gestures. When a man uses these gestures, he is stereotyped as gay and, in most situations, judged negatively.

In a recent study (Thomas & Ravlin, 1995), employees of the U.S. subsidiaries of Japanese manufacturing firms viewed and evaluated a videotape. There were two versions of this tape—in one, the Japanese manager interacted with American subordinates based on the U.S. normative management style; in the other, the Japanese manager acted according to the Japanese style. The result showed that the culturally adaptive behaviors of the Japanese manager were not uniformly evaluated positively or negatively. Therefore, when people who move outside their cultural group behave like those of the target culture, they may not receive positive evaluation for the hard work of making the adjustment. Thus, the common saying, "When in Rome do as the

Romans do," may not always be the best advice. Research has shown that androgy-nous women managers (i.e., those behaving with a balance of masculine and feminine styles) are often more effective than ones who behave in too masculine a fashion (Korabik & Ayman, 1989; Korabik, 1990). One should remain cautious, however, because two questions remain unanswered. To what extent do these processes have similar effects for men and women crossing the boundaries? To what extent are these issues present for Americans and non-Americans of different cultures? A review of the literature may provide some understanding of the implications of stereotypical mental maps and people's reactions toward nontraditional leaders.

Relating these two exercises to the glass ceiling experience is partially based on the fact that women and people of color are nontraditional leaders in the United States. The majority of nontraditional leaders are confronted with conflicting expec-tations (Ayman, 1993), and usually they are physically different from their traditional counterparts, white males. Research has shown that physical appearance is a strong salient cue in social perception (Chemers & Murphy, 1995). Therefore, the nontradi-tional manager invariably tries to adapt to the style of management in the organiza-tion while the employees notice that, for example, she is a woman, and expect her to be more feminine than the male managers have been in the organization.

Consider the case of a woman manager in a manufacturing plant. Her appearance will remind the observers (e.g., employees, clients, or peers) of a wife, a mother, or a daughter, but she is the boss. Depending on the observer's cognitive map regarding women's traditional roles and managers' traditional behaviors, the conflict between the two expectations can be high or low. Such a conflict, referred to as role conflict by gender-leadership researchers, has been demonstrated to be one of the main sources of job stress. So, although the effects of these conflicting expectations on the manager's subsequent behavior and on observer's evaluations are not totally clear, it is clear that the manager will experience some level of job stress that may negatively effect her behavior. There is some evidence that the more salient cue will activate the mental image. Therefore, it is possible that in organizations where the leaders' roles are designated by their outfit (e.g., military, police, and fire departments), the physi-cal cues may not be strong.

A summary review of research on implicit leadership theory follows, providing some findings that substantiate the effect of a schema on information processing and the presence of a masculine schema for managers or leaders. This review is followed by a brief discussion of the role of these processes and the glass ceiling.

Research has demonstrated that people remember information about a person in action based on the cues they receive. Studies by Lord and Maher (1991) have tested this process, demonstrating that when individuals were told that the person they were observing was effective, this triggered their mental image of an effective person. Therefore, in the report of what they had seen the person do, observers mentioned behaviors that the actor had not exerted but that were consistent with being an effec-tive leader.

Research conducted with managers and nonmanager samples of men and women in the past two decades (Schein et al., 1989) has shown that in the United States, people have a mental image of a manager's behaviors that is often quite distinct from women's and more similar to men's behaviors. This general distinction was also evi-dent in a recent study with school-age children in grades K-6. That is, children draw-ing leaders leading drew significantly more male figures than female ones (Ayman-Nolley, Ayman, & Becker, 1993).

As already mentioned, nontraditional leaders' physical characteristics are usually the salient cues that guide observers' information processing. For example, when an employee sees a female manager, the saliency of the fact that she is a woman will activate the employee's mental image of a woman. Because the traditional image of a woman is that she is nurturing and emotional, this expectation will influence the employee's interpretation of the woman's managerial behaviors. That is, if she demands something from the employee, she will be described as the "dragon lady." If the woman manager is persistent, she will be described as a "pushy broad." These mental processes become invisible hindrances that women face in the workplace. A clear example is a recent Price Waterhouse incident that created a major controversy. In this case, a woman consultant was denied promotion to partnership because she was persistent and a bit abrasive. These behaviors, though not necessarily advocated, had provided success for the men in the company. However, when she engaged in them, they were used against her. This case is not unique.

The term *glass ceiling* contains two images. One, a barrier through which those who are behind see what they are missing. Two, a barrier that is ellusive and invisible. The invisible characteristics of the glass ceiling make its elimination challenging. Usually the factors that contribute to its presence are subtle but can be eliminated by both the nontraditional individuals who are pursuing the leadership positions and the mainstream people who occupy these positions. Consider a white male CEO who has to choose a replacement for one of the members of his management team. This particular individual wonders who could handle the situation and do as good a job as himself. He is more likely to choose another white male over a woman or a person of color because on the surface the white male candidate resembles himself. In an article titled "Nun But the Brave" (Trillin, 1996), the author reported that the CEO of a high-tech company has "argued that virtually all people who are qualified to be directors of a major high-tech company happen to be white males and that putting people on the board for any other reason is stupid" (p. 14). Therefore, although research has demonstrated that there is no significant difference between men and women leaders in either leadership style or effectiveness (Eagly & Johnson, 1991; Eagly et al., 1995), the mental image some people have of managers still seems to maintain the gender stereotype.

In the past, research in which differences between men's and women's leadership styles have been found has been mostly associated with mixed-gender group settings. In mixed-gender groups, men emerge more often as leaders. Women seem to defer more to men. These two processes show that women are faced with some discrimination by others and that they are internally hesitant.

Awareness of Norms Limiting
Women's and People of Color's Behavior

Authors of popular books as *Men Are From Mars, Women Are From Venus* (Gray, 1993) and *You Just Don't Understand: Women and Men in Conversation* (Tannen, 1990) have argued that men and women have distinct cultures. That is, words mean different things to men and women, they approach situations differently, and what motivates them might, likewise, be different. These norms govern the way people feel and the way they behave. In the group exercise that follows, participants can experience what happens in a mixed-gender or -ethnic discussion group. They can also experience how they feel when their expressions are controlled by the norms of the culture.

Activity

The following is a two-phase activity that replicates organizations with different departments (e.g., Marketing, Finance, Production, Human Resources, Public Relations) faced with a problem. The problem needs to be designed to require the input of all departments. The directions to each department should highlight their focus and possibly put them at odds with one or more of the departments. An exercise that is frequently used is "Zenoland: Managing Culture Clash" (Pfeiffer, 1992). In phase one, groups of three to five participants representing a department discuss the problem and solutions for 15 to 30 minutes. At the end of their discussion, they ask the department head to convey their decision to others and to defend the group's position. In phase two, the heads of each department meet. They represent each of their constituencies as they solve a collective problem.

To provide insightful feedback, you can have independent observers keep a record of the interaction in the small groups or videotape the groups' interactions. To discuss the groups' processes, the observers need to keep track of the following behaviors for each participant: give information, ask for information, withdraw, elaborate, review the discussion, dominate, use humor, focus the group on the task. In addition, the observers are to assess if there were interruptions. Who interrupted? Who was interrupted? Were anyone's comments ignored? The feedback is not given until the entire activity is completed. A useful exercise is to make a matrix of these behaviors on the left side of a page and list the participants' names as columns on the top of the page.

In the management team meeting with all department heads present, two stacks of cards are placed in the middle of the table. Each member of the group is given a blue or a yellow badge. The group members are instructed to take a card that corresponds to their badge color before they say anything.

There should be half as many yellow cards as blue cards. On the blue cards the instructions should be for readers to speak forcefully or present their statements with absolute certainty (use styles of communication more descriptive of men). The yellow cards should direct readers to be tentative, to ask questions as a way of presenting their perspective, to include others' contributions when stating their own, or to defer to the ones with blue badges (use styles that are more common to women).

While the leaders of the small group are meeting in the middle of the room, the rest of the participants act as observers, standing around the leaders' table. They will each receive an observation sheet. They are not informed about the role of the two stacks of cards.

Depending on the number of leaders in the meeting, the discussion can go for 20 or 30 minutes with a goal to reach consensus. Afterward, the debriefing is conducted.

Debriefing

There are two categories of discussions. One, related to the first phase, might address the following questions.

1. How did the communication pattern affect the problem-solving process and the outcome?
2. Who spoke most often? Who spoke less often? Why?
3. What do you think contributed to the choice of the leader?

If the session is videotaped, the members of the team can later watch the tape to observe the process. If observers were present, they can present their observations to these questions.

In phase two, debriefing focuses on the leaders' meeting. First ask the observers to present their perspectives because they are naive about the instructions given to the members. They should provide responses to the following questions.

1. Did you notice a difference in the communication patterns among members?
2. Who were the more informed and stronger members of the team?
3. Who would you think is the leader of the team? Why?

The members of the leaders' team are then asked the following questions.

1. How did it feel to be restricted?
2. What did you learn about yourself?
3. What did you learn of the role of cultural expectations for men and women or other social groups?

If there is a diverse group of participants, the initial small groups could be formed by having all-male, all-female and mixed-gender groups. Also, if there are other ethnic groups or age groups present, the trainer can use these characteristics and form the teams with them in mind. The presence of diversity will enrich the discussions. The discussions will also allow the participants an opportunity to use their experience to reflect on the facts provided by the trainer in the presentation.

The debriefing discussion should bring awareness that the behaviors of women, men, and people of color are to some extent governed by norms and expectations that have been internalized by generations of socialization. Usually the participants will contribute their own life experiences regarding the restrictions they have felt. They also can tell stories of what happened to them when they tried to ignore the norm. For example, most professional women have experienced being in a meeting among a majority of men where, when they spoke, their comments were ignored, but when a male member of the team reiterated their point, it was heard and approved. This discussion leads to the last part of the session.

Field Exercise

Following are two lists (adapted from Chemers & Murphy, 1995; Haslett, Geis, & Carter 1992; Ragins, 1995). One is a list of situations to look for in an organization and the other a list of solutions to the situations. Individuals can consider themselves or their own organization when responding to the following.

1. What is the central theme or schema of your impressions and thoughts about women colleagues?

2. Do you expect the women you encounter at work to behave professionally, but then find yourself feeling annoyed or affronted and feeling that they have been domineering or arrogant when they fail to act in a feminine manner?

3. Do you sometimes find yourself searching for legitimate facts to justify a hiring, promotion, or evaluation decision?

4. Are the rules and policies strictly enforced for women but not for men?

5. Are women continually assigned routine, unrewarding work that is stereotypically considered "appropriate for women"?

6. Do women have salary equity with male colleagues?

7. Are women promoted as fast and as far up the ranks as men?

8. Are women frequently interrupted by male colleagues at meetings before they complete their question, comments, or presentations?

9. When a woman does manage to speak in a group, do other participants frown, scowl, or look displeased, compared to when a man speaks?

10. Are you aware of subtle verbal and nonverbal communication differences between men and women?

11. Does the manager introduce male visitors, job candidates, or new hires with praise and a personal endorsement, but introduce female visitors, job candidates, or new hires with only perfunctory facts?

12. Are sexist jokes told at staff meetings?

13. Does a male colleague continually bump into a woman or drape his arm around her shoulders when she does not want him to?

14. How is evidence or data interpreted? For approximately equally good reports, is a woman's work criticized for minor mistakes and its substance ignored, whereas a man's work is praised for the substance and its minor mistakes ignored? Is a woman's work always found wanting, no matter how good it is?

15. Are women's travel or training requests rejected because their work is "so important" that the organization could not spare them? Are they rejected because the departmental budget is tight? Do women not request funding support for professional conferences because they think there is no travel money? Were you surprised when a male colleague decided he wanted to go to a conference and, even though he was not on the program, the manager found the funds?

16. Were you surprised that a male colleague was not reprimanded for greatly overspending his budget for his latest project and was complimented for the fine results, when a female colleague kept within her budget and produced an equally good result but received no commendation?

17. Have women been receiving consistently high job evaluations and praise for their work from their manager, but no corresponding salary increase?

18. Have you wondered why some people are evaluated much more highly than others? Is the evaluation instrument full of subjective personal opinions disguised as seemingly objective appraisals?

19. Is there a risk for a woman who is the only woman in an area or who works in an organization with few, if any, woman in high-level positions?

Solutions: Some of these solutions are for women and people of color to consider implementing, some are activities that their colleagues can do, and some are the function of management.

1. Understand the process of sexism and sex discrimination
2. Increase the number of female authority role models
3. Educate your colleagues
4. Support women at all levels
5. Collaborate with others
6. Understand the organizational culture
7. Understand the organizational structure and goals
8. Establish credibility
9. Participate actively
10. Deal with the "damned if she does, damned if she doesn't" dilemma
11. Handle criticism
12. Avoid emotional labels
13. Know when and how to negotiate
14. Develop a range of communication and power styles
15. Analyze before acting
16. Assume power
17. Develop networks
18. Take calculated risks
19. Develop self-confidence
20. Persist
21. Recognize the bottom line

In closing, participants are asked to provide insight or ideas on how to break the glass ceiling. What things can the organization do? What can nontraditional professionals do? Recommendations are recorded on a flip chart.

Case Studies

This exercise is designed to encourage analysis of problems and practice in implementing the recommendations presented in this chapter. Depending on the size of the group, it could be done in small group discussions with a final general debriefing. During this exercise the participants are encouraged to look at each situation from all perspectives. Therefore, the facilitator should encourage the group to be considerate of each person and to reflect on each element in the situation. In this way, the discussion will not lead to male-bashing or racism, and problem-solving will be done collaboratively rather than one element becoming the focus for change. Usually such situations occur because of many different contributing factors. Therefore, the suggested change also should be multifaceted and the burden of change carried by all.

Case 1

Julie and Tom are both university graduates participating in a study to determine how people are viewed during the job interview process (Robbins, 1996). Among the many situations that were available, they responded to an ad for a territory manager at a lawn-care company. When their resumes were compared, it seemed that Julie had a bit stronger background for the job. However, the interviewer immediately began talking with Julie about a secretarial/receptionist opening (paying $300 to $500 a week). In spite of her qualifications for the managerial job, the interviewer wanted to give her a typing test. In the case of Tom, the interviewer focused on the managerial position and even provided encouraging comments and leading questions to make him interested in considering the job. In the study's follow-up, the interviewer admitted that his judgment was based solely on the gender of the interviewees.

_____

Discussion Questions

1. What do you think perpetuated the gender stereotype?
2. What would you recommend be done to illuminate the problem?

Case II

_____

Six people were present in a cross-functional team meeting at a manufacturing firm. These individuals represented various functions within the organization, including manufacturing (John), engineering (Lisa), marketing (Tom), finance (Mary), distribution/sales (Jerry), and human resources (Bob). As the discussion progressed, Lisa felt that the design issues were not being taken into account. However, she felt uncomfortable interrupting others to present her opinion. During the couple of hours that the meeting lasted, she tried to present her concerns by apologizing and then stating them in a very soft and tentative voice. Her statements were brief and inconclusive, such as, "I don't think the type of production technique we are implementing will allow for the flexibility of the design," or, " I feel that the existing design needs to be examined in relation to the durability of the metal." For the most part, her comments were ignored, and the meeting went along with no acknowledgment of her contributions. However, Tom, without acknowledging Lisa, restated what she had said a bit later in the discussion: "Based on our market survey, the customers have found that durability is important so we should look at our choices of metal and design." His voice was strong, and he stated his position with conviction. Mary interrupted the discussion and said, "We need to be attentive to cost. Our cost analyses have demonstrated that we are over the budget. These proposals I hear are totally without sound fiscal foundation. It cannot work." Mary had a loud voice and spoke forcefully. What she was saying was critical to the survival of the project. However, she was ignored by the group every time she interrupted and tried to bring the attention of the team members to the fiscal issues.

The team broke for lunch, and Mary and Lisa ran into each other in the cafeteria. The men had decided to go off-site for lunch and did not invite the women. As they sat to eat, Lisa and Mary commiserated about how they were treated in the meeting.

_____

Discussion Questions

1. What do you think was going on in this situation?
2. What would you recommend?

Note to the instructor: If no one mentioned how the men could have acted differently, you can encourage people to discuss this possibility.

Case III

In a staff meeting consisting of the director Paul (African American), and program coordinators Tom (European American), Mary (Italian American), and Bob (European American) of the county social services department, a discussion about annual strategic planning was initiated. Paul opened the session and said, "We need to get a closure on this plan today." Bob gave a lengthy, logical presentation of the direction the strategic plan should take. Mary passionately disagreed. The meeting turned into a half-hour debate between Mary and Bob. Tom was sitting quietly but was suddenly asked what he thought. Each time he would begin to speak, Mary or Bob would jump in. Then Paul would say, "And Tom, do you agree or would you like to add anything?" As the meeting progressed, Tom spoke less and less and deferred to others when asked what he thought. He was well connected to the community and, had he had a chance to present his thoughts, could have provided a valuable perspective to the plan. The meeting came to a close, with Paul thanking each one for their input. He added, "Bob, since you have so much interest in the topic, why don't you draft the plan? I am sure Mary and Tom would be happy to help you."

Discussion Questions

1. What do you think will happen?
2. What do you think could have been done in the meeting?

Discuss how each person's behavior contributed to the situation and what could have been done to avoid this situation. Try not to put the responsibility on any one person.

Comments for the Debriefing. In leading the debriefing discussions, what is important is for the participants to have the list of guidelines with them and to try to include as many of them as possible. The aim is not to victimize anyone or to put blame on any one individual, but to look at these situations as a system and acknowledge what each member in the situation could have done to avoid the mishap. To help the discussion move in this way, the facilitator may want to ask the group to first acknowledge all of the factors that could have contributed to the problem. Then the discussion could include what went wrong and how it could be remedied or avoided.

For example, in the first case, what could the female interviewer have done to bring the employer/interviewer back on task? What could the employer/interviewer have done to avoid letting his stereotypes affect his professional judgment? What role does employment law play in this situation?

In discussing mixed-gender or mixed-ethnicity cases, the following are more specific questions to help the group be more analytical: What might the meeting facilitator do to set the tone of the session? What can be done to prepare all participants for better discussions during meetings? How might the meeting have been conducted better? What might each member of the meeting have done to make the session run more smoothly?

Conclusion

The important thing to recognize is that breaking the glass ceiling is a complex process that requires consistent collaboration between men and women of all backgrounds as they discuss institutional policies in the work setting. Having fair policies that incorporate EEO and affirmative action guidelines opens the doors for all people. However, women are encouraged to take responsibility for their own situation. For instance, research has provided evidence that women who are more androgynous seem to be more successful as managers. That is, behaving either too feminine or too masculine is out of the range of acceptable behavior for a manager or for a woman (Ayman, 1993; Korabik, 1990).

The way to break the glass ceiling is by first becoming aware of how each person contributes to its presence, and then to set a system in place in which such behaviors are discouraged. This effort must be made by all men and women, including white people and people of color, until the mental maps that govern people's behaviors have altered. Success and achievement should not depend on color or gender—it should be available to all who can to achieve. Thus, breaking the glass ceiling requires the cooperation and efforts of all. As Effendi (1939) said, "The ceaseless exertions which this issue of paramount importance calls for, the sacrifices it must impose, the care and vigilance it demands, the moral courage and fortitude it requires, the tact and sympathy it necessitates, invest this problem, . . . with an urgency and importance that can not be over-estimated" (p. 28).

References

Abdu'l-Baha. (1982). *Promulgation of universal peace* (2nd ed.). Original work published 1922. Wilmette, IL: Baha'i.

Ayman, R. (1993). Leadership perception: The role of gender and culture. In M. M. Chemers & R. Ayman (Eds.), *Leadership theory and research: Perspectives and directions* (pp. 137-166). New York: Academic Press.

Ayman-Nolley, S., Ayman, R., & Becker, J. (1993). *Gender affects children's drawings of a leader.* Paper presented at the 5th annual convention of the American Psychological Society, Chicago, IL.

Batdorf, E. (director), & Salemme, K. (producer). (1991). *The watcher and the watched* [Video.] (Available from E. Batdorf, 324 A Street 4th Floor, Boston, MA 02210.)

Chemers, M. M., & Murphy, S. E. (1995). Leadership and diversity in groups and organizations. In M. M. Chemers, S. Oskamp, & M. A. Costanzo (Eds.), *Diversity in organizations: New perspectives for a changing workplace* (pp. 157-188). Thousand Oaks, CA: Sage.

Eagly, A. H., & Johnson, B. T. (1991). Gender and leadership style: A meta-analysis. *Psychological Bulletin, 108,* 233-256.

Eagly, A. H., Karau, S. J., & Makhhijani, M. G. (1995). Gender and the effectiveness of leaders: A meta analysis. *Psychological Bulletin, 117,* 125-145.

Effendi, S. (1939). *The advent of divine justice.* Wilmette, IL: Baha'i.

Foti, R. J., Fraser, S. L. , & Lord, R. G. (1982). Effects of leadership labels and prototypes on perceptions of political leaders. *Journal of Applied Psychology, 67,* 326-33.

Gray, J. (1993). *Men are from Mars, women are from Venus.* New York: HarperCollins.

Haslett, B., Geis, F. L., & Carter, M. R. (1992). *The organizational woman: Power and paradox.* Norwood, NJ: Ablex.

Heilman, M., Block C., Martell, R., & Simon, M. (1989). Has anything changed? Current characterizations of men, women, and managers. *Journal of Applied Psychology, 74,* 935-942.

Korabik, K. (1990). Androgyny and leadership style. *Journal of Business Ethics, 9,* 9-18.

Korabik, K., & Ayman, R. (1989). Should women managers have to act like men? *The Journal of Management Development, 8,* 23-32.

Lord, R. G., & Maher, K. J. (1991). *Leadership and information processing: Linking perception and performance.* Boston: Unwin Hyman.

Morrison, A. M., & Von Glinow, M. A. (1990). Women and minorities in management. *American Psychologist, 45,* 200-208.

O'Connell, M. S., Lord, R. G., & O'Connell, M. K. (1990, August). *An empirical comparison of Japanese and American leadership prototypes: Implications of overseas assignment of managers.* Paper presented at the meeting of the Academy of Management, San Francisco.

Pfeiffer, J. W. (Ed.) (1992). *The 1992 annual: Developing human resources.* San Diego: Pfeiffer.

Ragins, B. R. (1995). Diversity, power, and mentorship in organizations: A cultural, structural and behavioral perspective. In M. M. Chemers, S. Oskamp, & M. A. Costanzo (Eds.), *Diversity in organizations: New perspectives for a changing workplace* (pp. 91-132). Thousand Oaks, CA: Sage.

Robbins, S. P. (1996). *Organizational behavior: Concepts, controversies, and applications* (6th ed.). Englewood Cliffs, NJ: Prentice Hall.

Runkle, J., & Ayman, R. (1996). *Relationship between racial and ethnic stereotypes and management characteristics.* Unpublished manuscript, Illinois Institute of Technology at Chicago, IL.

Schein, V., Mueller, R., & Jacobson, C. (1989). The relationship between sex role stereotypes and requisite management characteristics among college students. *Sex Roles, 20,* 103-110.

Schein, V. E. (1973). The relationship between sex role stereotype and requisite management characteristics. *Journal of Applied Psychology, 57,* 95-100.

Tannen, D. (1990). *You just don't understand: Women and men in conversation.* New York: Ballantine.

Thomas, D. C., & Ravlin, E. C. (1995). Responses of employees to cultural adaptation by a foreign manager. *Journal of Applied Psychology, 80,* 133-146.

Trillin, C. (1996, August 12). Nun but the brave. *Time, 148,* p. 14.

PART II

Education

6

Introducing Active Exercises in the College Classroom for Intercultural and Cross-Cultural Courses

Richard Brislin

The purpose of this module is to introduce an approach to, and the rationale behind, the creation of teaching exercises in courses such as intercultural communication and cross-cultural psychology. An exercise will be introduced that has been designed to capture key concepts in an important topic area frequently covered in college coursework: the challenges to people's preexisting thinking when they interact extensively with people from cultures other than their own. As part of the presentation of concepts and methods, applications will be drawn to the work of cross-cultural trainers who might use exercises in their programs for diverse audiences such as businesspeople, health care workers, and social service workers.

Contents

Critical Incident

Some of the issues that professors face when introducing exercises into the classroom are captured in this critical incident.

Are There Penalties for Being Innovative?

_____

Dr. Delores Wilson had taught intercultural communication at the junior-senior level on three previous occasions. Although teacher ratings had been adequate, they did not put her on the list of "the most popular teachers" in her department. She felt that one reason for the merely adequate ratings was that students had not always seemed engaged in her presentations of material. Although nobody yawned with great frequency, there had been enough blank faces to suggest that some of the material was not being communicated effectively.

Delores thought that the introduction of some classroom exercises would be one way of involving students. Thinking back on her previous three classes, she asked herself, "What presentations could have been improved if students had actively worked with the material?" She decided that her previous class sessions devoted to "understanding stereotypes" could be improved. One of the concepts she had introduced to students was that, at times, stereotypes reflect poorly understood aspects of a cultural group's history or adaptation to its environment. Unknowing outsiders see behavior consistent with a stereotype but interpret this information in a careless way because they don't analyze reasons for the behavior in anything approaching a complex manner. Delores had lectured on this point but felt that students would understand it better if they worked with it in an active manner.

Delores divided the class into groups of four or five. She asked each group to follow these steps:

1. List cultural groups that you know—this can include your own.
2. Write down the stereotype of the group. If possible, distinguish between the stereotype held by culturally different others, and the stereotype group that is held by the group's own members.
3. Wherever you can, write down the reasons why the stereotype came into existence.
4. Where possible, write down various explanations of the stereotype that may lead to less negative conclusions about the cultural group if these other explanations are understood by people.

Students had no trouble with steps (1) and (2). Discussions within the groups were animated, and Delores was pleased that students could think of adjectives that described both other cultural groups and their own groups. Students were having less success with steps (3) and (4). So Delores took the information students listed for steps (1) and (2), wrote summaries on the chalkboard, and prepared to assist students in thinking about steps (3) and (4) by asking the groups to break up and to re-form as an entire class.

One of Delores's colleagues, Dr. Peter Armstrong, was a senior professor in her department. He was known to be a good lecturer and felt that the purpose of college classes was to instruct students in the key concepts of the discipline. His feeling was that professors know the concepts, and students do not, so the professor should prepare lectures about the concepts. He happened to pass by Delores's classroom while the students were chatting in an enthusiastic manner within their small groups. Wondering what they were talking about that was so interesting, Peter picked up his mail and went to his office.

Just as Peter was reading the fifth letter he had received that day, Delores began a discussion of the complex reasons behind oversimplified stereotypes. She pointed to the chalkboard and said, "Several groups listed the stereotypes 'Mexicans are lazy' and 'African Americans are musical.' Where might these have come from?" Observing that students' faces were puzzled but interested, she decided that she would give an explanation for one in the hopes that it would stimulate student thinking about the other. "The stereotype that Mexicans are lazy could have come from observations of the cultural customs surrounding siestas. Cities and towns in Mexico become extremely hot at midday. It makes sense to stop work for a few hours so that people do not become dehydrated or succumb to heat exhaustion. But if people from colder climates who are visiting Mexico notice only that shops are closed at midday, they might make the attribution of laziness. When this attribution becomes shared by a number of outsiders, it can become part of a stereotype. One of the cognitive processes behind this attribution is that people frequently make conclusions based on their firsthand experience (shops closed at midday) and rarely consider the possibility that there are other behaviors that are outside their personal observations. Mexicans may have been working very hard early in the morning in their shops (e.g., securing fresh food from wholesalers), but this work is beyond the observations of outsiders who may still be in bed!"

Given this stimulation, one student (a music major) raised her hand and said, "Maybe this type of reasoning can be applied to the example of African Americans. Africans, captured as slaves, brought complex rhythms with them as part of their culture, much like the Irish brought certain tunes in their heads when they emigrated. But after emancipation, African Americans were not allowed into many of the professions such as law, medicine, teaching, and so forth. Using the music of their culture and becoming entertainers was one of the careers open to them. People observe the success in music and conclude 'musical,' not thinking about the fact that using their cultural heritage was a way of supporting themselves and their families."

Three events then happened at about the same time. Delores said "good analysis" to the student. The rest of the students in the class laughed, not to make fun of the presenter, but to share in the excitement of discovery and insights and to laugh at themselves for previously holding the unanalyzed stereotype. Peter Armstrong left his office and passed by the classroom while students were laughing. Peter thought, "Chatting and laughing. Is this all that Dr. Wilson expects of her students? I hope she has more substance to report when she comes up for yearly departmental evaluations."

Discussion Questions

This critical incident brings up a number of questions that will be faced by professors who want to introduce active teaching exercises. These questions include,

1. What are the goals of any exercise?
2. What types of course content are best addressed in exercises?
3. What are some steps to consider in the development of classroom exercises?
4. What are the difficulties that should be considered, including both the responses of students and colleagues?

Possible answers to these questions will be suggested in this module.

College Coursework: The Challenges of Intercultural and Cross-Cultural Courses

For some years, professors who have taught courses in intercultural communication, cross-cultural psychology, and applications such as cross-cultural counseling and social services have recognized that these are difficult teaching assignments (Brislin, 1975; Spodek, 1983; to avoid repetition of words, these terms will be collectively referred to as *intercultural coursework* in the rest of this module). There are several reasons for this. One is that many students have not had significant intercultural experiences in their lives and so have a difficult time conceptualizing the fact that many people have been socialized into a very different culture. The returned Peace Corps volunteers of years past, who used to bring vivid personal experiences to class discussions and who were classroom stars, are fewer in number today. Concepts such as "differing nonverbal behaviors" and "direct and indirect communication styles" are consequently difficult to introduce because students have few personal experiences they can attach to the newly introduced concepts. This difficulty contrasts sharply with other courses in communication and psychology, such as public speaking, mass media, and social psychology. In these courses, concepts such as "organization of ideas in public presentations," "the effects of violence on television," and "interaction in small groups" are relatively easy to introduce because students have had relevant experiences in their everyday lives. This distinction between intercultural coursework and courses in which students can readily apply their memories of previous experiences has led to mentoring advice. Untenured assistant professors are frequently advised to put off teaching intercultural courses until they have tenure. Because students have to work with many unfamiliar concepts, they often do not give high teacher ratings at the end of their intercultural course. A glance at some "teacher evaluation" questions gives some reasons why. A question such as "did the instructor help me apply the concepts learned to my own life?" will not yield the answers of "definitely yes" from many students because relevant life experiences have been rare. It is relatively easy, of course, for students to see the relevance to their own lives of courses in public speaking.

This lack of previous experience might lead automatically to recommending the introduction of classroom exercises that substitute, as much as possible, for actual intercultural experiences. Indeed, recommending the use of such exercises is one of several themes in this module. However, the use of classroom exercises brings up a second reason why teaching intercultural courses is difficult. In many important circles, classroom exercises have a bad reputation. They are known as "frivolous," "touchy-feely wastes of time," "the product of intellectually bankrupt instructors," "time-fillers that have no place in an accredited curriculum," and have been given other descriptions that cannot be shared in polite company. Even if such objections are not applicable, another problem is that some exercises (however effective) have been used for so many years that many students have already participated in them. On three separate occasions recently, I have received memos or verbal communications warning me that I should be certain people have not already participated in some well-known exercises (e.g., BAFA BAFA; Albatross; filling out the Myers-Briggs inventory; applying Maslow's hierarchy of needs to one's own life). This means that if professors are going to use exercises, they should have command of many so that they can move quickly to an alternative if they discover that there will be problems with their initial choice.

Although acknowledging the excesses that have given some exercises a bad reputation, I believe that they can be valuable additions to intercultural coursework if careful thought is given to a number of steps in their development. In addition, if these or similar steps are used to help develop multiple exercises, professors will have access to a wide range and can make substitutions when appropriate. These are the steps I have followed in developing exercises I have used and have shared with others.

Steps in the Development of Classroom Exercises: Some Recommendations

To begin their analysis, professors need to be very clear about the purpose of their proposed exercises. They can ask themselves, "What is the purpose of the exercise I am planning to use? Is it to make students *aware* of some basic cultural differences? Is it to introduce *concepts* such as culture shock? Is it to give students some experiences with *affective* reactions to intercultural interactions, such as loneliness or feeling uncertain about the appropriateness of one's behavior? Is it to introduce students to the necessity of modifying *behaviors* in other cultures, such as communicating one's suggestions in an indirect rather than direct manner?" (This four-part approach in intercultural communication of awareness, concepts/cognitions, affect, and behavior is covered in Chapter 1 and presented in more detail in Brislin & Yoshida, 1994).

After these general questions are answered, a more specific set of issues needs to be addressed. These are the steps I consider when making a decision on the development or use of a classroom exercise.

1. Can the material be covered in lecture format or would students learn the material better by engaging in an exercise? Not all material needs to be covered through exercises, and too many exercises can become as tiring as too many lectures. In my own decision making, I ask myself, "Is there material I cover in lecture that students are grasping well, as shown by their nonverbal reactions, contributions to class discussion, and performance on tests?" Examples might be the physical symptoms of culture shock or the meaning behind gestures in a culture when those gestures can be translated with the equivalent of a full sentence. If I conclude that students are grasping the material less efficiently, I then consider the possibility of introducing an

exercise. A key point in these considerations, which will be referred to several times in subsequent discussions, is that the exercises should be designed to communicate important course material. This material will often deal with the central concepts of a discipline, such as intercultural communication (there are exercises in the following sources and throughout this volume), individualism and collectivism (Brislin, 1994), nonverbal behavior (Singelis, 1994), and bilingualism and interpretation (Freimanis, 1994). I often say to myself, "I *could* cover this material in a lecture. But I think I can do a better job, such that students will learn the material more effectively, if I spend classroom time on an exercise." If I can't convince myself that classroom time will be better spent on an exercise instead of a lecture, I don't use an exercise.

2. If my conclusion is that course material is not being communicated well through a lecture, I then ask, "Why is this material difficult for students to grasp?" The reason often involves an aspect of the general issue discussed previously: Students in intercultural courses often have not had significant experiences in cultures other than their own. I then try to think of ways to engage students in activities that allow them to grapple actively with the course materials. In addition, as much as possible, the activities in the exercise should substitute for a lack of significant intercultural experiences.

3. The next step is to consider the well-known advice to teachers, "Start students where they are at." I ask the question, "What *aspects* of the course materials I am covering have students had experience with?" For example, in the discussion of stereotypes in the critical incident, students could be encouraged to think of a time when they were treated as a member of some *category,* not as individuals. Many students can become involved in this discussion because they can think of examples; for example, tall men reporting that lots of people presume that they are basketball players. Women often report that "dates from hell" sometimes involve men treating them as members of the category "potential bed partners," not as individual human beings. The point can then be made that stereotypes are one example of the categorization process, and that they are categories about people. The move can then be made from this relatively familiar material to the less familiar—an understanding of stereotypes demands analysis of how they came into existence in a culture.

4. The technical details associated with the exercise can then be considered. Questions to ask include, "How long will the exercise take? Have I allowed enough time for debriefing? If the exercise will take more than one class session, is there a smooth transition between the point where the exercise has to be interrupted and then picked up again? What are the costs of the exercise in terms of time needed to break from a lecture format into the beginnings of the exercise? Will time be needed for students to become comfortable with certain aspects of the exercises, such as working with relative strangers?" I often pretest exercises with a group of students with whom I meet weekly—these are students who identify themselves as wanting to emphasize cross-cultural and intercultural studies in their education and who consequently are willing to meet on a voluntary basis.

5. Whenever I give presentations on classroom exercises at professional meetings, colleagues often ask the excellent question, "Where are the trouble spots? Can you prepare us for any potential difficulties using the exercises you are describing?" Informally, these trouble spots are sometimes referred to as "the atom bombs" that can occur when exercises are used. Different exercises have different potential trouble spots, and so answers of general usefulness will be uncommon. One answer

is that professors might consider not using certain exercises until they have seen them used by experienced colleagues. Furthermore, professors should not develop new exercises until they have a great deal of experience using published exercises. Another answer is to always keep in mind the point made earlier. The purpose of these exercises is to communicate course content, with attention to important concepts in the field. When the communication of important concepts is constantly kept in mind, professors can be flexible when they encounter difficulties. For example, they can switch to a more lecture-oriented format, as the professor did in the critical incident on discovering that students could list the content of stereotypes but were less successful in analyses of the stereotypes' origins.

Some advice deals with a specific exercise. For the exercise dealing with stereotypes, for example, my colleague B. James Starr at Howard University cautions that discussions dealing with certain groups are guaranteed to cause intense reactions. In the case of Howard University, that group (as the focus of the question, "What is the current stereotype?") is African Americans. I'm glad that he pointed this out because, in Hawaii, I haven't had the problem of intense reactions as long as all groups in Hawaii are considered in the exercise. For example, there *is* a stereotype of Caucasians from the continental United States and even a term for them—*mainland haoles*. The stereotype includes "pushy," "insensitive to local culture," "loud," and so forth. Knowing the potential problems allows professors to make informed decisions. They would not deal with stereotypes of certain groups if students are likely to react intensely *unless* the professor wants to generate and then guide such reactions. This means, of course, that the professor must be skillful when dealing with angry, shouting students, and so insight about one's abilities is an extremely valuable feature that professors should bring to decisions about exercises.

6. Another question deals with issues surrounding what might be called "public relations." Professors can ask, "Is there anything about this exercise that can lead to problems with colleagues? Might it be perceived as frivolous?" I begin by thinking about the recommendation already made. The purpose of the exercises is to communicate important concepts in a discipline. I convince myself that certain content lends itself to an exercise (as discussed previously). Then I imagine myself as an untenured assistant professor, in his late 20s, at a university with a reputation for academic conservativeness. Furthermore, I imagine that I am presenting an exercise, and one of the oldest, most powerful, and most conservative professors passes by and sees students laughing and enjoying themselves. At a later time in the faculty lounge, I envision myself explaining to this professor that I had important concepts to communicate. I could have lectured on this content, but I thought carefully and decided that an exercise would be most appropriate. If the senior professor I am imagining has the slightest sense of humor, I would then make a wager with him that the students who participated in the exercise now know the concepts as well as students who were exposed to the concepts in lecture format.

These points will be touched on during the following description of an exercise I have used successfully. The discussion prior to the introduction of the actual exercise comes close to the content of the short lecture I use to set the stage for the exercise. I also hope to communicate the point that I try to begin with examples with which the students will be familiar, and then move to applications to the special case of intercultural communication.

An Exercise: Cognitive Processes During Intercultural Interactions

Previously, colleagues and I identified commonalities in the experiences of people who engage in extensive intercultural contact, regardless of the exact form the contact takes (Brislin, 1981; Brislin, Cushner, Cherrie, & Yong, 1986; Cushner & Brislin, 1996). That is, we looked for commonalties in the experiences of overseas businesspeople, international students, immigrants, technical assistance advisers, and people who extensively interact with people from other cultural groups within a large and complex country, such as the United States or Australia. One set of commonalities centered on people's everyday thought processes: There are challenges to people's thinking, and these can overwhelm people and contribute to culture shock.

Categories

The starting point for any analysis of thought processes is to consider the concept *category* (Triandis, 1972). People cannot respond to every individual piece of information to which they are exposed. They have to put the information into a category and then respond (or not respond) to the category. Coming to work in the morning, people don't respond to "that new green Nissan," "that beat-up yellow Ford with the crummy paint job," and "that classic 1957 blue Chevy." Rather, they place cars into categories, such as "cars that can be totally ignored" and "cars that are in my way and to which I must pay attention." If they reacted carefully to each individual car, they would give insufficient attention to important matters and would crash! As another example, consider students walking across a college campus from one class to another. They cannot respond to each individual person they see. Rather, they place individuals into categories such as "people I don't know and can totally ignore," "people I know a little bit and can acknowledge with a head nod or wave," "people to whom I have to say 'hello,'" and "people for whom I must stop and chat." If they responded to every person, students would not get to their next class and would probably also be considered mentally unstable by observers.

People have categories about many aspects of life. Examples are "proper behavior in the workplace," "what a good boss does," "good schools," "edible food," "good family activities," and so forth. During extensive intercultural contact, these categories are challenged. Consider the example of Americans working in Japan (Yoshida, 1994). The Americans will be unfamiliar with cultural differences in workplace expectations and the behaviors typical of a good boss. In Japan, the workplace is a place where unmarried men and women meet and start romances leading to marriage. Good bosses in Japan introduce unmarried subordinates to potential spouses, a behavior considered totally "out of line" in many American companies. Schools for children demand much more rote memorization, drill, and long hours of homework than is common in America. The Japanese cuisine is very different from that commonly experienced in America, with far less red meat and far more raw fish. Family activities can suffer because of the expectations for after-hours socialization among coworkers in Japanese organizations.

No one of these challenges to people's preexisting categories will overwhelm people. After all, we make changes in our categories all the time. What we viewed as "advanced computer technology" 5 years ago seems hopelessly dated and quaint today. The total set of adjustments, to a set of category challenges is what contributes to tension and stress during extensive interactions. These stresses and tensions have been given a special name, *culture shock,* and can lead to physical symptoms, such as headaches, upset stomach, nausea, reduced energy, problems with sleep, and reduced sex drive. Culture shock can also lead to psychological problems, such as depression and self-perceived helplessness.

Insights Into Thought Processes

The conclusion to be drawn from this discussion is that people learn to process information in certain ways in their own cultures and learn that certain information is conveniently placed in certain categories. When these categories are brought to other cultures, they are likely to be challenged.

Another complexity may have already occurred to readers. The process of placing information into categories is not perfect in our own culture, and is likely to be even more imperfect when living in another culture. If the process of putting information into categories was perfect, we would not misunderstand people similar to ourselves in our own culture. For example, we say something that we place in the category of *compliment.* But the person we are addressing (from our own culture) interprets it differently. Has this happened to people? The answer is, "Of course." At this point in any formal presentation, students are usually able to give an example of a misunderstanding they have had when they tried to say something that was part of one intended category, but another person placed the same comment in a different category.

Important research has been undertaken for various reasons to discover why information processing is imperfect and why people can have misunderstandings when they are presented with (what they think is) the same information. Much of the relevant research has taken place as part of efforts in the discipline known as cognitive psychology, and there are now entire books devoted to the topic of human information processing (Janis, 1982; Kahneman, Slovic, & Tversky, 1982; Fiske & Taylor, 1991; Plous, 1993). The following discussion draws from these sources and applies key concepts to the special case of intercultural communication.

Imperfections in Information Processing:
Interpersonal and Intercultural Communication

Misunderstandings often stem from differences in the way information is processed. Eight concepts exist that are helpful in analyzing these misunderstandings. The examples given should be familiar to students, given their everyday experiences involving interpersonal communication in their own culture. Later, in the actual exercise, students will analyze these same concepts as they apply to people engaged in intercultural communication.

Object Construal

The type of information processing phenomenon that most closely resembles the placing of similar information into a different category is called *object construal.* The question is, "How do people construe different objects?" and the term *objects* is used broadly to refer to physical objects (an attractive piece of art, a comfortable workplace) and more subjective categories (good manners, physical attractiveness). Issues surrounding object construal are captured in popular folk sayings, such as "Beauty is in the eyes of the beholder," and "One person's meat is another person's poison."

For example, one student skillful in statistics offers to help another student who is obviously struggling with the material presented by the professor. The first student may construe this as helpfulness; the second student may construe this as condescension. As an intercultural example, an American student who asks a penetrating question of the teacher will often be perceived as sharp and involved. An Asian student who engages in the same behavior may be seen (by other Asians) as showing disrespect for the high-status professor.

Attention to the Concrete

People's attention drifts toward concrete and specific behaviors rather than to abstractions. Furthermore, people make conclusions about objects in their lives based on concrete experiences. Students may have heard that a certain professor is highly approachable and is good at answering questions in ways that students can understand. However, if a given student makes an appointment with that professor and finds the professor somewhat distant and uninterested in answering questions, the student is likely to make his or her own conclusion based on this specific, personal experience. Sojourners in France may have heard that the French don't like to speak their language with others unless it is used perfectly. However, if an individual sojourner interacts with French people who are happy to keep up conversations after hearing mangled utterances, the sojourner is likely to conclude otherwise. That is, they may conclude that the French are like most people and appreciate people's attempts to use their language.

Scripts

Scripts summarize common sets of behaviors, learned in a culture, that help people meet their goals. Shared scripts allow people to predict the behaviors of others and to have smooth interpersonal interactions. The opening phrase, "Hi, how are you?" is far more often followed by "Fine, and you?" than by a recital of troublesome physical symptoms. How do people meet each other at a reception? They introduce themselves or are introduced by someone else, shake hands, and engage in pleasant exchanges of innocuous information. This is a script: If someone broke the script, for instance, by immediately presenting intense political views, he or she would be considered deviate. A person goes to McDonalds at 8:00 p.m. and is seated by the maitre d'. No, wrong; that's not part of the script for a fast-food restaurant, and people expecting this script will be disappointed. In many Asian countries (e.g., Japan, Korea), meeting others at a reception involves the exchange of business cards, and sojourners who don't have such cards should not expect to be remembered the next time they see people who were at the reception.

Ignoring Base Rates

Discussions of base rates means that there are *numbers* in the background of any interaction people are having. This imperfection in information processing is related to "attention to the concrete" because the concrete example overwhelms the less visible and less accessible background numbers. The fact that people ignore base rates is a major reason why many multimillionaires have made their fortunes in the gambling industry. I hope it is clear from the discussion to date that the millionaires run the casinos and games and are themselves not the gamblers. The base rate, or numbers in the background, is that most gamblers lose money. The casino owner and game operators, with statistical odds on their side, make money in the long run. The individual gambler who wins becomes the concrete exception, and this person becomes the evidence for the reasonableness of gambling among friends, relatives, and people who read about winnings in the newspaper. Casino owners are happy to encourage publicity about a big winner because this becomes free advertisement for them and contributes to their incomes in the long run. The base rates are on the side of the casinos.

Another example, sometimes touched on in the mass media, involves air travel. The crash of an individual jet airplane is sensational and memorable, and hearing the news of such a crash can lead people to cancel trips. However, the base rate statistics are that air travel is the safest form of transportation (fewest accidents per mile). People have a greater chance of injury driving from their homes to the nearest airport than they do while actually flying in the commercial airliner.

Fitting Into Stereotypes

This type of imperfect information processing needs the least amount of introduction here because of the previous discussion. A stereotype is a special kind of category that involves people—an individual is given a group label and then descriptors associated with that group label are attached to the person. The group label can be based on gender, ethnicity, political persuasion, occupation, age—in other words, people put individuals into some kind of group. The use of stereotypes can be self-fulfilling. Assume that a professor feels that women are not quite as good at mathematics as men. The professor has an assignment involving mathematics that can be given to one of several student research assistants. If the professor behaves according the stereotype, the assignment might go to a man. The man might do well on the assignment. At a later time, this same man might get other assignments. The man might become quite good at mathematics because of all the practice he is getting. The woman may never have the opportunity to show her skills because the initial assignment was based on a stereotype.

Primacy/Recency

In processing complex information concerning issues with multiple competing viewpoints or possible conclusions, is the initial information given more weight, or are people more influenced by the last information they hear? These competing possibilities are captured in folk wisdom. Many of our mothers told us that, on meeting others for the first time, "first impressions are lasting." In contrast, experienced politicians warn newcomers that "people are interested in what you have done for them recently." A reasonable conclusion from research on primacy and recency is that if the subject matter is complex and has little structure to it, people who first present the information in an organized, clear way have an advantage. On the other hand, if the subject matter is familiar and audience members already have a well-developed structure for it, the last person presenting information and arguments may have an advantage because of imperfections in people's memories. People will better remember what was presented last, just as we remember better what we did yesterday than what we did 3 weeks ago.

Mistaking Knowledge for General Expertise

When people are not knowledgeable about a topic area, a person who knows one or a few things about the area may be seen as an expert. That is, a person may make one or two remarks that are perceived as intelligent, and subsequently general expertise may be attributed to this person. Assume, for example, that a group of people knows little or nothing about the World-Wide Web. If these people meet an individual who knows how to type in and enter requests for a certain web page, the individual may be seen an expert. Only later do the people learn that typing in web page requests is extremely easy and by no means indicates expertise. One reason for this information processing error is that, when making the initial attribution, people do not have additional information beyond the observation that the individual can make web-page requests. They have limited information and they make their conclusion based on what they know at any one point in time. There is no great motivation to look behind the information they have and to ask, "Is there more I should know before making the attribution of expertise?" At this point, students might be asked to think of an example in their own lives when they mistook a piece of knowledge for more general expertise. At times, students will come up with the example of their parents. "When I was young, I thought my parents knew everything because they were certainly good at some things. Part of growing up is learning that parents don't know it all and are imperfect, like all of us!"

Vague Knowledge Into a Strong Category

Once people have a strong and well-developed category, they are likely to put vague information into that category. They are likely to see *aspects* of the vague knowledge that fit into their strong category. In many cases, this information processing error is similar to the everyday observation that "people hear what they want to hear." The information they hear may be vague, but if they want to hear something that fits into their existing categories, they are likely to hear it. For example, the vague statement that "if you knew a politician personally, you would know why politics is in the state it is" can be interpreted negatively or positively. If people dislike politics, they can interpret the statement as describing sleazy politicians. If people believe that politics is society's arena, where people with conflicting positions can argue their viewpoints and compete for resources guided by laws, norms, and rules, then they can interpret the statement positively.

Exercise: Working With Limits to Information Processing

After the professor has presented a short lecture on the eight limits to information processing, students should be ready for an exercise in which they work with concepts that capture these limits. Students also work to apply the concepts to the special case of intercultural interactions. The assumption is that they are ready for this step given (a) the previous presentation that included examples with which they are familiar, (b) the inclusion of some familiar examples in the exercise, and (c) the assumption that there are *elements* in the intercultural examples to which students can relate. For example, incidents include the elements of meeting people for the first time and the feeling that one is not being understood. The exercise assumes that everyone has had these experiences in their own culture.

Step 1. Students receive 1 of 16 short vignettes that involve misunderstandings or mistakes in analyzing information. There are two vignettes for each of the eight information processing errors. They are asked to read the vignette and to determine which of the information processing biases it may contain. If there are more than 16 students, duplicates can be made so some students will have the same vignette. If there are less than 16 students, some students receive more than one incident.

Step 2. Students then move from their seats and interact with other students in the class. The object of the interactions is to find matches in the underlying concepts. If one student has a vignette that is an example of primacy/recency, he or she seeks out a student with *another example* of primacy and recency. As part of their interactions, if students find someone who has their same incident, they simply are told to move on to someone else.

Step 3. Even after students have found a match, they can continue interacting with others because some of the incidents contain more than one of the information processing errors. For example, a student might identify one person who has another primacy/recency example. But in addition, because this student's incident might also contain a stereotype, he or she might find another match based on this second information processing error.

Step 4. The students report back to the entire class. Students report on the matches they found, review the two vignettes, and explain why they feel the same information processing error is part of both. At times, they will come up with reasons for matches (e.g., two examples of following scripts) that the professor has not considered. This is fine, as long as they make a good case and are accurate in their thinking about the underlying concepts. The professor then expands on the students' reports to make sure that the concepts are clear in students' minds.

Here are the 16 incidents. Of course, students do not see the last few words that provide the label for the type of information processing issue contained in the incident. The information processing issue I emphasized in writing each incident is italicized. Other issues students have found and have defended well are also listed after this italicized concept.

1. An exchange student from the United States, living in Germany, is invited to an informal social gathering at a pub; does not contribute to discussions about U.S. foreign policy in Europe; is rarely invited again to such gatherings. *scripts*

2. A student from Japan in the United States chats with fellow students for the first time after a class early in the semester; Japanese student agrees with American students on their views concerning current movies, rock stars, and things to do on

weekends; Japanese student steers conversations around to what American students want to talk about; Japanese student finds himself uninvited by Americans to informal weekend activities. *scripts*

3. Looking for a car, a person reads *Consumer Reports* and decides on a Honda Civic because of its reliability; person runs into friend who says, "A Honda! My wife's cousin had nothing but trouble with one." Person does not buy Honda. *ignoring baseline*; attention to the concrete

4. In Japan, an American goes to a popular movie. There are few seats in the theater. When he tries one that seems to be empty, Japanese national uses gesture of flicking wrist away from self. American upset by rudeness of gesture. *attention to the concrete*; object construal

5. Busy student, working way through college, has to miss many classes because of job demands. This student is especially interested in working with a certain professor because of her expertise, but professor concludes that student is not serious about education. *object construal*

6. Male American in Beijing, China, asks attractive woman to dinner and the opera. He is surprised when other Chinese people he knows think that this male-female pair is romantically involved. *object construal*; script

7. Caucasian Americans meet African Americans on campus. They chat about athletics. In getting a diverse group of people together to go to a documentary movie being shown on campus about developments in Eastern Europe since the fall of the Berlin Wall, they don't invite African Americans. *fits stereotype*

8. American professor asks students to form teams to work on group projects. This professor happens to be a vivacious, exciting lecturer. Each group will give oral presentation on its work to rest of class in a month. American students are reticent about having Japanese nationals on their team. *fits stereotype*; object construal

9. Male student, as part of weekend social activities in college dorm, agrees to go to a "mixer," which means being linked to a female student in a "blind date" arrangement. Roommate also agrees to go to mixer. First student finds out little about his date. Second finds out that date is a double major in political science and environmental sciences, works her way through college, and is an honors student. Second student says, "It looks like I'm going to be stuck in a dull evening with a 'save the whales through government policy' feminist." First student says, "Yeah, I guess I've gotten the better deal." *ignoring base rates*; stereotype

10. President of a not-for-profit social services organization is hired because of her considerable fund-raising, organizational, and political skills rather than her knowledge of social services. One staff member wants to start a social services program in alcohol rehabilitation. This staff member introduces the president to potential clients, influential people in the community also in favor of the alcohol rehab program, and even sits the president down at a computer terminal and takes her through a program that assists in individualizing treatments to clients. The president chooses to support the program and turns down others (e.g., shelters for runaway teens) put forward by other staff members. *concrete*

11. American exchange student wins scholarship to Paris. Very shortly after arrival, meets other French students who share interest in playing 1950s rock and roll (Buddy Holly, Elvis, Chuck Berry). In sharp contrast to other Americans, this student has very fond memories of Paris years after the study year abroad. *primacy*

12. Both prosecution and defense finish their presentation of evidence in a murder trial where virtually all the evidence is circumstantial. The courtroom reporters, after the presentation of evidence, cannot predict what the jury will do. In their summations, the prosecution (going first) presents a compelling scenario of how the murder was committed that is consistent with all the evidence. The defense tries to punch holes in this scenario during its summation. The jury votes to convict the defendant of murder. *primacy*

13. Not speaking any Swedish in Sweden, an American says "Hello, how are you" to several Swedes (who look like they are college students) during intermission of a concert. One answers, in a shy manner, "We're fine, thank you." The American then asks this Swedish person if there is someplace he can find Indian food and where the best place to buy tickets for alternative rock concerts is. The American is then met with a blank stare from the Swede. *knowledge/expertise*

14. It was the 20th high school reunion for the class of 1975. As is human nature, many people thought about who had been successful and who had been less successful with their lives. In a conversation, several attendees noted that the two people who got the best grades, and who were the two speakers at the graduation 20 years before, seemed to have very ordinary jobs and had not followed through on the promise they had shown in their previous academic performance. *knowledge/expertise*; scripts

15. After 2 years in Africa, the Peace Corps volunteer was anxious about returning home to Wisconsin. "Maybe I can rekindle that old romance," the volunteer thought. The volunteer didn't expect many problems in moving back home because a number of friends had written letters saying "nothing much has changed around here." But after arriving home, the volunteer experienced a great deal of stress—everything seemed different, especially the old flame! *vague knowledge into strong category*

16. It had been a hard 3 years for the research organization, with government cuts making contracts hard to come by. The organization's largest number of contracts were in the area of national defense policy. Still, a number of employees thought that the organization would prosper if only a few specific policy changes were made that would allow competition for contracts in health care policy research. A new president was hired and in her first few weeks made statements such as, "We cannot be wedded so strongly to the past that we miss possibilities for growth." The employees interested in health care were optimistic at first but gradually became disillusioned when the organization continued its emphasis on defense contracts. *vague knowledge into strong category*

Notes on Application of Information Processing Errors to Vignettes

In vignettes 1 and 2, hosts expect visitors to behave according to *scripts*. The Germans expect the American to engage in discussions of foreign policy and politics. In the second incident, the Americans expect the Japanese visitor to talk about himself or herself. This will allow the American to identify activities (movies, concerts, athletic events) to which they might invite the visitor. When people don't follow the scripts, hosts have a difficult time including visitors into their activities.

In vignettes 3 and 9, people are *ignoring baselines*. When reacting to the one friend's report about a Honda, the person is ignoring the thousands of people who indicated satisfaction, as reported by the highly respected publication, *Consumer Reports.* Incident 9 is admittedly more difficult. When people combine descriptors of individuals they have not met, they ignore the fact that very few individuals could possibly have a highly specific combination of traits, habits, and qualities. They are ignoring the baseline that very few people have the combination (in this incident) of "dull, feminist, ecologist, political activist, and proponent of government intervention into policy decisions." Even if there was a one in two chance of each single descriptor being correct, the probability of all being correct is $\frac{1}{2}$ to the 5th power, or 1 chance in 32!

In incidents 4 and 10, people are reacting to very *concrete* events. These events are more memorable than abstractions. In incident 4, the gesture seems rude (actually, it is a polite sign that the seats are taken). In incident 10, the president has participated in concrete events related to a proposal and is consequently going to have specific memorable experiences when he or she reviews various proposals for funding.

In incidents 5 and 6, people are *construing objects* in various ways. The professor has a construal of the concept *serious student,* and the busy individual with job demands does not fit this construal. The American construes the evening with the Chinese woman as a nice first date. The woman, coming from a culture where any one-on-one interaction of this sort is taken very seriously, construes the date as a major move toward an exclusive dating relationship. In China, men and women socialize in large groups, and much later there may be "pairing off" after people get to know each other through interactions as group members.

Incidents 7 and 8 should be relatively easy for students. *Stereotypes* are being applied to individuals. Caucasian Americans think that the African Americans will not be interested in a documentary movie about Eastern Europe. The American students feel that the Japanese students will not be dynamic team members who can participate in an interesting oral presentation.

In incidents 11 and 12, people are responding according to the *primacy* effect. In Paris, the student had a positive early experience with French nationals and consequently has fond memories of his or her sojourn. In the courtroom example, the case is obviously difficult and confusing if experienced reporters can't make a prediction. In such cases, there will often be a primacy effect if the prosecution can present a clear scenario that integrates all information presented about the murder. Returning to incident 11, living abroad is confusing because people don't know what to expect. If they have pleasant experiences early in their sojourn, these are likely to be weighted heavily in their overall feeling about the host country.

In incident 13 and 14, people are *mistaking pieces of knowledge for expertise.* Just because a Swedish person knows a few English phrases, careful consideration should lead to the conclusion that they are not necessarily fluent. But sojourns are confusing, and so people latch on to isolated bits of knowledge and, relieved to hear something familiar, may conclude that people know much more English than they do. In incident 14, the people with the best grades demonstrated command of certain knowledge. But this does not mean that they have developed the type of expertise to have important careers. Such expertise often demands social skills, creativity, political sensitivity (see module by Brislin and Jane, this volume), and other qualities, not just knowledge as indicated by high school and college grades.

Incidents 15 and 16 represent the placement of vague knowledge into strong categories. The Peace Corps volunteer responds to the vague phrase "Nothing much has changed around here" and puts it into the strong category of "romance to be rekindled." As many returnees discover (see module by Wang, this volume), events at home change far more than is usually predicted. In incident 16, the president made a vague statement. People who had the strong category, "move toward health care policy research," interpreted the president's statement as supporting their desires.

Are There Potential Trouble Spots?

The only trouble spots in this exercise stem from the fact that it deals with difficult material. The professor has to know the material well to give the initial lecture and to then respond to students' reports of matched vignettes. Students have no trouble interacting and attempting to find matches, but will often come to the professor during the exercise and ask the questions, "Is this a reasonable interpretation of this vignette? If so, then this information processing error is involved." For example, one student interpreted incident 14 as involving a script: "The student did not follow through with people's expectation of a life script: do well in school, then do well in a career." I felt that this was a creative and accurate use of the concept *scripts*. A related potential trouble spot, then, is if students want to have "absolute answers" in the form of one absolutely correct information processing error attached to each incident. Professors have to remind students that human behavior is complex, and that interactions and challenges to our thinking are not collections of perfectly clear incidents and perfectly clear, precise, single solutions. This potential trouble spot will actually be a strength for professors who emphasize critical thinking in their classes and who encourage students to analyze problems according to many different viewpoints and through the use of multiple concepts.

Conclusion

When professors begin thinking about exercises with the question, "What difficult material, such as advanced concepts central to the discipline, do I want to cover?," certain problems begin to be addressed. There is immediately a move away from "fun and games" if the task is to communicate important concepts. Given this focus, colleagues in the professor's department can be invited to the presentation and asked to participate in the exercise. As in vignettes 4 and 10 (and also covered in the module on political skills by Brislin and Jane), giving wary people firsthand, concrete experiences is an effective tactic. In this case, colleagues may move from the abstraction "fun-and-game waste of time" to the more specific, "I've seen at least one exercise that communicates important concepts as well as a lecture would."

References

Brislin, R. (1975). Teaching cross-cultural psychology, with special reference to seminars involving participants from Asia and the Pacific. In J. Berry & W. Lonner (Eds.), *Applied cross-cultural psychology* (pp. 277-282). Netherlands: Swets and Zeitlinger.

Brislin, R. (1981). *Cross-cultural encounters: Face-to-face interaction.* New York: Pergamon.

Brislin, R. (1994). Individualism and collectivism as the source of many specific cultural differences. In R. Brislin & T. Yoshida (Eds.), *Improving intercultural interactions: Modules for cross-cultural training programs* (pp. 71-88). Thousand Oaks, CA: Sage.

Brislin, R., Cushner, K., Cherrie, C., & Yong, M. (1986). *Intercultural interaction: A practical guide.* Newbury Park, CA: Sage.

Brislin, R., & Yoshida, T. (1994). *Intercultural communication training: An introduction.* Thousand Oaks, CA: Sage.

Cushner, K., & Brislin R. (1996). *Intercultural interactions: A practical guide* (2nd ed.) Thousand Oaks, CA: Sage.

Fiske, S., & Taylor, S. (1991). *Social cognition* (2nd. ed.). New York: McGraw-Hill.

Freimanis, C. (1994) Training bilinguals to interpret in the community. In R. Brislin & T. Yoshida (Eds.), *Improving intercultural interactions: Modules for cross-cultural training programs* (pp. 313-341). Thousand Oaks, CA: Sage.

Janis, I. (1982). *Group think: Psychological studies of policy decisions and fiascoes* (2nd ed.). Boston: Houghton Mifflin.

Kahneman, D., Slovic, P., & Tversky, A. (Eds.). (1982). *Judgment under uncertainty: Heuristics and biases.* Cambridge, UK: Cambridge University Press.

Plous, S. (1993). *The psychology of judgment and decision making.* New York: McGraw-Hill.

Singelis, T. (1994). Nonverbal communication in intercultural interaction. In R. Brislin & T. Yoshida (Eds.), *Improving intercultural interactions: Modules for cross-cultural training programs* (pp. 268-294). Thousand Oaks, CA: Sage.

Spodek, H. (1983). Integrating cross-cultural education in the postsecondary curriculum. In D. Landis & R. Brislin (Eds.), *Handbook of intercultural training, Vol. 3: Area studies in intercultural training* (pp. 81-101). Elmsford, NY: Pergamon.

Triandis, H. (1972). *The analysis of subjective culture.* New York: Wiley.

Yoshida, T. (1994). Interpersonal vs. non-interpersonal realities: An effective tool individualists can use to better understand collectivists. In R. Brislin & T. Yoshida (Eds.), *Improving intercultural interactions: Modules for cross-cultural training programs* (pp. 243-267). Thousand Oaks, CA: Sage.

7

Reentry and Reverse Culture Shock

Mary Margaret Wang

You *can* go home again . . . so long as you understand that home is a place where you have never been.

Ursula LeGuin, The Dispossessed (p. 48).

University exchange programs, multinational corporations, and programs that send volunteers for work on international projects generally do a far better job preparing sojourners for entry into a foreign culture than they do preparing those sojourners for reentry into their own culture. One of the most frequently heard statements about extensive intercultural interactions is that, "compared to living in another country, there is more culture shock when returning home." This module explores definitions of reentry and the preparation of sojourners for their return to their home culture. Concepts covered include challenges to preexisting self-concepts, integration with friends and family once people return home, value change and choices, the length of the reentry process, and the sense of loss.

Contents

Author's Note: The author wishes to thank Supin Pfatsch and Melinda Wood for their assistance and insights on the issues presented in this chapter.

The Realities and Goals of Reentry Training

The reality of reentry training is that it is usually too little too late, if one can convince administrators and sojourners that it is needed at all. After all, what's so hard about coming home after a year or two abroad to a country and culture where one has lived for 20, 30, or 40 years? Ideally, reentry training should be integrated into an ongoing program that prepares sojourners for the cross-cultural experience and then helps them process the experience, in terms of the reality of life in the home culture, after their return. In other words, reentry training should begin before the sojourner ever leaves home and should continue throughout the sojourn and for years after the return to the home country.

Because it is so difficult to convince people that reverse culture shock will happen to them, it is necessary to find ways to persuade sojourners to attend reentry training sessions, at least until there has been time for word-of-mouth to establish the usefulness of the training. Initially, trainers need to look for people in the targeted audience who have had reentry experiences and enlist their aid in bringing in members of their group (administrative division, nationality group, age peers). Peers who have undergone reverse culture shock validate the trainers' assertions and can supply culturally relevant illustrations of generalities. Failing the availability of individuals with reentry experience, trainers may simply have to prevail on friends to bring in members of their group to the first few training sessions.

In general, the goals and reentry training include (a) convincing participants that reverse culture shock is real, that it affects every returning sojourner to some degree, and that it usually goes unrecognized; (b) encouraging participants to think about changes in themselves, changes at home, and what effect those changes are going to have on their reentry experience; (c) suggesting that participants start worrying about their return; and (d) convincing participants that there are measures they can take to assure that their own reentry is *relatively* painless in the short run, and a positive growth experience in the long run.

Critical Incidents

Incident A: The Reluctant Wife

Ellen hadn't been too happy when Jerry was given a 2-year assignment in Indonesia, even though it meant a lot of responsibility and welcome challenges for him. Two and a half years later, however, though she still complained a lot to her friends about the host culture, Ellen had become quite comfortable. She had made many close friends among the other expatriate wives; her kids—15-year-old Jake and 13-year-old Ted—loved the American school and had many friends there, and Jerry had thrived in his new job. There had been opportunities for travel to other countries in Southeast Asia, and servants to help with the cooking and cleaning. All in all, as much as she looked forward to returning to their home in suburban Chicago, Ellen had to admit that the family's experience in Indonesia had been a good one.

After nearly a year back in Illinois, Ellen seemed to be constantly depressed. She didn't enjoy the company of her old friends very much and found herself missing her friends in Indonesia. Initially she was happy to return to her part-time job, but soon found it dull, and anyway, she was so exhausted from doing the shopping, the cooking, and the housework that she didn't have the energy for work. She couldn't quit because money was tight; everything seemed more expensive than she remembered. The kids were unhappy at school; they found the suburban junior high school too big, unfriendly, and impersonal, and neither of them could seem to break into a group of friends they liked. Their grades were slipping, and Ellen worried about what to do to help them. And Jerry was no help at all. He came home every night and complained that his supervisors didn't appreciate and make use of the skills he developed in Indonesia, and that he was being given odd jobs to do while the company found a new position for him. He talked about looking for a new job, which just made Ellen more nervous.

Discussion Question

What is going on with Ellen and her family?

1. Ellen and her family were having typical, predictable problems of readjusting to their home culture.
2. Ellen and her family were suffering from unusually prolonged and severe reverse culture shock.
3. Reverse culture shock affects everyone, but it lasts only a few months at most, not a year. The problems Ellen and her family were having most likely have to do with the individual personalities of the family members.
4. The difficulties Ellen and her family were experiencing have nothing to do with their overseas experience. Teenagers often have problems at school, and job frustrations occur in everyone's career.

Incident B: Home to India

Miroo felt very fortunate to have received a full scholarship to do a Masters of Public Health degree at a good American university. Even with the scholarship, her extended family had to make considerable financial sacrifices to support her through the 2 ½ years it took her to finish her degree, and she was very grateful to them.

Miroo was looking forward to going back to her home city, where her mother was a prominent government official. In the U.S. she had to get used to doing many odious tasks that had been done for her by servants all her life in India, and she was glad to think that she would no longer have to do laundry or demeaning work-study chores. She expected that, because of her parents' connections, she would find an good job shortly after her return.

Things did not go as Miroo had expected. She fell ill shortly after her return to India and was sick for several weeks. After she was well enough to go out, she began to realize that her parents still treated her as a child. She was not allowed to go out and do things on her own; her parents insisted that a sister, brother, or cousin accompany her everywhere. When she argued that she had lived on her own in an American city for more than 2 years and had earned a degree with honors, they chided her for being arrogant and disrespectful. Miroo was further dismayed to learn that her parents, rather than occupying themselves in finding a good job for her, were busy looking for a suitable husband. Miroo was very unhappy with her family and was thinking of applying to Ph.D. programs in the United States and Canada, just to get away again.

Discussion Question

What might explain Miroo's problems with her family?

1. Miroo was experiencing typical problems associated with cultural reentry.
2. Miroo's family was being unreasonable. Having spent time and effort on getting an education, Miroo was naturally frustrated at not being given the opportunity to use her new skills and at being treated as a child.
3. Miroo was being unreasonable. Of course her parents feared for her safety. India is not the United States, and it is not safe for a young woman to be going out on her own. Miroo should try to be more understanding.
4. The behavior of Miroo's family is not typical. Most Indian families would be delighted to have a daughter who was willing to work to contribute to the family income.

Incident C: The Turners Return

Ed and Mavis Turner were glad to get back to their spacious midwestern home and their friends. They had been very pleased to have a chance to go to China shortly after Ed's retirement from his university position, even though it was hard to leave their comfortable home, their many friends, and their children and grandchildren. The Shandong Provincial Government had hired Ed as an agricultural expert, and Mavis, who had taught high school English for more than 30 years, taught English conversation and reading at a suburban hydraulic institute. Their Chinese colleagues and students had been kind, hardworking, enthusiastic, and appreciative of their expertise and commitment. The fact that Ed and Mavis were both flexible, tolerant people who enjoyed experiencing something a little different, made their experience in China quite a positive one, in spite of undeniable physical hardships.

For the first 2 weeks or so, Ed and Mavis felt nothing but joy. Their grandchildren had changed much in the 2 years that they had been gone, and catching up with their friends and kids had been fun. They began to notice, though, that although everyone had much to tell them, no one was especially interested in hearing about their experiences in China. When their church arranged for them to show their slides of China, Ed and Mavis were dismayed by the shallow questions and the negative attitudes toward China. Ed and Mavis were also distressed by the portrayal of China and the Chinese in the media and in the willingness of their friends and family to believe Ted Koppel rather than themselves.

Even though they were financially secure, Ed and Mavis found themselves troubled by how expensive everything was, and at the opportunities to spend vast sums on nonessentials. They had always enjoyed going out to eat, but now it bothered them to think about how much they spent on a single meal, especially when they recalled how life was so hard for their friends back in Shandong. In general, they found it hard to find activities that didn't seem pointless, or even worse, destructive and wasteful. Ed played golf a couple of times, and then stopped. They joined an environmental action group, but it seemed more social than political and they quit. Local politics were a constant source of irritation to them. Both of them suffered from stomach trouble for several months after their return, but both of them began to feel better when Mavis started to serve rice and vegetables almost every day.

Rather than becoming more comfortable in the town where they had lived for nearly 40 years, they seemed to withdraw from many of their old friends and to wait, instead, for letters from friends in China. When Ed suggested, 8 months after their return to the United States, that they look for another opportunity to return to China, Mavis agreed immediately.

Discussion Question

How can you explain Ed and Mavis's sudden unhappiness in a town where they have spent almost all their lives?

1. Ed and Mavis are at an age where it isn't very easy to adapt to changes anymore. They just need to give themselves a little more time.

2. It's not uncommon for people to become more critical of everything after their retirement, or to find that their views on things change. Their trip to China is only a small part of their difficulty with their friends and family.

3. Ed and Mavis are atypical. Most people their age not only would never even leave the country for such a long period as 2 years, but they would also be delighted to return and would never want to leave again.

4. Ed and Mavis are experiencing common symptoms of reverse culture shock. Their decision to return to their host country is not an uncommon solution to the discomfort of reentry stress.

Incident D: Back From a Semester in London

Jason had a great time on his semester abroad. London had been perfect for him. He'd never had an ear for languages, so he was relieved that it was possible for him to go to an English-speaking country. Living in a big city suited him, too. He had grown up in Chicago and felt comfortable with the varied night life, cultural opportunities, and bustle. He got along great with his flatmate, a student from Germany, and they had explored the city together, commiserated about the strange British university system, and exchanged impressions of their British hosts.

On returning to Chicago to begin his senior year, Jason felt unaccountably depressed. He felt that people were very interested in hearing about the adventures of students who had been to India and Japan, but everyone felt they knew all about England. No one seemed to be very interested in his experience. Sometimes he had difficulty understanding what people were saying to him, but he wasn't quite sure why. When he occasionally used a Briticism instead of the corresponding Americanism, his classmates thought him affected, or just odd. Things that he had never even noticed before began to irritate him, such as the fact that supermarkets were so enormous, that he had to drive to get to them, and that the public transportation was so impossible. He had never been much interested in politics, but now he found himself very critical of the government, particularly of foreign policy. He felt impatient with his friends because they didn't seem to care. He missed London and his flatmate Wolfgang more than seemed reasonable.

Jason started skipping classes, something he had almost never done before. He showed little interest in going out in the evening with his friends. Some of his closest friends started to get a little worried about him, and suggested that he see a student counselor.

Discussion Question

As a student counselor, what would you say Jason's problem is?

1. England is too similar to the United States for Jason to have experienced much culture shock in going there, let alone reverse culture shock on reentry. More likely there is something else going on in Jason's life that the counselor needs to learn about.
2. It's perfectly normal for a person who has been out of the country for 4 to 6 months to experience reverse culture shock. Jason needs to talk about and process his experience in England before he can get down to the business of course work and feel comfortable back at school.
3. Jason is experiencing problems common to many senior students. He is reluctant to graduate and is subconsciously sabotaging himself.
4. It is common for students returning from a semester abroad to take a few weeks to get back into the swing of things, but there is no need for him to see a counselor. All he needs is a little time. He should be encouraged to go out with friends and to attend his classes, even if he doesn't feel like it.

Discussion of Critical Incidents

Each of these four critical incidents is designed to highlight one or more aspects of reverse culture shock. Incident A illustrates how reverse culture shock may affect people of different ages and occupations in different ways. All the problems that Ellen and her family members are experiencing are common manifestations of reentry shock. In addition, Incident A addresses the issue of time; reverse culture shock may be most intense immediately after reentry or it may develop, becoming more and more pronounced over time. Sojourners who do not recognize their reverse culture shock, and who do not have an opportunity to process their experiences in a positive way, commonly continue to exhibit symptoms of reverse culture shock—depression, disorientation, inability or unwillingness to fit in—for years after reentry.

Incident B focuses on the problems faced by female sojourners returning home from cultures in which they had comparatively greater freedom and responsibility. Another issue is that of physical adjustment; like many returnees, Miroo becomes sick, possibly because of a change in diet or because of less hygienic conditions than those to which she has become accustomed. Physical problems can exacerbate or become confused with other reentry issues, such as emotional conflict with family members or difficulties finding a job.

In Incident C, Ed and Mavis Turner, though mature and very well established in a community in their home culture, experience profound reverse culture shock. Reverse culture shock, it must be stressed, affects nearly every sojourner, regardless of age. For many people, the only solution—and often a quite happy one—may seem to be another sojourn, perhaps a temporary or permanent return to the country from which they have recently returned.

Incident D addresses the particular problems of sojourners who are returning from a culture that is generally assumed to be not very different from the home culture. Precisely because reentry problems are not anticipated and will not be identified as such, reverse culture shock may be especially severe. Language alone does not define culture. Also important in this incident is that Jason feels no one is interested in hearing about his experiences. This is a very common complaint of returning sojourners. The feeling that one must not talk about the sojourn, or that no one is really listening and understanding, can make it very difficult for a returnee to process the overseas experience and move on from it.

Skill Concepts: Defining Reverse Culture Shock

Definitions

Adler (1976) defines *reentry* as "the transition into one's home culture after having lived and worked abroad" (p. 7). Oberg (1960) describes *culture shock* as "an occupational disease precipitated by the anxiety that results from losing all familiar signs and symbols of social intercourse" (p. 177). Reentry shock, or reverse culture shock, is losing the signs and symbols of social intercourse during the transition into one's home culture after living and working in another culture.

Those who must deal with reverse culture shock include returning students, faculty on exchange programs, researchers, anthropologists, population control workers, public health workers, international medical relief teams, artists, athletes, agronomists, journalists, environmentalists, Peace Corps volunteers, Hunger Relief volunteers, employees of multinational corporations and their families, Foreign Service officers and their families, military personnel and their families, UN Peacekeeping Forces, repatriated refugees, missionary families, and occasionally even short-term tourists.

The three terms most commonly used in the discussion of the reentry experience are (cultural) reentry, reacculturation, and reverse culture shock. *Cultural reentry* is the most neutral, a purely descriptive term that tells us nothing about the quality of the experience. Reacculturation suggests similarities to the initial cross-cultural experience, the process of adapting to the host culture from which the sojourner is now returning. The term *reacculturation* suggests possibilities for returnees to view reentry as a second cross-cultural experience, which may suggest helpful coping strategies. On the other hand, with its implications of getting back to normal, or re-acclimating to the norms of the home culture, it may mask the potential for growth that results from contact with other cultures. The phrase that remains in most common popular use, however, is reverse culture shock. Reenterers, their families, and their friends, are most likely to use this term, because with all its negative implications, it describes their experience very well.

Martin (1984, 1986) recognizes the crucial role of communication in coping with reentry and in turning it into a growth experience. She suggests that it might be better to conceptualize reentry as a process of sojourners' struggling with changed communication patterns: changes in the symbols, their meanings, and the rules that govern interaction. Through the process of acculturation to the foreign culture, the sojourner may "acquire new patterns of communicating, both verbally and nonverbally, and often internalize them as well" (Martin, 1986, p. 5). Martin stresses the importance of "communication with others" as a tool for reorientation and for learning to interpret changed patterns of interaction and changes in the sojourners themselves.

Martin (1986) quotes Upobor as saying, "The severity of reentry shock is proportional to the magnitude of change in the individual or the environment" (p. 123). Not only the individual has changed during the sojourn, but also the home culture and the people there. Therefore, it is the relative difference between the changes in the individual and in the environment to which that person is returning that is important.

If we consider reverse culture shock as a reaction to the cumulative changes in self and home during the sojourner's absence, it is not so surprising that recovering from reentry often takes much longer than the sojourn itself. In some cases, reentry is really never complete, because some changes—particularly changes in values—will affect the whole course of the sojourner's life. Reverse culture shock, then, may be considered a long-term process of coming to terms with oneself as a more complex, more multicultural individual in a changed but familiar setting.

Subjective Accounts: What Reverse Culture Shock Feels Like

Accounts of the reentry experience consistently emphasize feelings that can be discussed in terms of the following four areas (Austin, 1986): challenge to self-concept, disconfirmed expectations, sense of loss, and value changes and choices.

Challenge to Self-Concept

Even before reentry to the home culture, most sojourners begin to become aware of—and often frightened by—profound changes in their conceptions of themselves. Returnees must face the fact that they are not the same people who left on the sojourn; that they have been forever changed. Sojourners frequently lose, or learn to question, patriotic feelings, and as a consequence their sense of identity as citizens of their particular country may be changed. "If I'm not American (or Indian, or Chinese)," they may ask themselves, "then what am I?" Sojourners will have acquired new non-verbal behaviors they may scarcely be aware of, and many will have learned, or improved their fluency in, a foreign language, thus acquiring a whole new way of thinking about and expressing things. Sojourners may be aware that their "old selves" would not have approved of these new ideas and behaviors, and that those left behind will also disapprove.

Time does not stand still while one is away from home, and young adults, in particular, will be making life choices, some of which may be at odds with the home culture into which they were originally socialized. A young adult in a multicultural setting is being socialized by two or more societies simultaneously. The values of the home culture are still very much present in one's memory and in the presence of other nationals, and at the same time there are pressures to conform to the expectations and values of the host culture. Sojourners may choose a career or a partner, make a religious conversion, or become politically involved for reasons that are inexplicable to the people among whom they received their earlier socialization.

In considering what "the folks back home" will make of the changes in them, sojourners often discover that they are rather proud of the very changes that are likely to cause problems with the people they care about. New values, new tolerance, and new insights may make the sojourners critical of their old selves and the people who nurtured those selves. In other words, sojourners come to realize that they no longer share the values of groups and individuals with whom they have identified in the past and among whom they must now live again. At the same time that family and friends are eager for returnees to "get back to normal," the returnees may suddenly realize that they have no intention of doing so, of undoing all the hard work of acculturation into the foreign culture. No longer surrounded by those in the host culture who were responsible for the development of the new self, and no longer completely comfortable with the friends and family to which they return, returnees often feel completely alone, at home neither in the host culture nor in the home culture, only at home in some nonexistent place in between.

Disconfirmed Expectations: The Sojourner's Expectations

Although nearly every traveler expects to experience culture shock while visiting an unfamiliar culture, very few are prepared for the culture shock of returning to their supposedly familiar home culture. Campus Crusade for Christ lists an impressive 45 "more commonly occurring situations" (Austin, 1986) when their fieldworkers return to the home culture. The disconfirmed expectation that almost defines reverse culture shock is, "I didn't expect to feel like a foreigner in my own country." Returnees nearly always report feeling out of place, as if they were not at home but in a foreign country that is something like home. They get sick. The food disagrees with them; often the very foods they have been longing for are indigestible or simply disgusting. They may have trouble understanding what others are saying, not just because of references to popular culture but because they have become accustomed to a different pattern of conversation, a different rhythm of discourse.

The returning sojourner's expectations for the home culture are often extremely unrealistic, based on an idealized vision of home. Unwilling sojourners—military personnel involved in foreign conflicts, partners and dependents reluctantly accompanying businesspeople on overseas assignments—are especially likely to cope with frustrations in the foreign culture by consoling themselves that "this would never happen back home" or "when I get home I won't have to put up with this anymore." This builds them up for an enormous letdown when they return to the home culture, which is naturally less than perfect. Even those for whom the sojourn has been a positive experience are likely to idealize the reentry so that it cannot possibly live up to expectations.

Some commonly disconfirmed expectations that can be extremely upsetting and difficult to resolve concern personal relationships. Returnees don't expect to feel so critical of their loved ones. North American returnees from sojourns to developing countries are often deeply disturbed by what they see as the complacent provincialism and wastefulness of their family members and friends. Returning sojourners are often disappointed because they cannot simply go back to the relationships that they had when they left. They anticipate that their friendships will be as intense and as daily as when they left. They may fail to realize that the holes they left in others' lives when they departed will be filled; their friends will have found new friendships and new activities to occupy them and may not have much time for them when they return. In addition, returnees find that they seem to have little to talk about with many of their old friends. The bonds of common experience have been dissolved and often both parties find that there is nothing left on which to build a relationship.

Particularly disappointing for returnees is what Brislin and Van Buren (1974) call the Uncle Charlie syndrome. No one wants to hear about their trip, their insights, their exotic experiences. Their friends and family members are more interested in local gossip and professional sports than in the returnee's life-altering sojourn. In fact, the sojourner's need to communicate the experience to loved ones is far greater than most people's capacity to listen, especially when the listeners have little experience with the foreign culture and can, therefore, barely comprehend—even with great effort and good will—what the sojourner is trying to communicate.

Disconfirmed Expectations: Others' Expectations for the Returning Sojourner

Not only the sojourner is likely to be upset by the failure of the return home to live up to expectations; family members, friends, coworkers, and supervisors will have built up expectations of their own about what the returnee will want to do, eat, and talk about, how glad the returnee will be to see them and to be back home, and how the returnee will fit back into their lives. These expectations, like those of the returning sojourner, are often unrealistic.

Family and friends can be very upset that the sojourner doesn't seem happier to be home. In particular, family and friends don't expect the returnee to be so critical of the home culture. They often don't anticipate that the returnee will be homesick for the foreign country, missing friends there, longing for a now familiar lifestyle. They may take the sojourner's unhappiness, and criticisms, more personally than they were meant.

Family and friends generally expect the returnee to be interested in catching up on popular culture and local gossip, which is the only aspect of culture in which the stay-at-home is likely to have noticed changes. On the other hand, they may fail to comment on, let alone explain, truly fundamental but gradual changes. Those who have been living in the culture have a hard time taking any sense of perspective about the changes in it and appreciating the returnee's disorientation with regard to perfectly "normal" situations.

People will be confused by the returnees' inability to understand what is said to them, and their lack of interest in things about which they once were passionate. Again, it is easy to take the rejection of a thoughtfully prepared plan for a fun evening, or of a lovingly prepared "favorite" meal, as a rejection of the person who offers it.

When the returnee talks at length about the sojourn, about what he or she misses from the host culture, loved ones may become very impatient with what they see as the sojourner's unwillingness to "get back to normal." They cannot understand what is taking so long, and why the returnee is dwelling on the past. Even people who use the term "reverse culture shock" generally have little idea that it is measured in years, not days.

Sense of Loss

Whereas sojourners to foreign cultures generally intend to return home in the fore-seeable future, those returning to the home culture frequently face a tremendous sense of permanent loss. They must say good-bye to close friends they may never see again. They may leave a home they have grown to love, a familiar landscape, a career, school, pets—a whole life to which they will never return.

Loss of the lifestyle enjoyed in the foreign culture often adds to the stress of return. Many sojourners enjoy enhanced status in their communities while abroad. They may have more decision-making power than if they were back in the home office. They may be "foreign experts" in the host country, whereas back home they are just another engineer or geologist. A recent college graduate is a revered teacher. Even the foreign student commands attention at high school, simply by virtue of being the foreigner. Thus, returnees frequently feel undervalued as people, unnoticed and unappreciated.

Not only status, but also salary and benefits may be greater while overseas. In other cases, even a salary small by home-country standards may buy a comfortable living in the host-country economy. Expatriates may become accustomed to having servants, eating out frequently, or living in luxurious surroundings, at least compared to the rest of the community. Returnees may be shocked by how much things cost; their memory of prices will not have made adjustments for inflation and fluctuations in the prices of such things as homes.

Returnees may feel a sense of loss in regard to cultural advantages. The sojourner may find the fine arts relatively more affordable than at home. Hosts may arrange a wide range of entertainment for the visitor, or other members of the expatriate community may go out and find interesting diversions for themselves. Even when there is no particular performance to attend, there is always something interesting to do in an unfamiliar culture. Even doing the grocery shopping is challenging and interest-ing. Many international travelers report that they feel more focused and alive when in an unfamiliar culture, and that they miss that feeling of focus or presence when they are in the home culture (Fontaine, 1993).

Many women, in particular, report the loss of a sense of freedom. For North American women in countries where most people of their class have servants, there has been freedom from household chores that allows them to work outside the home and still spend relaxed time with their families and friends. They may be exhausted by the double burden of household chores and work, on top of the physical strain of reentry. Women returning to other countries from Europe and North America often complain that they must listen to their elders, especially the men, and that they miss the freedom to make their own decisions, to go out on their own, and to choose their own friends.

Even unwilling sojourners who have resisted acculturation into the host culture may miss the closeness of a small expatriate community. Seeing friends only once or twice a week—or month—can be very lonely for someone who is used to dining daily with groups of friends. The experience of being together in the foreign country, of puzzling out local customs and odd experiences, and of dealing with crises within the expatriate community, creates a closeness that may seem suffocating at the time but that is very much missed in the home country when everyone else seems too busy with their own lives to have much time for the returnee.

Finally, the returnee will miss many aspects of day-to-day living, things that may have initially irritated or bewildered them. Sojourners returning to developing countries may have become more dependent than they realized on technology that is unavailable at home, or on big research libraries. Returnees may miss mass transit systems or having their own cars. They miss sleeping in beds, or on the floor, or in hammocks. They may miss eating rice or seaweed or fish or cabbage on a daily basis. They may long for a view of the mountains or the sea, the skyscrapers or the forest.

Value Changes and Choices

Perhaps the greatest challenge to all returnees, especially those who have become very much acculturated into the host culture because of the length or the intensity of the cross-cultural experience, is to find a happy middle ground between the home culture and the host culture. Returnees need to consider how to integrate their international experience with the day-to-day realities of life in the home country without compromising important values acquired in the host culture. The challenge to returnees is to *recognize* the changes in their values and attitudes and *decide* which are worth pursuing and preserving and which to abandon in the interest of conformity and harmonious relations with significant others. Recognition of the changes is crucial to redefining self-concept in a positive way. At the same time, returnees need to realize that they do have choices, that there are decisions to be made about which values of host and home cultures to nurture, which to reject, and which to reconsider and recombine.

One choice to be made is whether, and to what extent, the returnee wishes to affect the attitudes and values of others. Unhappy, confused returnees all too commonly criticize indiscriminately, antagonizing the very people they wish to communicate with, win the affection of, or even persuade to accept their point of view. If returnees are going to affect the attitudes of others, if they are going to "share the wealth" of their cross-cultural experiences, they need to choose the issues that matter most to them and then consider how to communicate the importance of those issues to those who have not had the benefit of their cross-cultural experience. ALL returnees, it is important to remember, will have undergone some changes in their values, and ALL returnees need to make choices; the challenge is to do so wisely, for the most positive effect on self and others. This can be very difficult when one is reeling from shock.

Returnees need to consider social, political, technological, physical, and ideological limitations on putting their new knowledge to use. They also need to think about how to deal with those limitations. Sometimes older colleagues feel threatened by a young "upstart" newly returned from overseas. Other times, the technology is not readily available to continue projects begun elsewhere, or the political climate makes pushing a particular project or point of view difficult or even dangerous. Judiciously choosing a few key issues to go to battle over will help avoid frustration and may be the only way to assure that some of the newly acquired knowledge gets put to use.

Returning sojourners will want to take the cross-cultural experience into account in considering their career plans. Many young sojourners find that the cross-cultural experience encourages them to prepare for a career working with other sojourners. Others choose careers that allow for, or require, subsequent sojourns. Some returnees find that experiences in the host culture have prepared them for, or interested them in, career options that would not otherwise have occurred to them. An example might be someone who became interested in environmental issues or human rights while in another culture; that returnee may never leave his or her country again, but the sojourn was the impetus for their career choice. Sojourners returning to the same workplace, or type of workplace they left, need to be especially careful to consider the goals of their employers and the limitations of coworkers and superiors in appreciating the value of a cross-cultural experience about which they may understand little. Such returnees need to decide how best to promote their new talents in the working environment as it is, not as they wish it to be.

Many returnees find that they can become cultural mediators, thus remaining involved with their host culture while providing a welcome service to the community. Even high school year-abroad students will find opportunities to teach others about the cultures in which they have lived. There are often chances to do volunteer interpreting or translating, or to help others prepare for a visit from people from the sojourner's home culture. Cultural mediation may or may not develop into a career.

Attempts at Isolating Variables That Correlate With Reentry Shock

A number of researchers have attempted to isolate variables that correlate with culture shock and reverse culture shock. Some of those variables include gender (Brabant, Palmer, & Gramling, 1990; Gama & Pedersen, 1977), age (Brabant et al., 1990; Gullahorn & Gullahorn, 1963; Uehara, 1986), academic level (Gullahorn & Gullahorn, 1963), location and duration of sojourn (Torbiorn, 1982), degree of interaction in and adjustment to host culture (Uehara, 1986), and frequency of home visits (Brabant et al., 1990). Nationals of certain countries, such as the Japanese, may experience more stress on reentry because of the homogeneity of their cultures (Enloe & Lewin, 1987; Kidder, 1992; White, 1992).

The only things that clearly correlate with reverse culture shock are female gender (positively) and frequent home visits (negatively). Both the intensity and the duration of difficulties with reentry are more pronounced for women, for reasons too numerous to discuss here. The negative correlation of frequent home visits with reentry problems seems fairly simple and obvious. Reverse culture shock is a surprise, with expectations unmet and the unfamiliar where the familiar is expected. If sojourners have frequent opportunities to see the changes at home, they will be less surprised by them. They will be able to make plans and decisions throughout the sojourn that take changing conditions into account, and they will note changes in their own behavior, values, and attitudes and have the opportunity to integrate those changes more gradually.

Research also shows that although family relationships are often strengthened by the separation and return, friendships less frequently survive the reentry process, and romances almost never.

Skill Application: Small Group Discussion Focusing on Particular Aspects of the Reentry Experience

If there is any topic that lends itself to small group discussion, it is reentry. Every trainee's situation is unique; even if host and home country are the same, families and friends will differ, as will specific economic situations. Small group discussion allows fruitful worrying to begin, and encourages participants to begin considering the issues that will confront them on their return to the home country.

Discussion in each group centers around aspects of the reentry experience: food (and possibly other physical issues, such as climate or hygiene), friends and family, jobs and networking, the local economy, and maintaining international interests. Groups are rarely able to generate discussion questions for themselves. Most often, imminent returnees cannot imagine possible areas of stress and conflict and will need quite specific guidance to get started. Each group sticks to issues related to the chosen topic but participants are free to change groups at any time, as long as the predetermined maximum number of people per group (usually 6) is not exceeded.

Peer moderators—ideally individuals with previous reentry experiences—can make sure everyone contributes, and identify and challenge participants who believe that reverse culture shock is not going to happen to them. They can also identify trainees whose needs would be better served in a different discussion group. Mutual trust among members of the group is essential if participants are to share their concerns and identify the key issues for their own reentry. Moderators can help to establish a trusting, comfortable atmosphere in the group. They need also be prepared for the likelihood that participants may get rather emotional, especially if their reentry is imminent, the sojourn has been a long one, and previous preparation for reentry has been minimal.

Session Focusing on Food

1. What is a typical day's diet for you here? What was your typical diet in your home country before you came here? Do you expect your diet in your home country to change to include items you have become accustomed to eating here?

2. What foods from home are you looking forward to eating? Do you anticipate any problems in obtaining or digesting them?

3. What foods from the host country will you miss? Is there any chance that you will ever be able to obtain them after your return? What foods from the host country will you definitely NOT miss?

4. Has your diet changed because of a change in your religious beliefs or for other moral or philosophical reasons? Will be you be able to maintain your new eating habits after you return home?

5. Have you considered the possibility that the change back to your home country diet may cause temporary discomfort or health problems? Can you plan a diet that will allow you to become gradually reaccustomed to your home country diet and help you maintain good health through your reentry process?

Session Focusing on Relationships With Family and Friends

1. Who among your friends and family members do you think you will be able to depend on? Who will you be able to share your feelings with? Why? What specifically do you think you will need from these people?

2. With whom do you think you will need to work out new ground rules for the relationship?

3. What are some things that you would like your parents, siblings, extended family members, coworkers, friends, to know about you as you are now?

4. Can you think of any changes in your values or behavior that are likely to create stress in, or improve, your relationship with your parents, siblings, extended family members, coworkers, friends?

5. If your family is here with you, (a) Why did your spouse [kids] join you? (b) What do they think of being here? (c) What do they think of going home? (d) Has being here changed your relationship? Will you go back to doing things the way you used to when you return, or will you continue in your "new" ways?

6. If you are single, will you be expected to marry or begin looking for a spouse shortly after your return? How do you feel about that? How will you proceed?

7. If you were married shortly before coming here, or while you were in this country, how will your relationship with your spouse be different in the home country? Specifically, how will others' expectations for your relationship and the demands of family, work, and society on each spouse influence the relationship?

Session Focusing on Jobs and Networking

1. If you are returning to the same organization you worked for before your sojourn, (a) What changes have there been in the organization since you left? How do you know about the changes? (b) Have you been in regular contact with your supervisor by mail or phone? What about contact with coworkers? (c) To what extent will your new degree, your international experience, and your newly acquired skills be assets, and to what extent liabilities, as you return to your job? (d) Do you have any reason to anticipate that coworkers will be jealous of your overseas experience? What about your supervisors?

2. If you will be looking for a new job, (a) How much do you know about the job situation in your country at present? Is there any way that you could learn more? (b) To what extent will your new degree, your international experience, and your newly acquired skills be assets, and to what extent liabilities, in finding and doing your new job? (c) What are the most important things you will be considering as you hunt for a job? If (extended) family members will be helping you in your job search, will they agree with these priorities?

3. Has the world of work in your culture changed much in your absence? If you have been working in this country, how do you expect the workplace atmosphere to differ in your home country?

4. Will your professional status be higher or lower in your home country than it is here? Are you prepared for that change?

Session Focusing on Living on the Local Economy

1. Have there been any profound changes in the local economy of your home country or area since you left (e.g., loss or addition of a major industry, recession, change of economic structure, runaway inflation)?

2. How much do you expect it will cost you to get an apartment or house? What sort of home do you envision for yourself? Are these expectations realistic? What can you do to learn more about rents and real estate prices before you return?

3. Is it easier or more difficult to find a job than when you left? Why do you think so?

4. Are there things you have become accustomed to using in your work or daily life that will not be available in the area where you will be living? What are you going to do about that?

5. Will your financial status be higher or lower than it is in this country? Are you prepared for the change?

Session Focusing on Maintaining International Interests

1. Does your institution have an alumni association in your home country? Do you know how to contact them?

2. Will you have access to information about this country after you return to your home country? How important is that to you? How might you arrange to get regular information after your return?

3. Do you know of organizations in the area of your home country in which you will be living that have an international focus? Are you interested in joining them?

4. Are there people from this country living in your home country? Do you anticipate that you will have opportunities to socialize with them? Do you think you will want to?

5. How will friends, family, coworkers, and the like view your efforts to make new international friends and maintain international contacts?

Self-Help Measures: Coping Strategies and Suggestions for Smoother Reentry, with a Focus on Sojourns for Academic Purposes

Ideally, the sojourner's life in the home country should be richer for the cross-cultural experience. Institutions that host foreign visitors, the cross-cultural sojourners themselves, and their families and friends can do much to make the reentry experience a positive one (also see Chapter 8 in this volume).

What Institutions Can Do

1. Begin preparing sojourners for reentry as soon as they arrive in the foreign country, if not before they leave.

   A. Remind students and researchers to keep the needs and limitations of their home situations in mind. Courses and research projects can be selected, and purchases and demands on professors made, to prepare students for work in their own country rather than for work in the foreign country. This is especially important for students who will return from technologically advanced countries to developing countries. Providing sessions in which newly arrived international students receive training in how to make good use of advising sessions, make suitable demands on advisors, and see to it that the advice they get about their studies really keeps their long term needs in mind might be useful.

   B. Holding regular sessions where students from the same country or region discuss changes in themselves wrought by the international experience, and how those changes will affect them when they reenter, can help prepare students for what to expect. If possible, such sessions should be attended by one or more people who have experienced reentry into that culture.

C. Just worrying has been shown to be helpful (Brislin & Van Buren, 1974). If students are aware that reentry may be problematic and think about it before it happens, they are likely to make plans that will preempt some of the problems and come up with solutions that work for them as individuals.

The National Association of Foreign Student Advisors (NAFSA) in the United States makes materials on reentry available to their members. If your program doesn't allow for reentry workshops, at least distribute a workbook (e.g., Denney, 1986) that can be used by students, working on their own, to provide ongoing preparation for reentry.

2. Help faculty and support staff assist sojourners in making appropriate adjustments and decisions during the sojourn.
   A. Faculty members and others who work with international students need to understand that it is not always in the best interests of all visitors from all countries to become as acculturated as possible to the host culture. Reentry will be easier if students have not been pressured too much to abandon the practices and values of their home country. Faculty can also be encouraged to be sensitive to the fact that the long-term goals and needs of international students may not be the same as those of local students.
   B. Language programs (e.g., ESL) can offer training for international graduate students in how to make the most of advising sessions, what to expect from such sessions, and what the student's rights and responsibilities are in relation to faculty for graduate courses.

3. Contact alumni associations.
   Returnees need people to talk to, and some of the most sympathetic listeners are other returnees, those who have experienced what they are going through. Alumni associations can put returnees in touch with people who know EXACTLY what their foreign experience was and who can help them understand the reentry process and avoid common areas of conflict.

What Returnees Can Do for Themselves

Before Reentry

1. Prepare those to whom you'll be returning. Relay your thoughts and concerns before you return. Write to those you will have most contact with when you return and express some of your concerns about reentry. Write about the changes in yourself, your expectations for your return, what you miss most from the home country. Allow others a chance to prepare for the changes in you. Invite them to express their expectations for you on your return.

2. Prepare yourself. Just as you would before making a foreign sojourn, find out all you can about the home culture. Ask questions of friends, tourists, the embassy or consulate—anyone who might know—about prices, the job market, changes in the local economy, technological innovations. Subscribe for a while to a newspaper or magazine that reports on the area in which you'll be living.

3. If reentry training is offered, participate as frequently as possible.

After Reentry

1. Take it easy, take it slow.

   A. If possible, sojourners should give themselves a few months, or at least weeks, particularly after an absence of years, before beginning to hunt for jobs or apply to schools. After all, there are physical adjustments to be made—recovering from jet lag, becoming accustomed to the diet and climate—in addition to the psychological adjustments.

   B. Many sojourners find it much easier to return in two stages, first to the country and second to family and friends. Especially if you are returning to a small town, a less international and cosmopolitan area, you may be well-advised to spend a week or 10 days in a big city before proceeding home. Other sojourners take an opposite approach and spend some time in a remote area with one or two friends, or perhaps in a temple. Whatever will give you a chance to get over the shock of reentering the culture before dealing with what may be very intense emotional encounters with family and close friends is to be encouraged.

   C. Don't be afraid to hide out where you feel safe and gather information for a while. You might try Oprah Winfrey therapy—watching talk shows, home dramas, or any TV program that reflects media perceptions of "everyday life" in the culture and gives you an opportunity to observe interactions between members of the culture without you having to participate or be responsible to the parties involved.

   D. Don't be afraid to make use of family members or friends who can come between you and less understanding individuals when you need them to do so.

   E. Ask questions when you don't understand what's going on.

   F. Avail yourself of professional services. Find someone in the local home culture to help you put together a professional-looking, culturally acceptable résumé. Ask your family doctor, minister, or priest for advice about places to meet similar, sympathetic others.

2. Find people to talk to.

   A. Other people who have had international experiences in the same country with the same organization are the best possibilities. Anyone with international experience is a possibility. There is evidence in the literature that family members are more likely than friends to stick with returnees through a difficult reentry process.

   B. Look for like-minded people among those who work or otherwise spend time with international students or immigrants in your country. Volunteer your talents.

   C. Find people with similar interests. Get comfortable with a small group of people who share your interest in music or an activity. Join a sports team.

3. Remind yourself that this, too, is a cross-cultural experience. When the going gets tough, try to see your home culture as a "foreign culture" to be studied. Do the things that you did to become acculturated in the host country, such as watch TV or find cultural informants. Also, remind or inform others that this is a cross-cultural experience for you and that you need help interpreting some of the signs and symbols around you. Be frank about what you don't understand and why.

4. Be conscious that you have choices. Decide what values from the foreign culture are most important to cling to, and consider how those values can be integrated practically with those of the home culture.

Understand that the ball is in your court. Your cross-cultural experience will be in your mind, in one way or another, for a long, long time. This is not true of the people to whom you are returning. Help them out by asking questions when you need to, and perhaps explaining why you needed to ask the question in the first place. If you feel that your talents aren't being put to good use, especially those talents you gained while away from a work environment to which you have now returned, give some thought to how you can help your employers understand how they can better use your special skills.

What Family and Friends Can Do

1. Listen and try not to judge. Remember, breakdown in communication is at the heart of reverse culture shock. Try to help the returnee communicate. Be sensitive to the fact that the returnee is struggling with conflict: the desire not to hurt others' feelings, an inability to express his or her own feelings, and the sense that others have long tired of listening.

2. Help the returnee find others to be with. Being the sole person on whom a returnee depends can be exhausting. Introduce the returnee to others who may share his or her interests, a sports team, people new in town, other interesting "misfits."

3. Don't take it personally if the returnee is no longer interested in the things you think he or she should be, or doesn't seem thrilled with a meal you have cooked or an activity you have planned.

References

Adler, N. (1976). Growthful re-entry theory. [Unpublished mimeo.] Graduate School of Management, University of California, Los Angeles.

Austin, C. (1986). *Cross-cultural re-entry: A book of readings.* Abilene, TX: Abilene Christian University Press.

Brabant, S., Palmer, C. E., & Gramling, R. (1990). Returning home: An empirical investigation of cross-cultural reentry. *International Journal of Intercultural Relations, 14,* 387-404.

Brislin, R. & Van Buren, H. (1974). Can they go home again? *International Educational and Cultural Exchange, 9*(4), 19-24.

Campus Crusade for Christ (1980). A guide to reentry: Field test copy. In C. Austin, (Ed.), *Cross-cultural re-entry: A book of readings* (pp. 239-250) Abilene, TX: Abilene Christian University Press.

Denney, M. (1986). *Going home: A workbook for reentry and professional integration.* Washington DC: NAFSA.

Enloe, W. & Lewin, P. (1987). Issues of integration abroad and readjustment to Japan of Japanese returnees. *International Journal of Intercultural Relations, 11,* 223-248.

Fontaine, G. (1993, September 22). Motivations for seeking and keeping international assignments: Why do people do it? Lecture at the East-West Center. Honolulu, Hawaii.

Gama, E. M. P., & Pedersen, P. (1977). Readjustment problems of Brazilian returnees from graduate studies in the United States. *International Journal of Intercultural Relations, 1,* 46-58.

Gullahorn, J. T., & Gullahorn, J. E. (1963). An extension of the U-curve hypothesis. *Journal of Social Issues, 14,* 33-47.

Kidder, L. H. (1992). Requirements for being "Japanese." *International Journal of Intercultural Relations, 16,* 383-393.

LeGuin, U. K. (1974). *The dispossessed: An ambiguous utopia.* New York: Harper and Row.

Martin, J. (1984). The intercultural reentry: Conceptualization and directions for future research. *International Journal of Intercultural Relations, 8,* 115-134.

Martin, J. (1986) Communication in the intercultural reentry: Student sojourners' perceptions of change in reentry relationship. *International Journal of Intercultural Relations, 10,* 1-22.

Oberg, K. (1960). Cultural shock: Adjustment to new cultural environments. *Practical Anthropology, 7,* 177-182.

Torbiorn, I. (1982) *Living abroad: Personal adjustment and personnel policy in the overseas setting.* New York: John Wiley.

Uehara, A. (1986). The nature of American student reentry adjustment and perceptions of the sojourn experience. *International Journal of Intercultural Relations, 10,* 415-438.

White, M. (1992). *The Japanese overseas: Can they go home again?* Princeton, NJ.: Princeton University Press.

8

Managing International
and Intercultural Programs

Kenneth Cushner
Charles Nieman

Increasing numbers of organizations are being called on either to host a group of visiting internationals, to organize and conduct a program that takes a number of individuals to an overseas destination to work collaboratively with others, or to bring together representatives from two different groups who may have had limited contact with one another (e.g., Arabs and Jews). There are generally two approaches that individuals and organizations can adopt when planning and executing international or intercultural programs. The more unilateral approach is characterized by rather narrow attempts to satisfy one's own needs, with little sensitivity paid to those of the other party. Guiding questions that might be heard when adopting such an approach include "What do we want to show or accomplish?" or "How much can we gain?" When one is more concerned with introducing one's own product into another's marketplace, or in bringing one's own group into another's environment without consideration for how the other will be affected, the chance of long-term benefit and collaboration is limited. One group may win—however, it is often at the other's expense.

An alternative approach, a truly bilateral or multilateral approach, demands recognition of all parties' backgrounds, hopes, and attitudes, while attempting to satisfy one another's needs. Such an approach frequently results in new ways of doing things as all parties move beyond self-interest and strive to find common solutions and ways of interacting that can be agreed on by all. In a very real sense, a synergy develops that merges certain elements of both cultures as they go about creating a new approach. Guiding questions might include "How can we embark on a long-term relationship that benefits all parties?" or "We cannot do this alone; how can we best work together?" Such an approach is characteristic of a win-win situation.

This chapter strives to explore key issues regarding how to best prepare for intergroup contact so that all parties benefit in the long run by their individual and collective efforts. Some of these key issues include the development of program objectives; balancing task, culture learning, and free time; preventing or managing intergroup conflict; and understanding the unique demands placed on directors and participants of international and intercultural programs in such a manner that all parties benefit in the long run. Following a brief self-assessment and critical incident review, the module will explore concepts and concerns that are evident across six phases of an intercultural program—preprogram design and planning, prearrival and predeparture preparation, arrival, team-building and collaboration, project completion, and postproject and reentry.

Contents

   I. Self-Assessment

  II. Critical Incidents

 III. Skill Concepts

 IV. Applications

  V. Concluding Thoughts

Self-Assessment

Imagine a situation related to your present work or intended work context. Your immediate supervisor has asked you to take responsibility to plan two international programs. The first requires you to organize a 2-week program for a group of visiting representatives from another country who expect to work closely with your organization over the next 5 years. The second requires you to lead a group of 10 members from your organization into an organization in another country for 4 weeks to develop a number of collaborative or joint programs.

Sketch out how you would go about planning each of these programs. What elements or activities are critical to the success of each? When would your work begin or how much lead-time do you need to prepare? What should occur, and when? When would your program end? Who should be involved?

Critical Incidents

Building Closer Ties

_____

Daniel's company had recently expanded to include a number of international firms that previously had been small, independent companies. This was to be the first attempt to bring together representatives from these firms to help them better understand the parent organization and to establish closer ties. Three representatives from each company in Indonesia, Japan, China, and Thailand were to be present. Daniel was asked to coordinate the 2-week program.

Except for a mislaid suitcase or two, most of the groups' arrivals and settling-in seemed to be satisfactory. The initial weekend orientation to the immediate surroundings and overview of the upcoming program, although tiring for Daniel, went as planned. Although a few of the people seemed to be uncomfortable at first, especially when interacting outside their immediate group, their use of English seemed satisfactory and their enthusiasm high.

Monday was to be the first time the visiting group would meet with their American counterparts. Initial introductions were smooth and quick. Mr. Johnson, the company president, spent a good part of the morning providing an overview of the company. He spoke proudly of the company's history, its growth, and of the many contributions it had made to the local community. He was excited about the opportunity to reach out around the world and promised continued attention to the new international affiliates.

The afternoon was to be the first real opportunity for group work. Daniel had carefully arranged the groups so that each had a representative from each country. He planned many small-group activities, the first of which had the American counterparts leading a discussion that centered on company goals, both for the home country and for the fast-growing international firm. Each individual was expected to make a brief presentation of his or her own company and propose how he or she might link with others around the world.

The session did not at all proceed as Daniel had expected. The American group leaders were frustrated in their role. The Japanese and Chinese participants seemed to be uncomfortable with one another and the Thais and Indonesians offered little to the conversation. By the end of the afternoon, it was clear that everyone had had enough and was happy to leave. All that could be done was to adjourn for the day and hope that, after a good night's rest, spirits would be renewed. Daniel was depressed and didn't know what to do next.

Discussion Questions

What is your analysis of the situation? From your understanding of the specific circumstances, what issues or factors might be operating here, and how might they have contributed to the tense situation? From your understanding of the various cultures involved, what factors or issues might have contributed to the present situation? What might Daniel have done to prevent such a situation from occurring? What would you suggest he do now to improve the situation?

The Overseas Program Director

The telephone woke Anne well past midnight on a Sunday midway through the semester. The voice on the other end was familiar, and panicked. "Dr. Jameson," the voice began, "This is Steve Marks, and I'm stuck over the border in France without my passport. The border officials will not let me reenter Switzerland. Friday night, after our day of skiing, I put my passport in Dana's backpack for safe-keeping. She didn't know it was there, and I guess she decided to return to Geneva earlier with a few others. My passport is in her backpack, and I'm not even sure she knows it is there. What am I to do? Can you speak to the border official and ask him to let me in?"

"I don't think so," replied Anne. "This seems a bit more serious than just going over to a neighboring college town for a drink with your friends as you might do back home. Let me speak to the official."

In halting French, Dr. Jameson managed to explain the situation to the official and inquired how best to solve the problem. A possibility, it seemed, was to bring Steve's passport to the border, and he would probably be allowed to reenter Switzerland. At 3:00 in the morning, Anne managed to drag herself from bed, wake Dana in the dormitory, locate the elusive passport, get in her little but dependable Opal, drive 45 minutes to the border, meet with the border officials, bring Steve back to campus, and organize herself just in time to teach her 8:00 a.m. class on International Relations.

Frustrated and tired, Anne wondered why she ever sought out this assignment in the first place. Since arriving in Switzerland with this small group of 23 university students, her life had been one mishap after another. She had already had her fill of problems: Two students had to be taken to the local hospital after they had an accident in a rented vehicle, and then she had to go to court with them to face charges of reckless driving; one student had to return to the States after weeks of threatening suicide; she had to plead constantly with students to drink less and keep quiet after 10:00 p.m.; she had to accommodate the different schedules of the resident faculty, including their plans to take students on various field trips and thus upsetting everyone else's schedules; and, she worried every weekend when students went traveling, especially since Jason's passport had been stolen while traveling in Italy. Anne barely had time to do her own writing, something she assumed she would have plenty of time to complete. Life certainly was much less hectic back at the home campus. At least there most problems could be handled quite effectively during her regular office hours, and she didn't have to cross international borders—merely the campus—when a problem arose! On more than one occasion, Anne considered returning home. But she could not. She had volunteered for the assignment, and the students and resident faculty depended her to at least finish the semester.

Discussion Questions

What is your analysis of the situation? From your understanding of the specific circumstances, what issues or factors might be operating here and have contributed to Anne's frustration? What issues should Anne have considered before beginning this assignment? What would you suggest she do now to improve the situation?

Skill Concepts

International and intercultural programs often present a myriad of problems and situations that can never be anticipated and certainly not planned for. From dealing with sudden medical or psychological emergencies from both program participants and family members who remain behind, to attempting to maintain some sense of stability in one's regular work routine, the demands that present themselves during an international program seem to require a high degree of flexibility, ingenuity, persistence, a certain skill in diplomacy, and a sense of humor. A director of a study-abroad program away from the home university, for instance, must wear the hat of professor, student service officer, disciplinarian, psychologist and counselor, travel consultant, supervisor of other instructors, and dormitory counselor, all while remaining as active as possible with what is going on at the home campus. Directors of international programs at home must be able to assist others with medical needs, banking needs, entertainment, and integration into a local community; deliver effective orientation and reentry programs; provide support during times of homesickness and culture shock; and be cultural mediators, paying particular attention to how colleagues from different countries or backgrounds can work most effectively with one another as they struggle to achieve mutual goals.

Successful intercultural programs simply do not "just happen." Rather, they are the result of careful preparation, close attention to detail, and prudent back-up planning. If the program is to be a success, the director, whether as host or guest, must be intimately involved in the entire process from preprogram design to postproject activities. Yet what exactly does this entail, and what does this really require from the director? This section seeks to answer these questions by providing a checklist for both the hosting and traveling director and by highlighting and expanding on key considerations within each of the six phases of the program: preprogram design and planning, prearrival and predeparture preparation, arrival, team building and collaboration, project completion, and postproject and reentry.

Before proceeding, it is important to make two general comments about the checklists. First, although there are many similarities between the two, the reader is cautioned that hosting is fundamentally different from traveling, and both require different emphases and degrees of control from the director. Second, the questions posed in each phase are not the only questions a director needs to ask but, rather, form an essential core from which further tailoring can occur. In addition to these two comments, the reader should note that these checklists can also be used, with some obvious modification, for intranational encounters between two significantly different and often opposing groups (e.g., Arabs and Jews; blacks and whites).

Preprogram Design and Planning

Planning for an intercultural program really begins well in advance of the actual face-to-face encounter and can encompass many months of work. The most difficult yet important item in this phase is a clear definition of the objective(s) for both groups. This is not a time for assumptions, because assumptions are fertile ground for embarrassment and failure. Such potential problems can be avoided by directors who foster a truly collaborative effort with their counterparts in the other group. Indeed, the degree to which one can collaborate with the other parties involved in the encounter during this phase will directly determine how smoothly the arrival, initial team-building sessions, and eventual project completion will unfold.

Although perhaps more effective when offered soon after contact, cross-cultural preparation and orientation in this phase is also critical (see Chapter 1 of this volume,

Table 8.1 A Program Director's Checklist for Hosting International Visitors

Preprogram Design

What are the objectives (for both parties, if possible)?
    What is the intent of the visit?
    What are the expectations, long- and short-term?
    What "message" needs to be transmitted and to whom?
Who are the members of the visiting party?
    Are there "separate agendas" or individual goals that must be accommodated?
    Are there any special issues that must be considered (e.g., physical, medical, gender role, dietary, etc.)? Who provides medical insurance during the visit? Who arranges for the visas?
    Who on our side is acquainted with the visitors?
Who should the participants be on our side? Who controls the selection?
    What do our visitors' customs and our protocol require?
    What level(s) within the organizational hierarchy must be present and at which times?
    Is everyone on our side acquainted with one another?
    What special skills are needed (e.g., legal, technical, etc.)
    What information is to be presented? How, when, and by whom?
What are the available resources?
    What is the allowable time period for the visit, and is it flexible?
    What is the budget, and are there provisions for side excursions?
    Is an interpreter required?
    Is there a country or culture expert on staff?

Prearrival

Have the objectives and individual roles and expectations been clearly communicated to our participants?
Have our key participants been provided an orientation of the visitor's country, to include its geography, history, culture, customs, dress, body language, food, and etiquette?
    Are areas of potential agreement (similarities) and conflict (difference) identified?
    Are suggestions and strategies offered to mediate as necessary?
    For important encounters, such as formal meetings, have our participants role-played the most likely scenarios with a country expert? Are issues of protocol and cultural expectation clearly understood?
Does the final schedule contain sufficient detail to facilitate individual preparations and answer most questions?
    Does the final schedule contain a comfortable mix of cultural, informal, and task items?
    Have sufficient accommodations been reserved?
    Are telephone and fax numbers, and e-mail addresses when appropriate, listed for all hotels and major stops?
Are back-up plans prepared, and have all plans been verified for access and transportation and timed for accuracy?
Are social events included? If so, have invitations been sent, location and menu selected, seating arrangements determined, program planned, and toasts and speeches assigned?
    Will gifts be exchanged? If so, what, when, how, to whom, and by whom? (With gifts, protocol and appropriateness are very important.)
Who will meet and escort the visitors? Are welcome packets desired?
Will photographic support be needed?
Will the news media be involved? If so, who will coordinate that session?

Table 8.1 *(Continued)*

Arrival

Who should meet the guests upon arrival?

Will the visiting group remain together or travel separately, as position may dictate?

Is everyone and everything accounted for, and are there any immediate concerns?

Is there an allowance for personal time each day before and after work, and sufficient time allowed to recover from jet lag?

Intercultural Team Building and Collaboration

Is there a prevailing attitude of mutual respect active among the team members, visitor and host?

Is there a consistent, visible, and honest attempt by the host team to understand the culture and perspectives of the visiting team members?

Are there opportunities for individual cross-cultural interactions outside of work? Are they encouraged and are they happening?

Is there a visible willingness to listen to and learn from the visiting team members as much or more than the willingness to teach or preach one's own "solution"?

Are cultural sensitivities carefully observed when "fixing" responsibility, designating subordinate leaders, and making corrections?

Are there some regularly scheduled opportunities for the hosting members to discuss events, reactions, concerns, plans, or further strategies?

Is the flow of information in these sessions open among all participants, and does the structure allow for discussion of intercultural issues and how the participants and group can more effectively interact with the visiting country members?

Can the group laugh together about individual frustrations?

Is there a regularly scheduled time for visitors to meet without the hosts to debrief, share their own stories and experiences, and air frustrations?

Project Completion or Actualization

Is there a visible "win-win" attitude and a "win-win" product?

In public, are the results praised, and is the emphasis kept on the intercultural team and collaboration?

In private, are there sincere assurances for continued assistance, data sharing, and followup professional development and exchanges?

Has the door been left open for further collaborative work?

Postproject and/or Postdeparture

Have the host participants reviewed the events, activities, and lessons learned during the visit?

Are these points shared with other coworkers?

Have the participants reflected on changes in personal attitudes and perspectives regarding the visitors?

In the case of collaborative work, what are the plans for sustaining the relationships built during the visit?

Is there a need to address issues concerning refresher training, professional exchanges, periodic return visits, and so forth?

Have letters of appreciation, as appropriate, been sent to members of the visiting team and key members of the hosting team?

---

and Brislin & Yoshida, 1994; Cushner & Brislin, 1996; and Gudykunst, Guzley, & Hammer, 1996, for more detailed reviews of approaches to cross-cultural training and orientation, and Landis & Bhagat, 1996, Part III, for reviews of training for culture-specific regions). Included in this early phase is a range of issues, from the more mundane things such as obtaining passports and any needed visas, assuring that all have adequate medical protection, and planning airport pickup and accommodations, to such factors as selecting participants, providing alternate strategies for dealing with culture shock, teaching "survival" language skills, determining common purpose, and forming and nurturing the cross-cultural team.

If an interpreter is required, the director must use great caution. On the one hand, interpreters can facilitate communication and aid in meeting the overall objectives. In such cases, interpreters can be a very positive enhancement to the director's team. On the other hand, interpreters can easily have hidden agendas and false loyalties that can distract, distort, and subvert a project. In sensitive meetings, the director is well advised to seek reputable, certified translators, or those well known and trusted by embassy, university, or company staff.

Also critical in this phase is the selection of, and decisions about, appropriate participants (Kealey, 1996). Ideally, selection considers such factors as special skills or knowledge required, determination of which levels of the organization should be included, and prior experience in intercultural affairs. This is not a time to repay favors or rely on nepotism. Tremendous attention must be given to the importance of building relationships of trust, reliability, and congeniality, if the proposed project is to be a success.

Prearrival and Predeparture Considerations

Unlike preprogram design issues, the prearrival (for hosting situations) and predeparture (for sending situations) phase occurs in a relatively brief period of time—generally within a week or two of the actual program. For the director and the participants in both groups, this is the "first impression"; consequently, it must be carefully constructed and carried out in a smooth manner, because it will have a profound effect on all remaining aspects of the program.

In many ways, actual orientation and preprogram issues continue to be important to consider well into an experience. At this stage, it is important to make certain that participants have a basic understanding of geography, history, customs, dress, food, and etiquette. Survival language can also be introduced at this time. Likewise, participants should have some practice role-playing important encounters, such as greeting behavior, formalities during meetings and meals, gift giving, and any other protocols unique to the situation. In-depth analysis of the more critical issues related to interpersonal interaction, including cross-cultural differences in communication and behavior, and areas of potential agreement and conflict, although surveyed at this time, need to be reinforced a few weeks into a program. Often it is best to wait until participants have had ample opportunity to interact extensively with others and thus experience the reality of cross-cultural differences before giving extensive attention to intercultural communication and behavioral issues. At such a time, the content of these sessions will be much more meaningful than it was before the encounter.

Table 8.2 A Program Director's Checklist for Overseas Travel

Preprogram Design

What are the objectives (for both parties, if possible)?

  What is the specific intent of the visit?

  What are the expectations, long- and short-term?

  What "message" needs to be transmitted and to whom?

Who are the participants? Who controls the selection?

  What international and intercultural experience do participants have?

  What special skills are required (e.g., language, legal, cultural, etc.), and are these available within the group of participants?

  Are there special issues (e.g., physical, medical, dietary, etc.) that must be addressed?

  Are there "separate agendas" or individual goals that must be accommodated?

  Do the participants know each other? If not, are there provisions to do so?

What are the available resources?

  What is the allowable time period for the visit, and is it fixed or flexible?

  What is the budget, and are there provisions for the unforeseen?

  Is there expertise in the target culture within the group?

  Is there cultural and survival language training available?

What additional resources are essential for success (both in the home and target countries)?

  Is an interpreter required?

Is a "dry run" advisable?

Is there a need for back-up or alternate planning?

Predeparture

Have the objectives and individual roles and expectations been clearly communicated to the participants?

Has the group been provided an orientation of the target country's geography, history, culture, customs, dress, body language, food, and etiquette?

  Are areas of potential agreement (similarity) and conflict (difference) identified? Are suggestions and strategies offered to mediate or accommodate these as may be required?

  Is "survival" language instruction available?

  Do the participants understand the phenomenon of culture shock and how to minimize its effects?

  For important encounters, such as business meetings, have the participants role-played the most likely scenarios? Are issues of protocol and expectation clearly understood?

Does the final schedule contain sufficient detail to facilitate individual preparations and answer most questions? Who will have a copy "back home"?

  Are telephone and fax numbers, and e-mail addresses when appropriate, listed for all hotels and major stops?

  Are the back-up plans, if prepared, also available "back home"?

Do the individual participants have the following:

  A positive attitude about the upcoming experience?

  Passports, visas, required immunizations, and medical insurance?

  Travelers' checks and small amounts of local currency to cover porters' tips, taxi fares, snacks, and so forth?

  Electrical adapters or multivoltage electrical personal appliances and professional equipment?

Does all luggage have some means of being quickly identified (e.g., colored tags)?

When appropriate, is there someone who is responsible for keeping track of people and records?

(continued)

Table 8.2 *(Continued)*

Arrival

Is everyone and everything accounted for and are there any immediate concerns?

Are the in-country contacts (hosts) to be at the airport or available at a prearranged meeting place?

Is there an orientation to the immediate surroundings?

Are critical events or activities in the upcoming schedule confirmed?

Is there an opportunity for participants to call home and communicate their arrival?

Is there some regularly scheduled opportunity for the entire group to discuss events, reactions, concerns, plans, or strategies?

> Is the flow of information in these sessions open among all participants, and does the structure allow for discussion of intercultural issues and how the participants and group can more effectively interact with the host country members?
>
> Can the group laugh together about individual frustrations?

Intercultural Team Building and Collaboration

Is there a prevailing attitude of mutual respect active among the team members, visitor and host?

> Is there a consistent, visible, and honest attempt by the visiting team to understand and enjoy the host country and culture?
>
> Is there evidence among the visitor and host team members of individual cross-cultural interactions outside of work?

Is there a consistent, visible, and honest attempt by the visiting team to seek solutions tailored to conditions in the other culture?

Is there a willingness to listen to and learn from the host team members as visible or more so than the willingness to teach "your" solution?

Are cultural sensitivities carefully observed when "fixing" responsibility, designating subordinate leaders, and making corrections?

Is there a regularly scheduled time for the team to meet alone without the host country members to debrief, raise issues, and share frustrations? Does this include an orientation, insights, and progressive training for cross-cultural skills?

Project Completion or Actualization

Is there a visible "win-win" attitude and a "win-win" product?

In public, are the results praised, and is the emphasis kept on the intercultural team, collaboration, and the host country?

In private, are there sincere assurances for continued assistance, data sharing, and other professional development and exchanges?

Has the door been left open for further collaborative work?

Postproject and Reentry

Have the participants reflected on changes in personal attitudes and perspectives regarding the host country, its people, and themselves?

Have the participants reviewed the events, activities, and lessons learned during the journ? Upon return, are these points shared with other coworkers?

If the conditions of the sojourn were especially demanding, are the participants encouraged to take some time off to readjust to family, catch up on personal needs, and rejuvenate?

Is there a plan for sustaining the relationships built during the sojourn?

In the case of collaborative work, what are the plans for sustaining the relationships built during the sojourn? Is there a need to address issues concerning refresher training, professional exchanges, periodic return visits, and so forth?

Have letters of appreciation, as appropriate, been sent to hosts?

Basic questions that might be asked during this phase include "What will people need to feel comfortable in the first few days of their arrival? How can we go about facilitating cross-cultural understanding during this phase? What kinds of activities will facilitate initial meetings between the working groups and new understanding of the new environment?"

Arrival

This phase, although the most brief, is no less important. Helping people make early transitions will facilitate later work. Beyond the first impression, it is important for the director to respond quickly to those issues participants face that, if attended to early in a program, will help ease anxieties, enable all to know their immediate surroundings, and enable individuals to solve the day-to-day problems and issues they are certain to encounter. While attending to such issues as food, banking, medical services, basic communication technologies (telephone, fax, computer, etc.), and the use of public transportation, participants slowly become familiar with their new environment and increasingly knowledgeable about the "new culture."

Initial introductions to host-country participants should also occur at this time. Encounters should be structured so that participants get to know one another in a relaxed atmosphere, while offering an opportunity to practice language skills. Time spent with hosts' families or merely together with the hosts in the local community will also assist early transitions.

Intercultural Team Building and Collaboration

The director's role as a cultural bridge-builder is most essential in this phase. There is always a tendency among people to focus on differences, yet the director must be able to balance that tendency with pointing out people's similarities. In this way, members of both teams will learn to appreciate the diversity within the larger group and can begin to use it to produce a powerful synergy for truly multicultural results; that is, for results that stand on a foundation of mutual respect and that represent "win-win" solutions.

This is an extremely intensive phase for the director. Often the most productive efforts are those invested outside the narrow confines of the project. Guided introductions into the other culture, explanations of "strange" customs and mannerisms, and insights into the very soul of the people will produce the deeper understanding and respect needed for truly collaborative efforts. At this time the most effective cross-cultural training can occur. Also, care needs to be taken to schedule time regularly for individuals to voice concerns and frustrations and to facilitate constructive discussions and learning.

A rich body of literature related to efforts designed to improve intergroup interactions and the importance of providing social support for people living and working in new settings has developed over the years and provides a good foundation for program design (see Adler, 1986; Brislin, 1994; Cushner, McClelland, & Safford, 1996; Fontaine, 1996; and see Singelis & Pedersen, this volume). Such research has identified criteria that can serve as guidelines to facilitate efforts to bring together people from different backgrounds.

From a programmatic standpoint, efforts designed to facilitate intergroup inter-action can be facilitated by addressing issues related to the conditions of contact. Gordon Allport (1958), in proposing the contact hypothesis, suggested that one way to reduce negative prejudice and thus facilitate interaction among people was to bring representatives of different groups into close contact with one another. Although sometimes this proves helpful, it is not always the case; occasionally negative preju-dice is reinforced or formed where it did not previously exist. An alternative hypothe-sis suggests that it is the conditions under which groups come together that is critical. Certain characteristics of contact situations are required to assure positive outcomes, and program developers are advised to consider such criteria when developing their own programs. Considerable efforts under many different circumstances (bilingual classrooms, integrated housing and schools, prejudice-reduction programs) have led to recommendations concerning the best conditions under which social contact can be improved. These include the following:

Equal Status Contact

Amir (1969), working in integrated school settings in Israel, found that if individu-als coming together perceive that they have equal status, or equal access to any re-wards available, conditions are set for improved relations. In Switzerland, for in-stance, French, German, and Italian are all recognized as official languages. Official documents are made available in all three languages. Speakers of these diverse lan-guages, therefore, are all appreciated, well informed, and encouraged to participate in the society at large. Applications of this strategy are evident in programs that con-sider all participants to have significant contributions to make and that provide ample opportunity for each to contribute to all phases of a project, from preprogram design to postproject integration.

Superordinate Goals

Having equal status alone is not sufficient. Individuals who come together and work toward achieving some superordinate goal or common task that could not be satisfied without the participation of all involved are more likely to feel empowered and personally involved in the process. This concept stems from the work of Sherif (1958), who, after successfully creating hostility and aggression between two groups of boys at summer camp, found it quite difficult to bring them back together again as one larger, cooperative group. Finally, after much trial and error, he was able to bring both groups together after staging an incident in which a bus got stuck in the mud while on the way to a camp outing. For the bus to continue on its way, all of the campers had to work together to push the bus back onto the road. This superordinate goal, that could not have been achieved without everyone's participation, enabled all to work together as a group toward some common goal. In the work context, super-ordinate goals are readily evident when individuals collaborate with one another to solve a common problem, thus crossing national, ethnic, racial, gender, and other cultural lines.

Administrative Support Must Encourage Intergroup Interaction

To be effective, efforts to be more collaborative must be seen as important at all levels of the organization. Such efforts cannot be seen entirely as the whim or "cause" of a particular individual or particular group. As many as possible, from all levels of the organization, must actively encourage and show support for such efforts.

Contact Must Encourage a High Acquaintance
Potential or Intimate Contact

A high acquaintance potential must exist, encouraging rather intimate contact between individuals in a given situation. In other words, people must have the opportunity to get to know the "other" as a person in ways that render the stereotypic image one might hold inappropriate.

In addition to the preceding suggestions, individuals should be placed in heterogeneous groups for a variety of purposes, and can be encouraged (or required) to participate in mixed activities—any scheme that will enable people to get to know others on a rather personal basis. Time for informal activity, perhaps even structured into the day or on weekends, must occur.

Project Completion

Having invested a tremendous amount of time and energy into creating a "win-win" attitude and producing a "win-win" product, it is natural for the director to be quite weary, and it is tempting to concentrate on concluding the visit or project as quickly as possible to return to other pressing requirements "back home" or "back at the office." Resist this temptation! The last hours of the visit or project are extremely important, and whatever legacy remains will be shaped almost exclusively by what occurs and is said at that time. This is a time to forget the many frustrations that have occurred. This is also a time to consider issues related to "transfer of skills," that is, the ability of the "locals" to obtain the requisite skills to maintain the system after the others depart. This is also a time to look beyond individual efforts and difficulties and to openly praise the teams as a whole. This is a time to publicly and sincerely state and demonstrate the value of the time spent working together. This is a time to project future visits, exchanges, and collaboration that will serve to build on and continue this new friendship or partnership. This is a time in which sincerity, quality, style, and appropriate symbols are critical. This is *not* a time to be in a hurry to say "good-bye."

Postproject and Reentry

As with many things in life, the value of an experience is not fully appreciated immediately; rather, the experience needs time to be mentally massaged and reflected on. This process of reflection is often more effective when guided by a teacher, mentor, or trusted friend.

So, too, is it with intercultural encounters, and once again, the director plays a decisive role. Whether or not the participants have been keeping a journal, they should be encouraged to record their final impressions, both positive and negative, and to begin organizing and summarizing their thoughts. Also, because it is very rare for everything to proceed flawlessly, it is important to record problem areas, lessons learned, and any recommended future actions to help or to prevent a recurrence of any problems. In doing this, the participant needs to distinguish between problem areas at the individual and system levels.

This is also a time when program participants undergo intercultural reentry or reintegration into their original society. Particularly if the experience has been lengthy, individuals may now face many unexpected readjustment issues, including factors related to family and employment status. Martin and Harrell (1996), and Wang in this volume, provide a thorough review of reentry issues.

Shortly after hosting or returning from the visit, the director should gather the team together for a general debriefing. At this time, the preceding items should be discussed, with the focus on changes in personal attitudes and perspectives, strategies for continued relationships, and recommendations for addressing systemic problem areas.

Applications

A director's first challenge often lies with the stated objectives for the cross-cultural encounter. In the first incident earlier in the chapter, Daniel had to ensure that two things were accomplished: first, that the representatives from the Asian companies understood the parent organization, and second, that closer ties were established. These two objectives, although quite familiar to an American, probably confused the Asian representatives and served to raise obstacles.

The Asian cultures listed in the incident are much more collective than their American counterparts. For the Asian representatives, balance, harmony, order, and correct relationships within the group are most important, and to achieve this takes time and patience (see the chapter by Bhawuk in this volume). Furthermore, each of the Asian companies represent quite different cultures, may have a history of conflict, and are competitors with each other; Daniel cannot assume they are a homogeneous group.

The establishment of healthy group relationships requires a subordination of the individual to the interests of the group and an understanding that consensus is very important. In the incident, Daniel plans an orientation weekend but the American counterparts are not present—they do not come until Monday, the beginning of the "formal" schedule. If the goal was to establish closer ties, the Americans are starting out with serious disadvantages. Furthermore, in his remarks, Mr. Johnson, the company president, emphasized his American-only perspective, much to the dismay of the Asians, who were probably wondering how this newly formed team will be able to function.

The afternoon was even more confusing for the Asians. The group was divided; the subgroups held discussions centering on company goals; and individuals were expected to "speak" for their companies. Although the Americans may have been comfortable in this type of setting, the Asians were probably not. Clearly such important issues required a slower, more deliberate approach, intense listening, broad and frequent consultation with members of each of their companies, a warmer personal feeling about the new group members, a beginning of mutual trust, and much patience. This was not something to be hurried.

How can Daniel salvage the week? This is a very difficult question to answer, considering the results of the first 3 days, but it is not impossible if Mr. Johnson is receptive to listening and learning about his new partners.

In the second incident, Dr. Jameson was reacting to many unexpected circumstances. For one, it is an often erroneous assumption that overseas programs are primarily vacations for the faculty members who are in charge. Nothing could be farther from the truth! For many students, this may be a first international experience, complete with the accompanying culture shock and relative freedoms, yet with the required completion of coursework, exams, and out-of-class assignments. Thus, a program director must help students learn to create a balance between work and play. There may be resident faculty and staff whose needs must also be accommodated. There is the added burden of the overseas assignment not being perceived as meritorious by others at home, and the fact that one may be out of the loop when potentially important decisions are made at the home institution.

What might Anne do? Many of the circumstances that led to Anne's frustration could be relieved by a more organized and ongoing orientation for students. Building trust and strong collaborative relationships with students early and throughout the program, and helping students view the director as a team member and player rather than strictly an authority figure, will go far in terms of preventing problems. Anne should also strive to develop and maintain relationships with colleagues back at home. Perhaps maintaining a collaborative writing or research agenda will serve to keep her in the minds of her peers. In addition, she should take full advantage of the technology available and maintain almost daily communication via faxes and e-mail if available.

At this point, return to the plan you developed in the self-assessment section of this chapter. Review your plan and evaluate it in terms of the content of the chapter. What changes would you make in the initial design? What elements have been neglected in this chapter that you feel are important?

Now, consider the following scenarios. What advice would you give each as they proceed to plan their respective programs?

1. Mark Thomas, acting director of International Affairs at Central College, was asked to assist four faculty members as they prepared to visit three colleges in France. Each participating French college had already agreed, in principle, to encourage the exchange of students and faculty between their respective English and French departments. Faculty members were to depart in 4 weeks for a 3-week visit—1 week at each college site.

What might Mark advise, given the current time frame and expectations at Central College?

2. Reverend Brennan and Rabbi Weinstein have been asked to coordinate a program designed to host a group of 10 visiting Arab and Israeli youths. The goals of this program include facilitating dialogue between the Arab, Jewish, and Gentile members in the community and providing a venue to better inform people about the conflict in the Middle East. The 10 young visitors will be present for 4 weeks and are to work closely with about 200 young people in the community.

What advice would you give Reverend Brennan and Rabbi Weinstein as they go about planning their program?

3. Gloria Feeney, director of Human Resource Management at I & I International, was asked to prepare a 3-week program for a group of visiting Japanese managers who would be establishing a division of I & I in Japan over the next 2 years. Gloria

understood company policy and procedures well enough to collaborate closely with any international colleague. She was also aware, however, that gender differences were certain to be an issue with this group, because the American managers were $\frac{1}{3}$ female, whereas the Japanese team was all male.

What advice would you give Gloria as she went about planning her program?

Concluding Thoughts

This chapter has focused on the director, for it is the director whose interest, position, and experience are most critical to successful intercultural programs. The checklists have been prepared as guides, and the questions, although not exhaustive, can serve as useful prompts for important considerations.

In a larger sense and beyond the single visit or project, the program director has been selected because of her or his ability to identify and evaluate opportunities from a global and often cross-functional perspective. This perspective demands the construction of global networks, the capacity and ability to lead multicultural teams, and the openness and tolerance to adapt and succeed in environments quite different from the home culture (Brake & Walker, 1995)

If you have been newly selected as director, congratulations! Although the days ahead will be challenging and often frustrating, the rewards will be with you for a lifetime, and the memories will be some of your most cherished!

References

Adler, N. (1986). *International dimensions of organizational effectiveness.* Boston: Kent.

Allport, G. (1958). *The nature of prejudice.* New York: Doubleday.

Amir, Y. (1969). Contact hypothesis in ethnic relations. *Psychological Bulletin, 71*(5), 319-343.

Brake, T., & Walker, D. (1995). *Doing business internationally.* Princeton: Princeton Training Press.

Brislin, R. (1994). Working cooperatively with people from different backgrounds. In R. Brislin & T. Yoshida (Eds.), *Improving intercultural interactions: Modules for cross-cultural training programs* (pp. 17-33). Thousand Oaks, CA: Sage.

Brislin, R., & Yoshida, T. (1994). The content of cross-cultural training: An introduction. In R. Brislin & T. Yoshida (Eds.), Improving intercultural interactions: Modules for cross-cultural training programs (pp. 1-14). Thousand Oaks, CA: Sage.

Cushner, K., & Brislin, R. (1996). *Intercultural interactions: A practical guide* (2nd ed.). Thousand Oaks, CA: Sage.

Cushner, K., McClelland, A., & Safford, P. (1996). *Human diversity in education: An integrative approach* (2nd ed.). New York: McGraw-Hill.

Fontaine, G. (1996). Social support and the challenges of international assignments. In D. Landis & R. Bhagat (Eds.), *Handbook of intercultural training* (2nd ed.) (pp. 264-281). Thousand Oaks, CA: Sage.

Gudykunst, W., Guzley, R., & Hammer, M. (1996) Designing intercultural training. In D. Landis & R. Bhagat (Eds.), *Handbook of intercultural training* (2nd ed.) (pp. 61-80). Thousand Oaks, CA: Sage.

Kealey, D. (1996). The challenge of international personnel selection. In D. Landis & R. Bhagat (Eds.), *Handbook of intercultural training* (2nd ed.) (pp. 81-106). Thousand Oaks, CA: Sage.

Landis, D., & Bhagat, R. (Eds.). (1996) *Handbook of intercultural training* (2nd ed.). Thousand Oaks, CA: Sage.

Martin, J., & Harrell, T. (1996). Reentry training for intercultural sojourners. In D. Landis & R. Bhagat (Eds.), *Handbook of intercultural training* (2nd ed.) (pp. 307-326). Thousand Oaks, CA: Sage.

Sherif, M. (1958). Superordinate goals in the reduction of intergroup tensions. *American Journal of Sociology, 63*(4), 349-356.

Additional Resources

Following are some of the resources to which a director may want to refer for additional information. The reader is cautioned that this listing is only a small part of the wealth of information published in the last 15 years; in other words, this listing should be viewed as an introduction.

Background notes series by the U.S. Department of State, published by the Government Printing Office.

Culturgrams: The nations around us, published by the David M. Kennedy Center for International Studies at Brigham Young University.

InterActs series of country-specific books, published by the Intercultural Press, Yarmouth, ME.

Preprogram Design

Althen, G. (1988). *American ways: A guide for foreigners.* Yarmouth, ME: Intercultural Press.

Axtell, R. (1990). *Do's and taboos of hosting international visitors.* New York: John Wiley.

Kohls, R. (1996). *Survival kit for overseas living* (3rd ed.). Yarmouth, ME: Intercultural Press.

Kohls, R., & Knight, J. (1994). *Developing intercultural awareness: A cross-cultural training handbook* (2nd ed.). Yarmouth, ME: Intercultural Press.

Morrison, T., Borden, G., & Conaway, W. (1994). *Kiss, bow, or shake hands: How to do business in sixty countries.* Yarmouth, ME: Intercultural Press.

Arrival/Protocol

Dresser, N. (1996). *Multicultural manners: New rules of etiquette for a changing society.* New York: John Wiley.

McCaffree, M. (1977). *Protocol: The complete handbook of diplomatic, official and social usage.* Englewood Cliffs, NJ: Prentice Hall.

Team Building and Collaboration

Cushner, K., & Brislin, R. (1996). *Intercultural interactions: A practical guide* (2nd ed.). Newbury Park, CA: Sage.

Farson, R. (1996). *Management of the absurd: Paradoxes in leadership.* New York: Simon & Schuster.

Project Completion and Reentry

Martin, J., & Harrell, T. (1996). Re-entry training for intercultural sojourners. In D. Landis & R. Bhagat (Eds.), *Handbook of intercultural training* (2nd ed.) (pp. 307-326). Thousand Oaks, CA: Sage.

PART III

Concerns in Various Types of Intercultural Experiences

9

Doing the Right Thing

A QUESTION OF ETHICS

Paul Pedersen

Doing the right thing is not always easy. Because of implicit cultural bias in our social institutions, professionals working in multicultural settings sometimes have to choose between following the prescribed ethical guidelines of their profession or being ethical in a particular cultural context. This module will clarify the ethical alternatives available to professionals working in multicultural settings so that they can become more ethically "intentional" in their decisions and actions. As a result of this module the reader should be able to clarify her or his own "implicit" ethical standards and evaluate the level of ethical decision making in the group or organization to which he or she belongs.

Contents

Self-Assessment Exercise

Respond to the following statements by indicating whether you agree very much, somewhat, very little, or disagree very much, somewhat, very little, or whether you are uncertain.

1. Actions are judged according to their good or bad consequences.

strongly disagree	disagree	disagree somewhat	don't agree or disagree	agree somewhat	agree	strongly agree
1	2	3	4	5	6	7

2. There is an appropriate behavior for every situation.

strongly disagree	disagree	disagree somewhat	don't agree or disagree	agree somewhat	agree	strongly agree
1	2	3	4	5	6	7

3. Some decisions must be in the best interest of the group at the expense of the individual.

strongly disagree	disagree	disagree somewhat	don't agree or disagree	agree somewhat	agree	strongly agree
1	2	3	4	5	6	7

4. The consequences of rules and regulations will change from one situation to another.

strongly disagree	disagree	disagree somewhat	don't agree or disagree	agree somewhat	agree	strongly agree
1	2	3	4	5	6	7

5. Decisions are made by balancing the good and bad consequences.

strongly disagree	disagree	disagree somewhat	don't agree or disagree	agree somewhat	agree	strongly agree
1	2	3	4	5	6	7

6. Public leaders make decisions according to the consequences of their actions.

strongly disagree	disagree	disagree somewhat	don't agree or disagree	agree somewhat	agree	strongly agree
1	2	3	4	5	6	7

7. There are basic moral principles to guide us in all our decisions.

strongly disagree	disagree	disagree somewhat	don't agree or disagree	agree somewhat	agree	strongly agree
1	2	3	4	5	6	7

8. It is essential to know a person's good or bad intentions to judge that person's behavior.

strongly disagree	disagree	disagree somewhat	don't agree or disagree	agree somewhat	agree	strongly agree
1	2	3	4	5	6	7

9. Individuals or groups acting in good faith are not responsible for the consequences of their actions.

strongly disagree	disagree	disagree somewhat	don't agree or disagree	agree somewhat	agree	strongly agree
1	2	3	4	5	6	7

10. Teaching the rules of morality will lead to higher levels of ethical behavior.

strongly disagree 1	disagree 2	disagree somewhat 3	don't agree or disagree 4	agree somewhat 5	agree 6	strongly agree 7

11. Moral decisions depend on encouraging people to be well-intentioned.

strongly disagree 1	disagree 2	disagree somewhat 3	don't agree or disagree 4	agree somewhat 5	agree 6	strongly agree 7

12. Public actions are typically defended by the high moral intention of the promoters.

strongly disagree 1	disagree 2	disagree somewhat 3	don't agree or disagree 4	agree somewhat 5	agree 6	strongly agree 7

13. Biological factors are likely to determine a person's behavior.

strongly disagree 1	disagree 2	disagree somewhat 3	don't agree or disagree 4	agree somewhat 5	agree 6	strongly agree 7

14. Culture has a limited role in justifying variation of behavior.

strongly disagree 1	disagree 2	disagree somewhat 3	don't agree or disagree 4	agree somewhat 5	agree 6	strongly agree 7

15. Similarities are more important than differences across populations.

strongly disagree 1	disagree 2	disagree somewhat 3	don't agree or disagree 4	agree somewhat 5	agree 6	strongly agree 7

16. Cultural differences are not important.

strongly disagree 1	disagree 2	disagree somewhat 3	don't agree or disagree 4	agree somewhat 5	agree 6	strongly agree 7

17. It is possible to compare measured levels of moral development across cultures.

strongly disagree 1	disagree 2	disagree somewhat 3	don't agree or disagree 4	agree somewhat 5	agree 6	strongly agree 7

18. A good test will be valid in different cultural settings.

strongly disagree 1	disagree 2	disagree somewhat 3	don't agree or disagree 4	agree somewhat 5	agree 6	strongly agree 7

19. Variations in behavior are usually the result of cultural differences.

strongly disagree 1	disagree 2	disagree somewhat 3	don't agree or disagree 4	agree somewhat 5	agree 6	strongly agree 7

20. Apparent similarities across cultures are misleading.

strongly disagree 1	disagree 2	disagree somewhat 3	don't agree or disagree 4	agree somewhat 5	agree 6	strongly agree 7

21. Each culture influences its members to behave in unique ways.

strongly disagree	disagree	disagree somewhat	don't agree or disagree	agree somewhat	agree	strongly agree
1	2	3	4	5	6	7

22. Each culture must be understood from its own indigenous cultural perspective.

strongly disagree	disagree	disagree somewhat	don't agree or disagree	agree somewhat	agree	strongly agree
1	2	3	4	5	6	7

23. It is usually not possible to judge a person's behavior outside that person's cultural context.

strongly disagree	disagree	disagree somewhat	don't agree or disagree	agree somewhat	agree	strongly agree
1	2	3	4	5	6	7

24. Measures always need to be generated or modified to fit each cultural context.

strongly disagree	disagree	disagree somewhat	don't agree or disagree	agree somewhat	agree	strongly agree
1	2	3	4	5	6	7

Scoring and Debriefing Guidelines

1. Derive a score for items 1 through 6 by adding up your scores from each item. A low score will demonstrate your affiliation with the "consequentialist" approach to ethical judgment.
2. Derive a score for items 7 through 12 by adding up your scores from each item. A low score will demonstrate your affiliation with the "nonconsequentialist" but intention-based approach to ethical judgment.
3. Derive a score for items 13 through 18 by adding up your scores from each item. A low score will demonstrate your affiliation with an "absolutist" approach to ethical judgment.
4. Derive a score for items 19 through 24 by adding up your scores from each item. A low score will demonstrate your affiliation with a "relativist" approach to ethical judgment.

If you were surprised by your ethical position, you may want to go back and examine the items themselves to make sure you scored each item correctly. You may want to discuss in dyads or small groups the similarities and differences in your ethical position compared to the ethical position of others. There are no right or wrong ethical positions among the four previously indicated; however, it is important that you be intentional in deliberately defining your position if you expect to "do the right thing."

Concepts Necessary for Skill Development Introduction

The first step in "doing the right thing" is making good choices (Pedersen, 1995). The first ethical choice is to select from the three ethical perspectives available of relativism ("to each his/her own"), absolutism ("mine is best"), or some combination ("you are similar in some ways but different in others"). Most theoretical alternatives in the literature about ethics will fit within one or another of these three categories. The second ethical choice is to become familiar with the research on cultural encapsulation and the exclusionary tendencies that have characterized professional counseling and that require meaningful change. Cultural encapsulation is a bigger problem now than ever. The third ethical choice is to critically examine the professional ethical guidelines for counseling that are available to identify the implicit, culture-bound assumptions on which those guidelines are based. The fourth ethical choice is to generate alternative guidelines for the future that are culture-centered, fair, equitable, and practical.

Although ethical principles generated in one cultural context cannot be applied to other substantially different cultural contexts without modification, cultural or ethical relativism is not free of problems either. "If moral ideas reflect nothing more than internalized cultural norms, are not the theories of the relativists themselves culture-bound and thus devoid of any general validity?" (Gielen & Markoulis, 1994, p. 75).

Essential, then, is to distinguish between "fundamental" ethical principles that are not negotiable and "discretionary" aspects that must be modified and adapted to each setting. If fundamental principles are compromised, the result will be a relativistic position in which justice is determined by whatever the common practice of a community may be. If the discretionary aspects are not modified, the result will be an absolutist domination by special-interest groups that benefit from the status quo.

By examining four of the many different orientations to ethical behavior and by responding positively or negatively to each orientation in different situations, it will be possible to become more aware of the implicit and indigenous ethical standards that guide your own behavior and your judgments about the behavior of others. This unit will provide a brief taxonomy of perspectives.

The first two categories of consequentialist and nonconsequentialist orientation are described in Kierstead and Wagner (1993). The second two categories of absolutist and relativists are described in Berry, Poortinga, Segall, and Dasen (1992).

Consequentialism

The idea that the moral rightness of an action depends on its consequences—the end justifies the means—has historically been a popular viewpoint. Hedonists believed that personal pleasure and satisfaction was the ultimate good, although in ancient Greece the hedonists tended to live very ascetic lives. They believed that people should pursue maximum pleasure as the right thing to do. Utilitarians believed that maximum usefulness was the ultimate good. Choices were judged on a balance sheet of positive and negative consequences to determine which choice would lead to the most positive consequences and thus be most useful. Fanatics and radicals might also justify any behavior necessary to accomplish their end goal. A terrorist might genuinely believe that terrorism has a greater ultimate purpose and positive consequence than conformity.

The problem with the consequentialist position is that violence against social, political, or economic minorities can easily be justified as serving the greater good of the majority culture. A second problem of consequentialism is the difficulty in discovering or measuring, not to mention anticipating, the consequences of any action.

Nonconsequentialism

Another popular ethical orientation is to judge behavior according to the intention of the individual or group doing that behavior. As long as people are well-intentioned, they should not be subject to criticism for what they have done. Because we cannot know the consequences of any action, we are forced to judge people according to their intentions. The German philosopher Immanuel Kant placed great emphasis on intention in judging ethical behavior. The end does not justify any means to achieve it. Punishing the innocent is always wrong, whatever the consequences. Elements of this ethical theme are apparent in the U.S. Bill of Rights and later in the 14th Amendment, the 1964 Civil Rights Act, and other legislation. Legislating ethical behavior according to intention is easier than legislating it according to consequences. Religious leaders have also depended on intention to justify their behavior by putting themselves in God's hands or by following God's will in their actions.

The problems of nonconsequentialism are evident in the pain or suffering caused by well-intentioned persons. By disregarding the consequences of one's behavior, the sought-for long-term ultimate good may be overshadowed by short-term harm. Judgments based on intention tend to ignore the people affected by behavior and disregard the sociocultural context in which that behavior occurs.

Absolutism

The absolutist position disregards problems of ethnocentrism and applies the same fixed evaluative criteria across all cultures in the same, more or less unchanging, perspective. The importance of cultural context is minimized. Comparisons across cultures according to universally applied standards are encouraged and the same measures, strategies, theories, and ethical standards are applied regardless of cultural differences. The dominant culture typically defines and dominates the criteria by which ethical behavior is evaluated. Cultural differences between groups are disregarded and cultural similarities to the dominant group are positively evaluated. Differences from the dominant group are typically described as deficits in intelligence, honesty, or right-mindedness, as defined by dominant group criteria.

Historically, psychology has often focused on narrowly defined absolute principles of psychological functioning across cultures. The psychological description of "normal" behavior typically coincides with the behavior of people in the dominant culture. Imposing an absolute standard of ethical behavior in a diverse plurality of cultural contexts typically creates conflict between the dominant group and minority groups.

Relativism

Relativism comes in a variety of forms. Relativism based on ethical egoism assumes that what is right for one person may not be right for anyone else. Relativism based on ethical egotism assumes that right is a function of reconciling each person's belief independently. Relativism that is based on ethical nihilism assumes there is no meaning to moral concepts. Cultural relativism assumes that right and wrong are determined exclusively by the culture of the individual. Cultural relativists try to understand each cultural group in its own terms, with a minimum of "contamination" by outside influences. Actions are not evaluated or even explained by outside criteria. Psychological differences are explained by cultural differences, with similarities being coincidental or inconsequential. Qualitative rather than quantitative measures are used to understand a people, and comparisons across cultures are discouraged.

The problem with relativism is that it discourages moral discourse and disregards ethical guidelines outside of each cultural context. Standards of moral behavior are tied to conventional behavior in each cultural context, which might change from time to time, place to place, and person to person.

Synthesis

Although these four extreme forms exaggerate the alternatives available in making ethical decisions, they demonstrate tendencies or predispositions that appear in more subtle forms within each indigenous synthesis of ethical alternatives. The synthesis between consequential and nonconsequential alternatives is called a *rule utilitarian* or *reflective equilibrium* position (Kierstead & Wagner, 1993), which seeks to combine the best aspects of the other two alternatives. This position asserts respect for individual human beings as a nonnegotiable and fundamental basis and universal requirement. Human respect is valued as an end and not a means toward any other end. Thus, ethical standards require more than good intention, but each action is also judged by its consequences, which might be different in each context, prohibiting acts that would result in showing disrespect for another person.

Berry et al. (1992) synthesize absolutism and relativism in a position they call *universalist*. The universalist position assumes that psychological processes such as pleasure and pain are universal and the way those processes are manifested will be different in each culture. These psychological processes provide universal guidelines for ethical behavior but are expressed differently in each culture. Comparisons across cultures become possible by separating the process from the manifestation. Judgments about ethical behavior require understanding both the underlying, fundamental similarities across cultures and the idiosyncratic and unique identity features of a culture. Ethical judgments depend on culture-general and fundamental values defined by psychological processes combined with discretionary and diversified manifestations of those values and processes across cultures.

The synthetic alternatives are much more complicated and inconvenient than the four exaggerated extremes, which also makes these syntheses less popular. Rather than impose absolute standards, disregard standards, focus on intentions, or depend on consequences, the syntheses provide another option. The syntheses allow each group to manifest its own cultural identity while at the same time acknowledging common psychological principles that connect the welfare of each group to every other group.

Critical Incidents

In the following case examples you will be asked to come up with four different responses that you believe would be the "right" thing to do, according to consequences, intention, absolute, and relativist perspectives. By identifying these alternative responses, you may gain awareness of your own indigenous standards for doing the right thing.

1. You are acquainted with a student whose lifestyle does not emphasize "time consciousness." The student's failure to meet deadlines has downgraded his otherwise adequate academic performance and has alienated the student from his teachers. Neither the student nor the school seem willing to adapt their style and standards to one another. The student's father asks you what to do.
   1.1. Consequentialist:
   1.2. Nonconsequentialist:
   1.3. Absolutist:
   1.4. Relativist:

2. You find that the inhabitants of a small village where you are staying resent Americans a great deal because of previous bad experiences with the U.S. military and tourists. You discover that you have been grossly overcharged at your hotel and taken advantage of in other ways. Your plan was to spend the whole summer in one place rather than tour around, so that you would get to know the people and not be an ordinary tourist. Now you find they are taking out their hostility toward Americans on you as an individual. Your friend asks you to evaluate the local inhabitants' ethical behavior.
   2.1. Consequentialist:
   2.2. Nonconsequentialist:
   2.3. Absolutist:
   2.4. Relativist:

3. The person with whom you are traveling, a friend from back home, turns into an "Ugly American," condescending in his treatment of others, suspicious that he is being cheated, concerned that nothing is "clean" enough, and generally obnoxious toward non-Americans. You want to help him make a better adjustment both for his sake and because his behavior is unethical and embarrassing. He asks you to explain what you see as the problem.
   3.1. Consequentialist:
   3.2. Nonconsequentialist:
   3.3. Absolutist:
   3.4. Relativist:

4. You are in a mixed group of new acquaintances in a foreign country. The elections have just been held, with the political parties divided according to Protestant and Roman Catholic lines. The discussion is extremely intense and likely to erupt into violence. You are not well enough acquainted with the issues to recognize which of the people in your group belong to which political party or religious group. One of the leaders in the group asks you for your opinion.
   4.1. Consequentialist:
   4.2. Nonconsequentialist:
   4.3. Absolutist:
   4.4. Relativist:

5. In becoming acquainted with your host family, you discover that the women in this society are in a very subservient role, working very hard and completely dominated by the men. Cautious inquiries suggest that this style of life is well accepted and normal, even though it seems extremely unfair to you, as a woman. Your anger over

this unfair treatment is beginning to show, and the members of your host family are starting to make fun of you for being a "women's libber." You feel a need to respond.

5.1. Consequentialist:

5.2. Nonconsequentialist:

5.3. Absolutist:

5.4. Relativist:

6. In spite of your best efforts to learn the foreign language, you find yourself very inadequate in your ability to express yourself. The people with whom you talk on the street seem very impatient and somewhat irritated by the way you do violence to their language. You refuse to use English, even though their English is adequate, but are beginning to resent their lack of sympathy with your attempts to enter their culture. You catch yourself becoming unreasonably angry with a complete stranger who doesn't understand you when you ask him a simple question. He asks you to explain your angry behavior.

6.1. Consequentialist:

6.2. Nonconsequentialist:

6.3. Absolutist:

6.4. Relativist:

7. You are Jewish and find yourself in a large German city where everyone seems prejudiced against you. You had many relatives who suffered under the Germans in concentration camps but you were never aware of any strong anti-German bias until now. Separating your feelings against them as a group from your relationship with them as individuals seems impossible. You can understand and explain your bias but you cannot seem to control your feelings, which are coming out in your behavior toward Germans. A German casual acquaintance asks you if you are Jewish because you "look" Jewish. You try to decide how to respond.

7.1. Consequentialist:

7.2. Nonconsequentialist:

7.3. Absolutist:

7.4. Relativist:

8. You are black and have been invited to speak before a class of secondary-school students in a foreign country who have never seen or talked with an American black before. A friend of yours invited you to come and explain to them about the racial problem in the United States and what is being done to combat racism. A student asks you why blacks are treated badly.

8.1. Consequentialist:

8.2. Nonconsequentialist:

8.3. Absolutist:

8.4. Relativist:

9. The leader of your group traveling abroad is a very authoritarian male who succeeds in dominating, planning, and controlling the activities of the group. He is very jealous of any threat to his control. Other members of the group are able to tolerate his domination but you find it increasingly impossible. The other members have begun looking to you, a woman with considerable international experience, for advice and guidance on what to do. You believe that the leader is doing a bad job and resents your threat to his authority. You have to decide what to do.

9.1. Consequentialist:

9.2. Nonconsequentialist:

    9.3. Absolutist:

    9.4. Relativist:

10. One of your friends is planning to marry a foreign national who is of a different religion and a different nationality. Neither set of parents agrees to the marriage and the engaged couple is not sure they will be able to overcome both the differences of culture and of religion. At the same time, they are unwilling to separate and are hopeful that once they are married their families will somehow come to agree. They ask your advice.

    10.1. Consequentialist:

    10.2. Nonconsequentialist:

    10.3. Absolutist:

    10.4. Relativist:

11. Your new friends abroad insist on borrowing things from you and neglect to return them unless you ask for them back. They appear much more casual about ownership of personal belongings than you would like and assume that they have a right to your things as your friends. You try to set an example by not borrowing anything from them but they continue to borrow from you and don't acknowledge the subtle hints you make. They seem to be using you to their own advantage, although among themselves they seem to be getting along well. You have to decide what to do.

    11.1. Consequentialist:

    11.2. Nonconsequentialist:

    11.3. Absolutist:

    11.4. Relativist:

12. You have been caught with a group of friends abroad who were in possession of marijuana. The police have placed all of you in jail and are not allowing you to contact anyone outside the jail. The conditions are impossible and you feel that you are entirely at the mercy of the jailer. You are ready to do just about anything to get out of the jail and are angry because you didn't even break the law in the first place. The judge offers you a chance to get off if you testify against your friends.

    12.1. Consequentialist:

    12.2. Nonconsequentialist:

    12.3. Absolutist:

    12.4. Relativist:

Review your responses to the preceding critical incidents, looking for patterns in your own indigenous ethical standards. Match the patterns you discover with your scores on the four alternative ethical orientations described in the self-assessment scores. Identify the advantages and disadvantages of each ethical orientation for you in your own personal situation.

Skill Applications

Skill applications of applied ethics focus on aspects of human behavior important both to cross-cultural research and to morally relevant perception. How do people process social and morally relevant events? What do they attend to and use to make choices? The literature on moral development presumes that preexisting cognitive structures—the levels of moral reasoning—affect the processing of events in moral stories and, more specifically, the recall of those stories. Narváez (1993) has written in the area of moral perception from a multicultural perspective, applied to the Kitty Genovese murder in the 1960s, where Genovese was stabbed to death in a residential neighborhood and, although the neighbors were aware of the ongoing crime, nobody interfered. Narváez also looks at the situation of Rodney King and the Los Angeles police officers in 1992, where police brutality was recorded on videotape and the jury still found the police not guilty of using excessive force. The daily newspapers report similar examples of human variance in moral behavior.

Moral rules are different from moral principles. *Moral rules* refer to actions such as stealing, killing, cheating, lying, and so forth. *Moral principles* integrate the rules in a broader context, referring to not using others for our own purpose or pleasure and respecting human dignity and human-heartedness. "Whereas Western secular ideals emphasize the dignity and personhood of individuals, religious Tibetans emphasize the Buddha-nature inherent in everyone, Hindus uphold ideals of universal nonviolence (*ahimsa*), and Confucianists focus on humanistic ideals of human-heartedness (*jen*). These cultural ideals are based on different metaphysical assumptions but they all emphasize a concern for human dignity, solidarity and justice" (Gielen & Markoulis, 1994, p. 87).

Kohlberg (1984) and Rest (1995) have proposed that moral reasoning moves from an initial concern with practical consequences or rules to the development of moral principles. Rest (1995) expanded the psychological research on morality from aspects of intention and judgment to a four-component model of moral behavior. Rest presumes four psychological processes in moral behavior: (a) moral sensitivity to the interpretation and conceptualization of events, (b) moral judgment to determine which potential action is the most moral, (c) moral motivation to prioritize moral action above personal values or needs, and (d) ego strength and implementation skills to carry out moral priorities.

Kohlberg (1984), in his theory of moral development, rejected the right of society to determine what is right and wrong for the individual. Kohlberg's cognitive approach presumed stages in moral judgment, like a staircase, based on responses to problems and observing the resolution of moral dilemmas. Different people were expected to solve moral dilemmas differently. He presumed that there are six problem-solving strategies or stages in a developmental sequence. The simple precedes the complex, so that each new stage elaborates previous stages. Rest (1995) summarizes these six stages in sequence.

1. Stage 1 emphasizes obedience. "Do what you're told."
2. Stage 2 emphasizes instrumental egoism. "Let's make a deal."
3. Stage 3 emphasizes interpersonal concordance. "Be considerate and you will make friends."
4. Stage 4 emphasizes law and duty to the social order. "Obey the law and it will protect you."
5. Stage 5 emphasizes consensus-building procedures. "You have a duty to follow the due process."
6. Stage 6 emphasizes nonarbitrary social cooperation. "Be rational and impartial."

Rest (1995) demonstrates how individuals are interconnected with other individuals through these six stages of cooperation and consensus building. The presumption is that the deep structure of Kohlberg's six stages transcends the appearance of superficial differences across cultures. In research cited by Rest (1995), moral development scores increased with age or education, even recognizing problems of translation and dependence on samples of opportunity.

Segall, Dasen, Berry, and Poortinga (1990) and Berry, Poortinga, Segall, and Dasen (1992) review the cross-cultural research on moral development to point out that the definitions of morality, the criteria of moral desirability, and prevailing moral dilemmas are likely to vary across cultures. In attempting to "do the right thing," it will be important to understand how culture can shape both perceptions and interpretations of morality.

More than 90 studies have investigated whether moral development moves from the preconventional to conventional to principled level (Gielen & Markoulis, 1994). "Most cross-cultural studies on moral reasoning have validated the existence and developmental properties of the preconventional and conventional levels of moral reasoning, but the cross-cultural evidence for the postconventional principled forms of moral reasoning has been weaker" (Gielen & Markoulis, 1994, p. 73).

Narváez (1993) divides moral sensitivity into moral perception through preconscious and unconscious processing of data and moral interpretation through a conscious and controlled processing of data. Perception and interpretation are treated as separate and distinct processes. Although the criteria of interpretation are guided by culturally learned patterns, the interpretative criteria themselves are also based on culturally learned perceptions of reality. Therefore, it is important to first examine the "interpretations" of moral sensitivity according to culturally learned patterns, and to then examine the culturally learned "perceptions" of reality on which those interpretations are based.

As an attempt to develop and differentiate perceptions from interpretations, it will be useful to demonstrate the interaction of these two processes. First, interpretations will be divided into sociocultural dimensions suggested by Geert Hofstede (1986,1991,1980) in his 55-country database. Pedersen and Ivey (1994) have developed a spectrum of four synthetic cultures based on one end of each of the four dimensions. According to this configuration, Alpha culture is a high power-distance culture. *Power distance* indicates the extent to which a culture accepts that power is unequally distributed in institutions and organizations. Beta culture emphasizes strong uncertainty avoidance. *Uncertainty avoidance* indicates the lack of tolerance in a culture for uncertainty and ambiguity. Gamma culture emphasizes individualism. *Individualism* indicates the extent to which a culture believes that people are supposed to take care of themselves and remain emotionally independent of groups, organizations, and other collectivities. Delta culture emphasizes masculinity. *Masculinity* indicates the extent to which traditional masculine values of assertiveness, money, and things prevail in a culture, as contrasted to traditional feminine values of nurturance, quality of life, and people. By examining these four synthetic cultures it is possible to synthesize extreme form examples from a wide range of different cultures.

Second, perceptions will be divided into the four underlying perceptions of moral sensitivity mentioned earlier according to the consequentialist, nonconsequentialist, absolutist, and relativist perspectives. The consequentialist perception determines right and wrong according to the consequences of an action. The nonconsequentialist perception determines right and wrong according to the intention of the actor. The absolutist perception of right and wrong depends on absolute and unchanging princi-

| | Interpretations | | | |
	Alpha	Beta	Gamma	Delta
Perceptions				
Consequentialist	1	2	3	4
Nonconsequentialist	5	6	7	8
Absolutist	9	10	11	12
Relativist	13	14	15	16

Figure 9.1. Ethical Perceptions and Cultural Interpretations

ples. The relativist perception of right and wrong depends on conventional thinking in each context. These four differentiated perceptions of moral sensitivity will each suggest a different set of underlying assumptions.

By combining the underlying perceptions with the alternative interpretations it is possible to demonstrate cultural variation in discretionary aspects of moral sensitivity while maintaining a constancy of moral principle.

Return to the 12 cases earlier in this unit and determine how each "perception" would be different according to each of the four synthetic culture "interpretations."

1. In a hierarchical culture such as Alpha, the important consequence would be to protect the power and authority structure.
2. In an uncertainty-avoidance culture such as Beta, the important consequence would be maintaining law and order by following the rules.
3. In an individualistic culture such as Gamma, the important consequence would be maintaining individual freedom.
4. In a high-masculine culture such as Delta, the important consequence would be winning every competition.
5. An appropriate intention for Alpha would be respect for hierarchy and authority, as through filial piety.
6. An appropriate intention for Beta would be following the stated rules and legal guidelines to the letter.
7. An appropriate intention for Gammas would be looking out for themselves.
8. An appropriate intention for Deltas would be survival of the fittest.
9. An absolutist Alpha would make moral judgments by recognizing the responsibility of leadership that goes with power.
10. An absolutist Beta would resist changing the rules for reasons of expediency.
11. An absolutist Gamma would place survival and self-protection over all other interests.
12. An absolutist Delta would see flexibility as a sign of weakness.
13. A relativist Alpha would respect authority in each social context, however that hierarchy is structured.
14. A relativist Beta would focus on the rules that define order in each social context.
15. Relativist Gammas would expect everyone to follow their own rules.
16. A relativist Delta would scope out the competition's rule in search of weaknesses.

Doing the right thing requires attention to both the similarities across cultures and the differences between cultures. This can be done by examining each situation according to perception and cultural interpretation. If cultural similarities are overemphasized, then the dominant or stronger cultural group will define those standards of similarity and impose them on minority groups without regard to cultural differences and at the expense of cultural identities. If cultural differences are overemphasized, then each separate cultural group will seek to survive on its own in competition with every other group, without regard for the common ground that links the welfare of each group with every other group (Pedersen & Pedersen, 1989; Pedersen, 1994).

Field Experiences

The best way to learn about making ethical decisions in multicultural settings is to look at actual incidents where decisions were made and then to evaluate whether or not those decisions were ethically appropriate. Case books on ethical decisions are available through the American Psychological Association (APA, 1987), the American Counseling Association (Herlihy & Golden, 1990), or books such as that by Corey, Corey, and Callahan (1993). Finding critical incidents in the newspaper or public media is also possible. Interviewing samples of providers and consumers of human services who have had experience in multicultural situations is another possibility. These incidents capture the complexity of multicultural relationships in which ethical decisions are made.

1. Gather examples of multicultural critical incidents that occurred in a brief 5-6 minute period of time, required a decision to be made, and had serious consequences if a wrong decision was made, but where no clearly right decision was obvious ahead of time.

2. Analyze each critical incident by identifying each behavior that might be interpreted in a negative or potentially hostile way by other individuals or groups but without judging or evaluating the behavior out of context.

3. Analyze each example of different and potentially negative or hostile behavior in terms of the possibility of shared positive common expectations between individuals or groups as a basis for comparing and evaluating one or both individuals' or groups' behavior.

4. Develop an intervention strategy for building on the common, shared perceptions of trust, respect, safety, success, or ultimate effective behavior, without disregarding the culturally learned interpretations by which those perceptions are manifested.

5. Collect a variety of 20 or 30 critical incidents, with a brief description of the incident plus your analysis of how the individuals or groups are both similar and different and your suggested strategy for evaluating the ethical behavior of the individuals or groups.

6. Apply your critical incidents to a training setting by dividing participants into several small groups of about five persons per group. Divide the critical incidents so that each group has copies of all the incidents to work with.

7. Give each group an equal amount of time (5 or 10 minutes) to discuss each incident and evaluate your intervention strategy in terms of its ethical adequacy. If the group believes it has a more adequate ethical intervention strategy for the critical incident, ask it to identify that strategy.

8. When all the groups have evaluated each critical incident and your intervention strategy in terms of ethical adequacy, introduce the four contrasting ethical extremes for (a) consequentialism, (b) nonconsequentialism, (c) absolutism, and (d) relativism, and

ask the group to discuss the perceptual strategy they judged as most ethically adequate in terms of these four interpretative dimensions.

9. Ask each group to report on how the same critical incidents were evaluated differently to demonstrate the influence of each individual or group's indigenous ethical standards.

10. Lead a general discussion on "doing the right thing" in multicultural situations, demonstrating that ethical decision making is not only "right" but it often is more efficient and leads to more effective action as practicing professionals make accurate judgments.

Conclusions

Ethical decision making is not a luxury. By "doing the right thing" in multicultural relationships, the practicing professional becomes better able to function in a meaningful and credible way, take on leadership functions in multicultural settings, and identify win-win outcomes of multicultural conflict. Doing the right thing is almost never easy, however. The simple answers to ethical decision making through focusing only on consequences, intentions, absolutes, or differences are not satisfactory. Multicultural situations are typically complicated and require the professional to consider both similarities and differences at the same time.

This module has focused on synthesizing several typical approaches to ethical decision making. By separating perceptions from cultural interpretations and by evaluating the ethical adequacy of each individual or group's behavior in its context, it becomes possible to compare the behaviors of individuals or groups without disregarding their cultural identities.

The ethical guidelines of the American Psychological Association and the American Counseling Association contain a systematic cultural bias that weakens their authority. Professional guidelines could be strengthened by (a) making explicit the implicit assumptions behind the code of ethics, (b) not assuming that the provider's self-reference-criterion is an adequate guide, (c) focusing more on protecting the consumer rather than the provider, (d) clarifying the boundary between ethics and law, and (e) reducing dependence on dominant culture values such as individualism as a universal norm and standard.

Guidelines are suggested in this chapter for training professionals in ethical decision making through the analysis of critical incidents in terms of four extreme alternatives emphasizing consequences, intentions, absolutes, or relative differences. There is no easy or simple solution to knowing what the right thing to do might be. However, the ongoing process of refining each person's indigenous ethical standards to fit a variety of culturally different situations will contribute toward more sophisticated levels of professional behavior.

References

American Psychological Association. (1987). *Casebook on ethical principles of psychologists.* Washington, DC: Author.

Berry, J. W., Poortinga, Y. H., Segall, M. H., & Dasen, P. J. (1992). *Cross-cultural psychology: Research and applications.* Cambridge, England: Cambridge University Press.

Corey, G., Corey, M. S., & Callahan, P. (1993). *Issues and ethics in the helping professions.* Pacific Grove, CA: Brooks/Cole.

Gielen, U. P., & Markoulis, D. C. (1994). Preference for principled moral reasoning: A developmental and cross-cultural perspective. In L. L. Adler & U. P. Gielen (Eds.), *Cross-cultural topics in psychology* (pp. 73-87). Westport, CT: Praeger.

Herlihy, B., & Golden, L. B. (Eds.). (1990). *AACD ethical standards casebook* (4th ed.). Alexandria, VA: American Counseling Association.

Hofstede, G. (1980). *Cultures consequences: International differences in work related values.* Beverly Hills, CA: Sage.

Hofstede, G. (1986). Cultural differences in teaching and learning. *International Journal of Intercultural Relations, Vol. 10*(3), 301-320.

Hofstede, G. (1991). *Cultures and organizations: Software of the mind.* London: McGraw-Hill.

Kierstead, F. D., & Wagner, P. A. (1993). *The ethical, legal and multicultural foundations of teaching.* Dubuque, IA: Brown & Benchmark.

Kohlberg, L. (1984). *The psychology of moral development: The nature and validity of moral stages.* San Francisco, CA: Harper and Row.

Narváez, D. (1993). *Moral perception.* Paper for the preliminary oral examination, Department of Educational Psychology, University of Minnesota.

Pedersen, P. (1994). *Handbook for developing multicultural awareness.* Alexandria, VA: American Counseling Association.

Pedersen, P. (1995). Culture-centered ethical guidelines for counselors. In J. G. Ponterotto, J. M. Casas, L. A. Suzuki, & C. M. Alexander (Eds.), *Handbook of multicultural counseling* (pp. 34-49), Thousand Oaks, CA: Sage.

Pedersen, P., & Ivey, A. (1994). *Culture centered counseling and interviewing skills.* Westport, CT: Praeger.

Pedersen, P., & Pedersen, A. (1989). The cultural grid: A complicated and dynamic approach to multicultural counseling. *Counseling Psychology Quarterly, 2,* 133-141.

Rest, J. R. (1995). Background: Theory and research. In J. R. Rest & D. F. Narváez (Eds.), *Moral development in the professions: Psychology and applied ethics* (pp. 213-224). Hillsdale, NJ: Lawrence Erlbaum.

Segall, M. H., Dasen, P. R., Berry, J. W., & Poortinga, Y. H. (1990). *Human behavior in global perspective.* New York: Pergamon.

10

Ethnocultural Identification
and the Complexities of Ethnicity

Ann-Marie Horvath

Increasingly, ethnic identity is playing a role in the professional and personal lives of individuals interacting with a range of people from various ethnocultural groups. As a result, there is a need for a means of understanding cultural differences. Recognizing the importance of ethnic or cultural identity is key to successful intercultural interactions. This module is designed to facilitate an understanding of ethnocultural identity as it relates to the reader's own experiences. Throughout this module it is hoped that readers will gain (a) an awareness of the complex nature of cultural identity, (b) increased knowledge of their own cultural identity and the multiple sources from which identities arise; and (c) guidelines for facilitating and promoting cultural identity in themselves and others. This module is presented in five sections: a self-assessment exercise, case studies, skill concepts, skill application, and field exercise.

Contents

V. Field Exercise

VI. Concluding Remarks

Self-Assessment Exercise

This exercise is designed to introduce some of the major components of ethnocultural identity and to provide a foundation of knowledge as participants expand their understanding of the various aspects of their own identity.

Instructions

The following questions are concerned with your identification with an ethnic or cultural group. There are many different words to describe the different backgrounds or ethnic groups that people come from. Some descriptions are based on heritage; others may come from personal choice often related to cultural exposure. Some labels are specific, whereas others are broad. Some examples of the names of cultural and ethnic groups are Mexican, French Canadian, Jewish, Hispanic, African American, Asian, Ethiopian, Korean American, Okinawan, Indian, and European American. Every person is born into an ethnic group or, sometimes, multiple groups, but people differ with regard to how important their ethnicity is to them, how they feel about it, and how much it affects their behavior.

Please fill in or check the spaces for the following items:

1. In terms of ethnic or cultural (ethnocultural) groups and labels, when referring to myself, I consider myself to be _____. (Note: more than one group name is acceptable.)

2. What ethnocultural group would other people classify you in based on your physical appearance? _____

3. Is there a discrepancy between the group(s) you identify yourself as and the group to which others would place you?

   Most of the time _____ Some of the time _____ Usually not _____ Never _____

4. How currently active are you in learning more about and becoming more attached to your ethnocultural roots and traditions? (Please think in terms of your answer to question 1.)

   Not interested or active _____ Interested but not active _____ A little active _____ Moderately active _____ Very active _____

5. Is your involvement in this group (refer to question 4) your own choice _____ encouraged by group members _____ caused by your family's involvement _____ other _____ (give reason) _____.

6. How much pride do you have in your own ethnocultural heritage and traditions? (Again, refer to question 1.)

   Example: Sara doesn't think about her ethnic heritage very much but her grandparents live with her and her family celebrates all of their ethnic holidays. She is happy to share in these cultural celebrations, though she ordinarily doesn't think about her ethnicity. Sara would answer that she has *a little pride* in her ethnocultural heritage. Now please rate yourself.

   A lot of pride _____ Some pride _____ A little pride _____ No pride _____ Shame _____ Dislike _____

7. Have you taught or would you (if you were to have children) teach your children about your ethnic group(s) and their cultural heritage?

    Probably not _____ I haven't thought about it _____ I will if they ask _____ I probably will teach them select things _____ I will definitely teach them as much as I can _____.

8. Some people are born into an ethnic or cultural group(s) and then later choose to identify with other groups in addition to or even in place of their original group. If your cultural identity has changed, please write down what caused the change (e.g., immigrated to Germany, married a Chinese woman, etc.).

    _____

9. Please write in all the ethnic groups that you and other members of your family (e.g., biological mother, biological father) are genetically a part of. Please keep in mind the percent of ethnicity (blood quantum) for each person, so that each person is 100% identified. You may write in any specific groups where applicable (e.g., Native American—Navajo; South American—Brazilian). You do not need to write in the percents but please try to be as specific as possible.

    Biological mother: _____

    Her mother: _____ Her father: _____

    Biological father: _____

    His mother: _____ His father: _____

    Yourself: _____

Workshop Leaders

Participants may then discuss their answers with others. This exercise is useful to demonstrate differences in identity within members of a cultural group and among different groups. Participants should be assured that various aspects of their identity may not be congruent. Persons identifying with multiple groups may wish to complete the questions separately for each group. Persons unable to choose a traditional ethnic group could be encouraged to choose any social group/reference group (e.g., Christians, surfers, lesbians) that is applicable.

Case Study: An Illustration of Multiple Group Identification

Katriona

This case study is presented as a narrative, told by Katriona, a 21-year-old who recently passed her final examinations and graduated with a degree in occupational therapy from a university in Australia (Mullavey-O'Byrne & Horvath, 1994).

_____

I guess I could be described as a bilingual, bicultural health science student. I think that is one aspect of me. I suppose a good place to start would be with my background. I'll talk about my parents first. They came to Australia, via France, in the '60s, when my brother was about 8. I was born here. They say they came because of the opportunities they heard were in Australia. My dad is a builder. When they came, he worked on building sites, then with a Spanish friend who had a small company. He then went into partnership with this friend and has been in this business ever since. My mum doesn't go to work—she's too busy at home. Now she also does some volunteer work with the local Spanish community, helping out with the old people at the day center.

Now, back to me and my school years. I started school in my neighborhood. There were a lot of kids from different cultural groups at the school. Then I went to high school at another school. That was the same; we had people from just about everywhere, and that was good. The friends I used to hang about with, though, were mostly from Australian backgrounds—that wasn't usual. Most people, both boys and girls, who came from different backgrounds sort of clung together at school, like the Italians went with the Italians, the Spanish went with the Spanish, you know. . . . But there was one group of us who were mixed, from all different backgrounds, including Australian. I went with that group, which meant I was different to begin with, I mean different from the other kids from ethnic groups . . . I don't know why I went with that group, maybe it was because my best friend when I was in primary school was Australian . . . I always had enough friends though, and I had different sets of friends.

I took Spanish classes all the way through high school, but these were separate from school. I had to go in the evenings, so I developed another set of friends who were all Spanish. That was always interesting, like living in two different worlds. I liked doing things with both groups.

I always had friends coming over to my house. That was interesting. In some ways things were pretty much the same as any home, except that I speak Spanish at home! My friends would go, "Woo! What is she doing?" I tend to mix it in a bit without knowing I'm doing it. I might be speaking to my mum and just throw in some words and my friends would say, "Woo! What's all that about?" I just slip in and out of Spanish and don't realize I'm doing it.

When I go out with my friends and meet new people, they are often surprised when they find out that I'm Spanish. I do think I look European; then when people ask me if I am, they look surprised when I say, "Yes I'm European; actually, I'm Spanish." I think some people have a hard time believing me. I don't know if that's because I've grown up here in Australia, I behave like an Australian . . . but I see myself as growing up with all the influences that have happened here, not only Australian. I mean things here are really diverse. . . . At least that's how I experienced growing up here.

Then it was strange when my cousin and I went to visit the family back in Spain and France. We went thinking, "Yes, we are both Spanish." We were very surprised when they saw us as very Australian. I was expecting that they would all see us as Spanish. My cousin and I didn't think we had accents . . . but the relatives all said we had Australian accents.

When I started occupational therapy, I was surprised that there were not more people from different backgrounds doing the course, as I'm used to being with heaps of people from different backgrounds. It was really pretty strange.

Since I've been studying here, I have lost contact with a lot of my Spanish friends; now most of my friends are Asians and Australians. A lot of my friends have gone back to Spain with their families, some have stayed, others have gone back to marry Spanish men. My parents don't want to go back except to visit. When I asked my mum why, she says Spain is different from when she was a girl; and besides that, she says she has spent more than half her life here in a country that has been very good to her, so why would she want to go back? She gets really angry when people say they have done their bit and are going back, because after all, Spain is their country. She always reminds them that this country has been good to them; they have been able to save money and have a good life. It seems strange to me that she doesn't agree with them. Maybe it is because she knows she has had a better life here than she would have had back in Spain. She always tells me that they would not have had the same opportunities had she and my dad not come here. I think my mum and dad have influenced my thinking on these matters quite a lot.

How do I see myself? Well I guess I see myself as really mixed in because I didn't stay in the same little clique with Spanish friends. In some ways it was worse for me, because when I was at school I never quite fit in either group. I mean my Spanish friends would accept me when I went out with them, but I was never one of the closer friends. It was the same when I went out with my Australian friends. With them there was just this one girl who would try to make me feel bad. She would be talking about something and then say something about "filthy greasy person" and look at me and say, "Oops, sorry, no offense, I didn't mean you." I tried to act as if I hadn't noticed, but it used to make me feel lots different, and I knew she was only saying it because I was there. But it is really stupid to get worried, because people are always stereotyping other people. Now we have more Asian migrants, the Europeans stereotype the Asians, not only the Australians. People are like that no matter where they come from.

I think my background is really an advantage to me now that I am older and have older friends. When you are a teenager, it's like you say to your parents, "Please don't do anything to embarrass me." All teenagers go through this anyway, but its worse if you are from a different background. I went through such a phase in my teens. When I was out shopping with my mum, I'd get really angry if she spoke to me in Spanish. I would feel really self-conscious. Now I really like it. I believe I have the best of both worlds. I've had the opportunity to see different ways of looking at things. I feel sort of half and half. I don't know that I would say that I'm completely Australian. I'd still say that I'm a bit of a mix. I think that is really good in relation to the career I have chosen—the health services need people working in professional roles who come from different ethnic and cultural backgrounds to ensure that everyone gets access to appropriate and quality care. As the generations pass though, things change. It's different for each generation—like me, I'm not completely Australian, but I'm not completely Spanish either!

Discussion Questions

1. What have been the main influences on Katriona's identity development?

2. Would you consider her bicultural? Would you say that Katriona identifies simultaneously with more than one culture or with one culture at a time?

3. What are the personal resources and strengths she has drawn on to help her deal with difficulties she has experienced? What external resources have helped her in these situations?

4. Do you believe there have been critical points in the development of her identity? In your view, were there any potential crisis points? What factors mitigated against their development?

5. What other critical points (relating to her identity) do you envision Katriona is likely to encounter in the future? In her career? In her private life?

Skill Concepts: The Complexity, Functions, and Variations of Ethnocultural Identity

Introduction

Why should we think about cultural or ethnic identity at all? One of the reasons why ethnic and cultural (*ethnocultural*) identity is important is because of a growing recognition that comparing people on the basis of race is illogical and based more on societal politics than on scientific merit. Often people do not have a sound rationale for choosing race as a variable. At the same time that people are moving away from the use of race as a variable, there is growing recognition of differences between people among differing ethnocultural groups. Although ethnicity may be more specific and thus a better variable than race in understanding cultural differences, it is still too broad to have practical use in many personal and professional interactions. Membership in an ethnic or racial group does not mean the same thing to all members.

The Complexity of Ethnocultural Identification: Clarification of Terminology

Although there is much discussion on the need for recognition of diversity, there remains inconsistency in the criteria and terminology used to categorize individuals. Persons are most often grouped according to their surnames or visible racial or physiological characteristics. Less attention has been paid to the diversity within cultural and ethnic groups or to people with multiple group heritage.

Understanding ethnocultural identification relies on an ability to define *culture, race,* and *ethnicity. Ethnic identity, ethnocultural identity,* and *acculturation* at times appear to refer to the same process, yet there are important differences among them. Let's briefly examine the basic meanings of each of these terms.

Culture

Culture has been linked to many ethnic and racial differences. But what is *culture*? Brislin (1993) suggests that culture ". . . consists of ideals, values, and assumptions about life that are widely shared among people and that guide specific behaviors" (p. 4). In conjunction with biological, environmental, and psychological determinants, it may be said that culture contributes to human behavior and the processes and biochemical reactions of the body (Marsella & Kameoka, 1989). Culture is perhaps the broadest way to refer to differences among people.

Race

The exact meaning of race remains controversial. Once race was thought to be a term used to explain genetic and physiognomic differences among four major groups of people: the white, yellow, black, and red (Spikard, 1992). Over time, additional categories have emerged for Native Americans, Pacific Islanders, and people of mixed heritage (Spikard, 1989; Root, 1992). Now, however, a growing body of literature characterizes race as a sociopolitical construct unrelated to biological heritage (Spikard, 1992; Root, 1992). Social scientists, mostly outside of the USA, have used the term *race* to represent a combination of biological and social traits. For instance, Rodriguez (1992) asserts that Latinos view race as biological inheritance and cultural variables and include such aspects as social class, behavior, and physical appearance. For our purposes, race is defined as individuals sharing a common ancestry who are distinguished from others by external features and traits (e.g., skin color, eye shape) (Wilkinson, 1993). Throughout history, differences in intellectual functioning, aptitude, athletic ability, mental illness, personality, and more have been linked to racial group membership. Racial identity refers to the extent to which individuals identify with their racial group. Despite the abundance of energy devoted to the study of racial differences and identity, the use of race as an explanation for differences among people (such as culture) is too vague and broad to be of use in guiding us in interactions within diverse societies.

Ethnicity/Ethnic Groups and Identity

The term *ethnic group,* used to refer to people sharing a common ethnicity or heritage, has not been much easier to define. Ethnicity and race are often used interchangeably, although the two terms are thought to represent different processes (Berry, Poortinga, Segall, & Dasen, 1992). Ethnicity does not depend solely on the use of external features or biology to distinguish groups, as does race. One useful guideline is to think of ethnicity as a smaller subunit of individuals within broad racial categories. Thernstrom's (1980) *Harvard Encyclopedia of American Ethnic Groups* records 101 ethnic groups defined by the following 14 factors: common geographical origin; migratory status; race; language or dialect; religious faith; ties that transcend kinship, neighborhood and community boundaries; shared traditions, values, and symbols; literature, folklore, and music; food preferences; settlement and employment patterns; special interests with regard to politics in the homeland and the United States; institutions that specifically secure and maintain the group; an internal sense of distinctiveness; and an external perception of distinctiveness. Religions, cultural organizations, and nationality all have been included as examples of ethnic groups in the literature. In its most simple form then, ethnic identity refers to the degree to which an individual self-identifies with a referent ethnic group (Phinney, 1990).

Ethnocultural Identity and Acculturation: A Subtle but Important Distinction

Ethnocultural identity and ethnic identity account for diversity within groups. However, ethnocultural identity moves beyond the attitudinal level of strength of attachment to the ethnic group. A simple definition of ethnocultural identity refers to the extent to which an individual endorses and practices a way of life associated with a particular cultural tradition (Marsella & Kameoka, 1989). The importance of multiple components of one's identity, such as behaviors and guiding values, is stressed in this definition. *Ethnocultural* also stresses the role of culture in the group and allows more readily for identification with groups not traditionally viewed as *ethnic groups* per se. Although *ethnocultural identity* refers only to one's identity with one's chosen groups, *acculturation* typically refers to the degree to which an individual identifies with or adjusts to the mainstream culture (e.g., Sodowsky, Lai, & Plake, 1991). Acculturation is only relevant when cultures come into contact (Berry, 1980). When viewed as an orthogonal construct (Oetting & Beauvais, 1991), acculturation refers to an individual's adjustment or "fit" with the referent minority and majority group cultures. Accordingly, "ethnic identity may be thought of as an aspect of acculturation, in which the concern is with individuals and the focus is on how they relate to their own group as a subgroup of the larger society" (Phinney, 1990, p. 501). Others have suggested that, following cultural contact, acculturation is the process of change that may occur in individuals within any of the cultures involved (Berry, 1980). As influenced by acculturation, ethnocultural identity is then viewed as being shaped by the cultural environment of the minority group, the majority culture, and their interactions (Berry, 1993; Bernal & Knight, 1993).

Choices in Identity Versus Forced Choice

Individuals have multiple options for conceptualizing their cultural identity. At certain times and in certain locations, one form of self-labeling or another has been favored. The choice of label is often influenced by the context of the situation and the individual's motives. Stephan and Stephan (1989), in interviews with students in New Mexico and Hawaii, discovered that even the wording of the inquiry can result in a changed label. Allowing individuals to freely choose their identity and labels tends to result in more accurate self-descriptions than forcing people to choose among predetermined labels. Individuals identifying with multiple groups or with groups not often listed in forced-choice inquiries often end up labeled as *other* (see Iijima-Hall, 1992) or *mixed,* and the purpose of elucidating specific and useful information is lost.

When given freedom to choose, individuals may choose an identity that reflects a broad category such as *nationality* (e.g., American, Mexican, Hungarian), *race* (e.g., Caucasian, African), or *pan-ethnicity* (e.g., Asian-American, Hispanic, Polynesian). Others may choose narrower terms, whether of a *specific ethnic group* (Native Hawaiian, Cherokee, Chamorro) or *hyphenated ethnic group* (e.g., French-Canadian, Greek-Australian, Italian-American). Individuals identifying with multiple ethnic groups have the preceding choices in addition to labels such as *mixed, mestizo, international person* (Lutzker, 1960), *universal person* (Walsh, 1973), or *multicultural person* (Adler, 1987). Ethnocultural identity may also be based on identity with a *religion* (e.g., Christian, Jewish, Muslim), *geographical region* (e.g., Southern, Texan, Pacific Islander) or *reference group* (e.g., college student, surfer, business executive).

Socialization and the Components of Ethnocultural Identity

At first glance, cultural identity appears to be a stable, diffuse, unidimensional entity composed of the ethnic group or groups of our heritage. In reality, ethnocultural identity is created by interconnected aspects of our socialization (values, beliefs, religion, language, social network, and exposure to other cultures).

Childhood socialization has been found to influence the development of cultural awareness and sense of ethnic identity (Knight, Bernal, & Carlo, 1990; Knight,

Bernal, Cota, Garza, & Ocampo, 1993; see also the edited volume by Rotheram & Phinney, 1987). Demo and Hughes (1990) measured the socialization of a subset of black American adults. In their study, they asked respondents to indicate what they had been taught by their parents about "what it is like to be black," and "how to get along with white people" (p. 368). Those respondents raised in an integrative/assertive manner or a cautious/defensive manner reported feeling closer to other blacks and more commitment to separatism (Demo & Hughes, 1990). Their findings support their assertion that early childhood experiences have a profound effect on later life identification. Adolescents and young adults, especially, may engage in cultural customs because they have been socialized to do so (Rotheram & Phinney, 1987) or are expected to do so by other members of their cultural group. Later in life, peer groups and one's social relationships may replace the family as a source of socialization. Socialization may occur later in life, as well, when individuals choose to be enculturated (i.e., voluntary socialization) into a cultural group other than their own. Ethnic group membership arising from socialization consists of the social networks an individual establishes and maintains, the ethnic affiliations upheld by the members of these groups, and the contacts the individual has with them. Three basic tenets of ethnocultural identity arise from the various influences of socialization: (a) ethnocultural identity is multidimensional; (b) ethnocultural identity is contextually based; and, (c) ethnocultural identity is dynamic and variable.

Multidimensionality

Identification with a cultural group is based on multiple facets, including attitude, value, and behavioral components (e.g., Knight et al., 1993; Marsella & Kameoka, 1989; Sodowsky, Lai, & Plake, 1991). The exact relationship among the various dimensions remains unclear. Some researchers assert that individuals who subjectively feel attached to a cultural group validate their attitude by engaging in practices or behaviors associated with the particular group (Berry, 1980, 1993). Equally plausible, however, is that individuals, for whatever reasons, engage in cultural practices and behaviors without a preexisting awareness of strong cultural identity (Burke & Reitzes, 1981). Identity with the group may develop from exposure to and involvement with these cultural practices. Regardless of the directionality of the components, behaviors and attitudes have been viewed as two distinct contributors and manifestations of identity with an ethnocultural group, and will be considered separately.

Behaviors

The interaction of the two opposing cultural forces is posited to determine culturally related behaviors: ". . . changes in a host of psychological qualities become possible (identity, values, attitudes, abilities, etc.) and are expressed in a large array of behavioral domains, such as language, dress, social relations and the like" (Berry, 1993, p. 273). These expressed behaviors, also referred to as *ethnic role behaviors,* involve participation in various behaviors that manifest "ethnic cultural values, styles, customs, traditions, and language" (Knight, et al., 1993, p. 106). Although Knight and colleagues discuss the acquisition of behavior through the formation of an ethnic identity, the manifestation of behaviors may be viewed, in turn, as a concrete representation of ethnic or cultural identity. For the most part, however, the continuation of one's cultural practices remains a viable aspect of cultural identity.

Results of a study by Kivisto and Nefzger (1993) on Jewish cultural behaviors suggests that many individuals do participate in activities associated with their heritage, rather than maintaining their ethnicity only symbolically, as has been suggested by other researchers (e.g., Gans, 1979).

Attitudes, Values, Beliefs

Behavior does not directly underlie cultural differences, but attitudes and values do. When framed as being based on values and beliefs, ethnic identity is concerned with an individual's perception of belonging to (identifying with) one group, as distinct from other groups. Ethnic attitudes and values encompass feelings about, pride in, and loyalty and attachment to an ethnic group and its particular ideals and values in comparison to other groups. In certain contexts, perceptions that discrimination and prejudice are directed against one's ethnic group also contribute to a sense of ethnic identity. Cultural pride or feelings of pride about one's ethnic group is another frequently seen, attitude-based component of ethnocultural identity (see Suinn, Ahuna, & Khoo, in press).

The Importance of Context

Like acculturation, ethnic identity is only meaningful for most individuals when two or more cultures come into contact (e.g., Phinney, 1990; Root, 1992). Yet an individual's sense of ethnocultural identity may not fall neatly into one ingroup and one outgroup. Rather, it is possible that the behaviors that individuals associate with ingroup membership may be quite different from behaviors that suggest attachment to cultural groups outside of one's primary identity. For instance, although speaking one's ethnic language and shopping at a store featuring products from one's culture of origin may be associated with an immigrant's sense of ingroup membership, going to school and shopping at the mall may trigger feelings of identification with the mainstream culture (Sodowsky et al., 1991). At the same time, participation in mainstream behaviors, such as being expected to voice one's personal opinion in large groups of coworkers, may heighten one's ingroup identification by providing a disconcerting reminder of one's personally preferred behaviors, or alternatively could lessen one's ingroup identification as one makes continual efforts to "fit in" with the other culture.

Context provides clues for behavior but does not eliminate individual choice in identification. People with multiple identities may select signs of the identity most appropriate to the situation. In a study of students of mixed heritage, students' responses regarding their identity differed depending on whether they were asked about their ethnicity in the context of an official form or by friends and family (Stephan & Stephan, 1989). Even for persons with one overarching ethnocultural identity, strength of identity tends to be more pronounced when in contact with persons holding vastly differing identities than when among culturally similar others. Also, some individuals may suppress or hide their identity to blend into a mainstream cultural society, although emphasizing their identity when doing so is more profitable or supported. An example would be a Nigerian-American businesswoman emulating her white peers at the office, but adopting Nigerian aspects of her identity when at home with her family Context should always be considered in the assessment of ethno-cultural identity.

Ethnocultural Identity is Dynamic

Ethnocultural identity is subject to modification over time, affected by the accul-turation process, and influenced by contextual factors. Developmental processes play a role in the salience and manifestation of ethnocultural identity. Whereas the influ-ences of socialization on behaviors tied to ethnocultural group membership become apparent in young children (Phinney & Rotheram, 1987), it is not until adolescence that cultural self-identity is thought to be realized (Phinney, 1992). Ethnocultural identity may become even more salient as we mature and the effects of earlier sociali-zation become internalized (Triandis, 1972). Among developmental transitions that may affect one's identity are marriage, when one's spouse may hold a very divergent identity, and the birth of one's children, with the accompanying need to make deci-sions related to raising children according to the norms of a particular culture's tra-ditions. The influences of family and friends on our identity will probably also vary according to our own social development. Thus, for some individuals, ethnocultural identity will wax and wane or even be transformed into new identities across the lifespan.

Functions of Ethnocultural Identity

Although a full coverage of this topic is beyond the scope of this module, to elu-cidate the relevance and potential applications of attention to cultural identity, let's examine two issues: racism and service delivery.

Reduction of Racism

Increased media and national attention to racial and ethnic conflicts and incidents on college campuses has led to an increased interest in staff being asked to offer education and training to students and staff, and to assist students in their efforts to understand the role of ethnicity and race in their lives (Pope-Davis & Ottavi, 1994). Still, the focus of most attention has been on racism or increasing cultural sensitivity, especially for whites, and not on the meaning of being a member of a particular cultural group (Carter, 1990; Helms, 1984; Pope-Davis & Ottavi, 1994). According to Helms (1984), higher levels of racial identity (a broader measure than ethnic iden-tity) relate to improved cross-cultural interactions, an increase in multicultural inter-actions, and better personal adjustment. Strong white racial identity has also been shown to relate to racism scores in a study conducted by Carter (1990). The reduction of racism is thus one goal of trainers, reached in part through the ability to build awareness and facilitate the development of positive ethnic identities in all members of the community.

Improving Service Delivery Within Diverse Societies

Cultural differences between service deliverers and consumers may interfere with effective service provision. Although many providers are conscientiously attending to culturally appropriate service delivery, it is less clear which consumers benefit from this attention. For example, providing Spanish-language advertising to a Cuban American who does not identify herself as a Spanish-speaking Cuban American may result in the loss of the sale and subsequent revenue.

Although the business community naturally has monetary incentives to understand the cultural identity of consumers, the health care services have additional motivators. Recent studies have begun to ascertain the importance of ethnic identity (often referred to as racial identity development) in choosing successful client-patient matches (Pope-Davis & Ottavi, 1994). For instance, understanding the cultural beliefs and practices of the culture with which an individual identifies can lead to improved compliance with treatment and better communication (Thompson, Thompson, & House, 1990). A number of studies have also examined ethnic identity as a mediating variable in the willingness of minority-culture individuals to seek mental health services (Atkinson & Gim, 1989; Gim, Atkinson, & Whiteley, 1990; Sanchez & Atkinson, 1983).

Applications of Ethnocultural Identity

Multiple Identities: Mixed Ethnicity and Multicultural Allegiance

Who are individuals with multiple ethnocultural identities? Anyone identifying with an ethnocultural group other than that of the "mainstream" society yet also choosing to participate in the mainstream culture is arguably bicultural (Berry & Kim, 1988). Yet some but not all of these individuals will identify themselves as a member of the mainstream culture and thus may or may not have multiple identities. In other words, it is possible to adapt one's behavior to function according to a culture's guidelines without identifying with the culture (Bhawuk & Brislin, 1992). Given prolonged exposure to the culture, however, some individuals may choose to identify with it. This type of identification is often described as a *reference group identity* (Sherif & Sherif, 1969) or a group to which one aspires to obtain membership. Some but not all aspects of an individual's life may be affected and the individual may or may not be recognized as a group member by others (Brislin, personal communication, July 1995). Peace Corps volunteers, people in intercultural marriages, and international businessmen with repeated or intense intercultural experiences may acquire multiple identities. Children of intercultural marriages (Stephan & Stephan, 1991b) or born and raised outside of their parents' culture will vary in the extent to which they are socialized in and identify with the various cultures to which they are exposed. There are no standard guidelines to determine rules for cultural identity and, given the subjective nature of identification, some individuals may acquire an ethnocultural identity based solely on learning a second language or childhood exposure to diversity within their community. In the diverse cultural environment of Hawaii, over 40% of a university student sample self-identified with more than one ethnic group (Horvath, Marsella, & Yamada, 1996).

Traditionally, despite having no well-founded evidence, the prevailing attitude of the popular and scientific press emphasized negative consequences arising from socialization with multiple cultures. Interestingly, a mental disorder is based on an inability to integrate multiple identities and, although based on disassociative behaviors, when described in general terms resembles the definition of an individual with multiple cultural identities. Ironically, in an article on cultural differences in the disorder, Spanos (1994) states, "People who enact multiple identities behave as if they possess two or more selves, each with its own characteristic moods, memories, and behavioral repertoire. Under different names, this phenomenon occurs in many cultures. In North American culture, it is frequently labeled multiple personality disorder" (p. 143).

Only in the past few years have the advantages of multicultural identity been discussed. Bhawuk and Brislin (1992) suggest that people with experience in more than one culture exhibit cultural flexibility that translates into intercultural sensitivity or the ability to behave in culturally appropriate ways in more than one culture. Although this study did not directly assess identification with multiple cultures, given their demographic profiles, their sample of university students in Hawaii and internationally experienced young scholars probably included people with multiple cultural identities. Using samples from Hawaii and New Mexico, Stephan and Stephan (1991a, 1991b) found evidence that individuals of mixed ethnicity and bicultural socialization did not exhibit negative personality traits or poor adjustment. Instead, these students demonstrated less ethnocentrism and more exposure to and liking of Hispanic and Asian cultures than students with single heritage or allegiance. Studies of the acculturation of immigrant groups have also supported the notion that identity with the mainstream culture and one's traditional ethnocultural group is indicative of positive well-being (Berry & Kim, 1988).

Ethnocultural Identity and "Americans": The "Not Applicable" Syndrome

There will probably be some readers thinking to themselves that this module may be of interest to "minorities" but not to themselves. Often these individuals identify with culture on a national or racial level rather than on a cultural or ethnic-group level. "I don't identify with a culture," "N.A.," and "American" are frequent responses when these individuals are queried about their ethnocultural identify. Given the subtle, "unspoken," taken-for-granted nature of culture (Brislin, 1993), this attitude is understandable in people with little exposure to diversity. After gaining some intercultural exposure to and awareness of the role culture plays in their lives, individuals who complain that they don't have a cultural identity may be surprised to see that they are guided by the widely shared assumptions of major or multiple groups.

Skill Development

Expanding One's Identity

The purpose of this exercise is to expand the concept of ethnic identity to include multiple aspects of the cultural influences present in our daily lives. This exercise is particularly useful for people who believe they lack an ethnocultural identity.

Instructions

Read through the following questions quietly on your own and formulate your responses. When you have completed this, select a partner and discuss your responses. Reflect on the experience of sharing your responses: what was it like for you, what did you learn about yourself, and what did you learn about your partner?

Questions

1. Think about the networks you have and the groups that make up those networks (e.g., church members, coworkers, relatives). Make a list of them and then construct a sociogram to illustrate the nature of the groups and their interrelationships. Are the members of these groups in any particular ethnic group? In what ways do they contribute to your ethnocultural identity and related behaviors? In what areas do they influence and guide you?

2. Do you see yourself as more or less like some groups (e.g., in appearance, the way you express your feelings, the values and beliefs you hold, your behaviors)? Which groups and why?

3. Identification with a cultural group often has implications for behaviors, attitudes, and values. Identification with two cultures can offer challenges. What challenges might occur for someone identifying with the following pairs of cultural groups? Which pairs might offer more challenges? What similarities in the pairs would be likely? Note: You may wish to select one pair and seek information from members of the group.

    A. Japanese and Mexican
    B. Korean American and Italian American
    C. French Canadian and British Canadian
    D. Eastern European and Western European
    E. Japanese and Chinese
    F. Hawaiian and Samoan

Translating Identity Into Behaviors

This is an exercise that demonstrates one method of assessing your degree of behavioral involvement with an ethnocultural group. This exercise is designed to allow you to explore your own participation in the activities or traditions associated with the ethnic group with which you identify. By completing the index and then answering the discussion questions, you will better understand the extent of your behaviors associated with this group.

Instructions

Write in the name of the ethnocultural group with which you *most strongly identify,* and then circle the number corresponding to the strength of your identification with this group. Next, answer each item according to how much you participate in the following activities or customs of the specific ethnocultural group you choose at the *present time* (e.g., Mexican American, Japanese American, Chinese, Irish American). We recognize that many people have a diverse ethnic background. For this exercise, if you feel you strongly identify with more than one group, choose the group you most identify with or choose one of the groups and record it on this page. You may wish to complete this exercise separately for each group you identify with.

1. Name of Group: _____

2. To what extent do you identify with the ethnic background you selected above (i.e., how strong is your identification with this group)?

very little	1	2	3	4	5	6	7	very much

Please respond to the following questions according to the scale.

never	sometimes	often	very often	always
1	2	3	4	5

_____ 1. Eat the food specific to the group (e.g., Korean kimchi, Mexican quesadilla, German bratwurst)

_____ 2. Watch movies (films, VCR tapes) that use the language of the group or that depict the cultural group

_____ 3. Watch TV programs that use the language of the group or that depict the cultural group

_____ 4. Shop at stores that feature products of the group (e.g., Chinese market, kosher deli)

_____ 5. Speak the language of the group with family or close friends

_____ 6. Dress in the clothes of the group (e.g., Japanese kimono, Scottish kilt, Indian sari)

_____ 7. Listen to the music of the group (e.g., traditional or popular music of the culture)

_____ 8. Read newspapers/magazines of the group (in English or in the ethnic language)

_____ 9. Active in a political movement or ideology of the group

_____ 10. Have some of the artwork of the group (e.g., decorations, artifacts in the house)

_____ 11. Date members of the group (or married to a member of the group)

_____ 12. Learn the dances and music of the group (e.g., Hawaiian hula, Japanese bon dance, Polish polka

_____ 13. Use the traditional medicines or treatments of the group (e.g., herbal medicines, acupuncture)

_____ 14. Listen to or hear others speaking the language of the group (even if you do not always understand)

_____ 15. Attend the traditional religious or spiritual services of the group (e.g., a Buddhist temple, Catholic Mass, Greek Orthodox)

_____ 16. Go to physicians, hair stylists, lawyers, or other professionals who are from the group

_____ 17. Spend time talking, gossiping, or chatting with members of the group

_____ 18. Spend time studying the history or culture of the group (alone or in voluntary courses)

_____ 19. Follow the political and other current events of the group (locally or in the home country/region)

_____ 20. Work in an organization that is owned by members of the group or in which group members are frequently seen

_____ 21. Belong to at least one cultural organization (e.g., Americans of Japanese Ancestry)

_____ 22. Interact frequently at informal gatherings with members of the group (e.g., parties, potlucks, picnics)

_____ 23. Participate in hobbies that are popular mainly within the group (e.g., origami, mahjongg, traditional musical instrument)

_____ 24. Interact with close friends from the group

_____ 25. Participate in sports popular within the group (e.g., bocce ball, cricket, curling)

_____ 26. Vote or would definitely vote for candidates from the group

_____ 27. Observe the holidays and celebrations of the group (e.g., Cinco de Mayo, Oktoberfest, Boys' Day)

Now please read through the following questions on your own and formulate your responses. It may be helpful to jot down a few of your thoughts as you go through the questions. When you have completed this, please select a partner and discuss your responses. Questions should be answered first individually and then in pairs or small groups.

1. Which of these behaviors/practices/activities do you engage in because of your identity with this group?
2. Which of these behaviors do you feel play a part in determining your ethnocultural identification (i.e., doing it enhances your identity)? Which of the items do you feel are irrelevant to your identification with your group?
3. Are the values or beliefs that underlie these behaviors specific to your ethnocultural group, or universal? Can you identify any of the values behind any of the behaviors?
4. What are some of the influences behind the behaviors you endorsed? Are these practices you learned from your family or other members of your groups? Do you engage in these behaviors because you choose to do so or because you have been socialized or encouraged to do so by members of our group? Do you do them alone or with other group members? Give examples.

Workshop Leaders

Although the items are meant to capture variation within individuals' personal identity, the items may be summed and the total scores compared along individuals identifying with the same group. Scores may be compared across groups with further discussion on reasons for differences among ethnocultural groups.

The Confused Martian: Finding a Shared Culture

The purpose of this exercise is to develop a sense of shared culture. This exercise is especially valuable for individuals who believe that they do not have a shared cultural identity. The concept of reference group identity is particularly relevant and participants are encouraged to go beyond typical categories of groups based on national and ethnic groups.

Instructions:

A Martian (the group leader) has come to Earth to study the cultural identity of Earthlings. Thus far, the Martian has been astonished by the inconsistency and lack of concrete categories used to describe Earthlings. The confused Martian comes to you for help with this project in exchange for taking you for a ride in the spaceship. You agree to help and are provided with these instructions. Participants are asked to form groups of individuals sharing common cultural features. The groups may be based on nationality, ethnicity, common life experiences, or other shared traits. Creativity is encouraged for including people who do not fit into existing groups. Each group should create a label for itself. Examples of previous groups include African Americans, white males, international travelers, women executives, Spanish-speakers, and English-language learners. Each group is then provided with a large sheet of poster paper and markers and asked to list the traits, behaviors, values, and other shared aspects of their group. Each aspect must be shared by all members of the group to avoid confusing the Martian any further. Participants may be given Thernstrom's characteristics of an ethnic group as a starting point. Once the groups are finished, they are asked to take turns posting their paper and presenting their culture to the Martian leader. Debriefing would include comments by the Martian on the process involved in the formation of the groups, discussing any difficulties in agreement or generation of cultural features. Participants should be encouraged to comment on any discrepancy between membership in a group and the group others would probably impose on the individual. Plenty of time should be left for discussion.

Field Exercise

This exercise is designed to increase your identification with a cultural group by increasing your awareness of the group's history, values, beliefs, and other dimensions. The following sources are suggested as avenues for further learning and exploration:

1. Read books on the historical experiences or migration of the group
2. Talk to elders or well-respected members of the group about traditional practices and values (you may wish to prepare questions in advance)
3. Talk to other members of the group about current issues and topics of interest to group members (the Internet offers a convenient forum for discussion)
4. Study the language or dialect of the group
5. Join or create a cultural organization with other group members
6. Celebrate a traditional holiday or ritual of the group
7. Seek out others who have had similar experiences (e.g., who have interacted in multiple cultures)

Concluding Remarks

The previous discussion and exercises highlight the complexity of ethnocultural identity and illustrate a few of the difficulties that could occur when we rely on ethnicity alone as a sort of magical formula to provide all information about a person. Measuring the strength of a person's identification with one or more ethnocultural groups allows a more accurate picture to be formed than using ethnic heritage alone.

Ethnocultural identity is composed of our beliefs, values, level of pride, and behaviors associated with the group or groups to which we identify. Despite the importance of ethnocultural identity for many individuals, we need to remember that this forms only one aspect of a greater identity that includes our family roles (e.g., mother, sister), occupation, personality, and physical being (e.g., blond, short, skinny). However, when living or working within a diverse society, knowledge of our own and others' ethnocultural identifications provides a greater chance of interacting and reacting in a manner appropriate to the cultural values, attitudes, and expectations of the person.

References

Adler, P. S. (1987). Beyond cultural identity: Reflections on cultural and multicultural man. In L. Samovar & R. Porter (Eds.), *Intercultural communication: A reader* (pp. 410-429). Belmont, CA: Wadsworth.

Atkinson, D., & Gim, R. (1989). Asian-American cultural identity and attitudes toward mental health services. *Journal of Counseling Psychology, 36,* 209-212.

Bernal, M., & Knight, G. (Eds.). (1993). *Ethnic identity: Formation and transmission among Hispanics and other minorities.* New York: State University of New York Press.

Berry, J. W. (1980). Social and cultural change. In H. C. Triandis & R. Brislin (Eds.), *Handbook of cross-cultural psychology, Vol. 5, Social* (pp. 211-279). Boston: Allyn and Bacon.

Berry, J. W. (1993). Ethnic identity in plural societies. In M. E. Bernal & G. P. Knight (Eds.), *Ethnic identity: Formation and transmission among Hispanics and other minorities* (pp. 271-296). New York: State University of New York Press.

Berry, J. W., & Kim, U. (1988). Acculturation and mental health. In P. J. Dasen, J. W. Berry, & N. Sartorius (Eds.), *Health and cross-cultural psychology* (pp. 207-236). New York: Academic Press.

Berry, J. W., Poortinga, Y. H., Sagall, M. H., & Dasen, P. J. (1992). *Cross-cultural psychology: Research and application.* New York: Cambridge University Press.

Bhawuk, D. P. S., & Brislin, R. (1992). The measurement of intercultural sensitivity using the concepts of individualism and collectivism. *International Journal of Intercultural Relations, 16,* 413-436.

Brislin, R. W. (1993). *Understanding culture's influence on behavior.* Fort Worth, TX: Harcourt Brace Jovanovich.

Burke, P. J., & Reitzes, D. C. (1981). The link between identity and role performance. *Social Psychology Quarterly, 44*(2), 81-92.

Carter, R. T. (1990). The relationship between racism and racial identity among White Americans: An exploratory investigation. *Journal of Counseling and Development, 69,* 46-50.

Demo, D. H., & Hughes, M. (1990). Socialization and racial identity among Black Americans. *Social Psychology Quarterly, 53,* 364-374.

Gans, H. (1979). Symbolic ethnicity: The future of ethnic groups and cultures in America. *Ethnic and Racial Studies, 2,* 1-20.

Gim, R., Atkinson, D., & Whiteley, S. (1990). Asian-American acculturation, severity of concerns, and willingness to see a counselor. *Journal of Counseling Psychology, 37,* 281-285.

Helms, J. E. (1984). Towards a theoretical explanation of the effects of race on counseling: A Black and White model. *The Counseling Psychologist, 12,* 153-165.

Horvath, A. M., Marsella, A. J., & Yamada, S. Y. (1996). Ethnocultural identity: Psychometric study of a behavioral scale. Manuscript submitted for publication.

Iijima-Hall, C. C. (1992). Please choose one: Ethnic identity choices for biracial individuals. In M. P. P. Root (Ed.), *Racially mixed people in America* (pp. 250-264). Newbury Park, CA: Sage.

Kivisto, P., & Nefzger, B. (1993). Symbolic ethnicity and American Jews: The relations of ethnic identity to behaviors and group affiliation. *The Social Science Journal, 30,* 1-12.

Knight, G. P., Bernal, M. E., & Carlo, G. (1990). *Socialization and the development of cooperative, competitive, and individualistic behaviors among Mexican American children.* Unpublished manuscript, Arizona State University, Tempe, AZ.

Knight, G. P., Bernal, M. E., Cota, M. K., Garza, C. A., & Ocampo, K. A. (1993). Family socialization and Mexican American identity and behavior. In M. E. Bernal & G. P. Knight (Eds.), *Ethnic identity: Formation and transmission among Hispanics and other minorities* (pp. 105-129). New York: State University of New York Press.

Lutzker, D. (1960). Internationalism as a predictor of cooperative behavior. *Journal of Conflict Resolution, 4,* 426-430.

Marsella, A. J., & Kameoka, V. (1989). Ethnocultural issues in the assessment of psychopathology. In S. Wetzler (Ed.), *Measuring mental illness: Psychometric assessment for clinicians* (pp. 231-256). Washington, D.C.: American Psychiatric Press.

Mullavey-O'Byrne, C., & Horvat, K.-M. (1994). *Ethnicity and ethnic identity.* Invited workshop module at the Third Annual Workshop for the Development of Intercultural Expertise, East-West Center, Honolulu, HI.

Oetting, E. R., & Beauvais, F. (1991). Orthogonal cultural identification theory: The cultural identification of minority adolescents. *International Journal of the Addictions, 25*, 655-685.

Phinney, J. (1990). Ethnic identity in adolescence and adulthood: A review of research. *Psychological Bulletin, 108*, 499-514.

Phinney, J. (1992). The multigroup ethnic identity measure: A new scale for use with diverse groups. *Journal of Adolescent Research, 7*, 156-176.

Phinney, J. S., & Rotheram, M. J. (Eds.). (1987). *Children's ethnic socialization: Pluralism and development.* Newbury Park, CA: Sage.

Pope-Davis, D. B., & Ottavi, T. M. (1994). The relationship between racism and racial identity among White Americans: A replication and extension. *Journal of Counseling and Development, 72*, 293-297.

Rodriguez, C. E. (1992). Race, culture, and Latino "otherness" in the 1980 census. *Social Science Quarterly, 73*, 930-937.

Root, M. P. P. (1992). Within, between, and beyond race. In M. P. P. Root (Ed.), *Racially mixed people in America* (pp. 3-11). Newbury Park, CA: Sage.

Rotheram, M. J., & Phinney, J. S. (1987). Ethnic behavior patterns as an aspect of identity. In J. S. Phinney & M. J. Rotheram (Eds.), *Children's ethnic socialization: Pluralism and development* (pp. 201-218). Newbury Park: Sage.

Sanchez, R., & Atkinson, D. (1983). Mexican-American cultural commitment, preference for counselor ethnicity, and willingness to use counseling. *Journal of Counseling Psychology, 30*, 215-220.

Sherif, M., & Serif, C. (1969). Social psychology. New York: Harper & Row.

Sodowsky, G., Lai, E. W. M., & Plake, B. S. (1991). Moderating effects of sociocultural variables on acculturation attitudes of Hispanics and Asian Americans. *Journal of Counseling and Development, 70*, 194-204.

Spanos, N. P. (1994). Multiple identity enactments and multiple personality disorder: A socio-cognitive perspective. *Psychological Bulletin, 116*, 143-165.

Spikard, P. R. (1989). *Mixed blood: Intermarriage and ethnic identity in twentieth century America.* Madison, WI: The University of Wisconsin Press.

Spikard, P. R. (1992). The illogic of American racial categories. In M. P. P. Root (Ed.), *Racially mixed people in America* (pp. 12-23). Newbury Park, CA: Sage.

Stephan, C. W., & Stephan, W. G. (1989). After intermarriage: Ethnic identity among mixed-heritage Japanese-Americans and Hispanics. *Journal of Marriage and Family, 51*, 507-519.

Stephan, W. G., & Stephan, C. W. (1991a). Intermarriage: Effects on personality, adjustment, and intergroup relations in two samples of students. *Journal of Marriage and the Family, 53*, 241-250.

Stephan, W. G., & Stephan, C. W. (1991b). Effects of bicultural socialization on personality and intergroup relations. *Journal of Marriage and the Family, 53*(1), 241.

Suinn, R. M., Ahuna, E., & Kho, G. (in press). The Suinn-Lew self-identity acculturation scale: Concurrent and factorial validity. *Educational and Psychological Measurements.*

Thernstrom, S. (Ed.). (1980). *Harvard encyclopedia of American ethnic groups.* Cambridge, MA: Belknap.

Thompson, W. L., Thompson, T. L, & House, R. M. (1990). Taking care of culturally different and non-English-speaking patients. *International Journal of Psychiatry in Medicine, 20*, 235-245.

Triandis, H. C. (1972). *The analysis of subjective culture.* New York: John Wiley.

Walsh, J. E. (1973). *Intercultural education in the community of man.* Honolulu: University of Hawaii Press.

Wilkinson, D. (1993). Family ethnicity in America. In H. P. Mckadoo, (Ed.), *Family ethnicity: Strength in diversity* (pp. 15-59). Newbury Park, CA: Sage.

11

Conflict and Mediation Across Cultures

Theodore M. Singelis
Paul Pedersen

With increased global urbanization and modernization, the traditional sources of help for mediating personal conflict through the village and family have been displaced by professional mediators, helpers, and counselors. The purpose of this module is to provide some awareness, knowledge, and skills that will be useful to mediators, helpers, and counselors in mediating intercultural conflicts. As a result of participating in this module, the reader should gain (a) an awareness that cultures have various assumptions that guide their behavior, (b) knowledge that will enable them to separate facts from inferences, and (c) skills built on this awareness and knowledge that will allow them to better manage intercultural conflicts. The module demonstrates how these skills can be applied through the use of the Cultural Grid for analyzing intercultural conflicts. Finally, an exercise for developing intercultural conflict and mediation skill is described.

Contents

Self-Assessment of Conflict and Mediation Attitudes

The purpose of this questionnaire is for participants to assess their own attitudes and approaches to conflict and mediation. There are no right or wrong answers, though cultures vary as to the emphasis that is placed on various aspects of conflict and mediation. The assessment can be used to determine one's cultural assumptions and compare them with other possible assumptions. Please answer as honestly as possible by indicating your agreement or disagreement with each statement by circling one of the responses.

1. In resolving conflicts, personalities are more important than facts.

strongly disagree	disagree	disagree somewhat	don't agree or disagree	agree somewhat	agree	strongly agree
1	2	3	4	5	6	7

2. A fair outcome requires a neutral mediator.

strongly disagree	disagree	disagree somewhat	don't agree or disagree	agree somewhat	agree	strongly agree
1	2	3	4	5	6	7

3. In resolving conflicts, the status of the parties is an important consideration.

strongly disagree	disagree	disagree somewhat	don't agree or disagree	agree somewhat	agree	strongly agree
1	2	3	4	5	6	7

4. It is normally possible to resolve conflicts if the people involved are honest and direct.

strongly disagree	disagree	disagree somewhat	don't agree or disagree	agree somewhat	agree	strongly agree
1	2	3	4	5	6	7

5. The best mediator is one who knows the parties well.

strongly disagree	disagree	disagree somewhat	don't agree or disagree	agree somewhat	agree	strongly agree
1	2	3	4	5	6	7

6. The first step to resolving a conflict is to get the parties to admit the conflict face to face.

strongly disagree	disagree	disagree somewhat	don't agree or disagree	agree somewhat	agree	strongly agree
1	2	3	4	5	6	7

7. If I were asked to help resolve a conflict, I'd want to know some history of the people involved before asking about the specifics of the present disagreement.

strongly disagree	disagree	disagree somewhat	don't agree or disagree	agree somewhat	agree	strongly agree
1	2	3	4	5	6	7

8. It is not right to apologize if you are not at fault in a conflict.

strongly disagree	disagree	disagree somewhat	don't agree or disagree	agree somewhat	agree	strongly agree
1	2	3	4	5	6	7

9. It is often wise to depend on someone else to work out your conflict for you.

strongly disagree	disagree	disagree somewhat	don't agree or disagree	agree somewhat	agree	strongly agree
1	2	3	4	5	6	7

10. If someone acts in an aggressive and hostile way, it is safe to assume they are your enemy.

strongly disagree	disagree	disagree somewhat	don't agree or disagree	agree somewhat	agree	strongly agree
1	2	3	4	5	6	7

11. Formal rituals are necessary to successfully resolve declared conflicts.

strongly disagree	disagree	disagree somewhat	don't agree or disagree	agree somewhat	agree	strongly agree
1	2	3	4	5	6	7

12. A mediator unknown to both parties is best because this assures neutrality and anonymity.

strongly disagree	disagree	disagree somewhat	don't agree or disagree	agree somewhat	agree	strongly agree
1	2	3	4	5	6	7

13. Conflict represents a challenge and an opportunity for change.

strongly disagree	disagree	disagree somewhat	don't agree or disagree	agree somewhat	agree	strongly agree
1	2	3	4	5	6	7

14. If people share the same positive expectations, their behaviors toward one another are relatively unimportant.

strongly disagree	disagree	disagree somewhat	don't agree or disagree	agree somewhat	agree	strongly agree
1	2	3	4	5	6	7

15. Sometimes the best way to deal with a conflict is to keep silent.

strongly disagree	disagree	disagree somewhat	don't agree or disagree	agree somewhat	agree	strongly agree
1	2	3	4	5	6	7

16. To insure fairness in mediation, communication rules must be applied in the same way in all settings.

strongly disagree	disagree	disagree somewhat	don't agree or disagree	agree somewhat	agree	strongly agree
1	2	3	4	5	6	7

17. Conflict can be a means to positive change.

strongly disagree	disagree	disagree somewhat	don't agree or disagree	agree somewhat	agree	strongly agree
1	2	3	4	5	6	7

18. One should look to the future and not the past when finding solutions to conflicts.

strongly disagree	disagree	disagree somewhat	don't agree or disagree	agree somewhat	agree	strongly agree
1	2	3	4	5	6	7

Score Sheet for Self-Assessment

Instructions

Write the number you indicated for each item in the location specified below. Then add the columns. There are four total scores.

Context. Higher scores indicate a tendency to view conflict and mediation from this perspective.

Low context. Low and high context refer to communication styles that are, in part, related to cultural background. These concepts will be explained more specifically in the text that follows. When in a conflict, those with higher scores have a tendency to be direct in communication, problem-oriented, and focused on the future. In addition, those scoring high also hold the belief that mediator neutrality is important to "fair" mediation.

High context. When in a conflict, those who score higher have a tendency to be indirect in communication, person-oriented, and aware of the past. In addition, those scoring high also prefer, or at least accept, a mediator from inside their group.

Expectation. Higher scores here indicate the normal tendency to attribute attitudes to behaviors according to one's own cultural assumptions.

Outlook. This represents your attitude toward conflict as a challenge or a failure. Higher scores indicate viewing conflict as a challenge rather than a failure.

High Context		Low Context		Expectations		Outlook	
Item#	*Score*	*Item #*	*Score*	*Item #*	*Score*	*Item #*	*Score*
1		2		10		13	
3		4		14		17	
5		6		Total =		Total =	
7		8		Max = 14	Min = 2	Max = 14	Min = 2
9		12					
11		16					
15		18					
Total =		Total =					
Max = 49	Min = 7	Max = 49	Min = 7				

Concepts Necessary for Skill Development

Introduction

The literature on mediation and, to a lesser extent, the literature on counseling carefully distinguishes between the more "objective" and "neutral" bases of mediation in contrast with the more "subjective" and "directional" bases of counseling (Landry, Kolb, & Rubin, 1991; Rubin, 1989). In this module, we wish to make no such clear distinction. Although strict "neutrality" and "objectivity" in mediation may be appropriate and desirable in certain conflicts, there are many more conflicts that can be successfully mediated by people who are known to the conflicting parties. For example, parents, coworkers, supervisors, teachers, or friends are often in a position to mediate conflicts, although they cannot make a claim to "neutrality" or "objectivity" because of their relationship to the conflicting parties. Furthermore, we question the ability of even highly trained mediators to be completely "objective." As we discuss in the following section, the way conflicts are viewed and managed is culturally based. All mediators, trained or not, bring biases, preferences, and attitudes toward conflict to the table with them (Augsburger, 1992). We believe that mediators, like counselors, need awareness, knowledge, and skills to work effectively in intercultural settings. Therefore, in this module, our approach to mediation is more closely linked to counseling than most. We begin the discussion of concepts relevant to intercultural conflict and mediation with a description of terms and assumptions that should make clear the approach and scope of the module.

Conflict

In this module, we are primarily interested in conflict at the interpersonal level. To this extent mediation will resemble the counseling process. At the same time, we wish to stress that these microlevel conflicts have profound implications on many macrolevels. In cultures where any conflict is a disruption of cosmic harmony, the way that individuals handle their interpersonal conflict has cosmic implications. Conflict is seen as rooted in incompatible goals but the incompatibility may or may not be real. This is to say that often what is perceived as incompatible is, in fact, only a misperception resulting from wrong inferences rather than accurate facts. Thus, although many conflicts may be inevitable and necessary, others are unnecessary because they are rooted in misinterpretations. Finally, we would like to make clear that conflict can be constructive or destructive. For example, conflicts stemming from misinterpretations of intentions, if managed properly, will lead to greater understanding and perhaps greater cooperation. Conflicts may also lead to innovation that provides both sides with more than was originally available to either (Jandt & Pedersen, 1996).

Mediation

We define *mediation* broadly as an ongoing process that aims at win-win outcomes in which all parties are helped. This is distinguished from zero-sum approaches that focus on win-lose outcomes. Mediation, then, is an approach to managing conflict that mobilizes opportunities for mutual growth similar in many ways to the goals of counseling. Often, but not always, there will be a third party involved in a mediation. However, we wish to emphasize that we believe it is virtually impossible for any third party to be completely neutral. Thus, it seems much more reasonable to acknowledge this lack of neutrality and follow the more common, non-Western, custom of using a mediator who is known and trusted by both parties. Mediation does not involve a set model or easy solution but is complex and dynamic in accommodating to each cultural context.

To be effective, mediation must be fluid and adaptable. We suggest that by stepping back from the conflict and observing themselves, mediation can even be accomplished—in what has been called a "second-party mediator model"—by the conflicting parties themselves. All counseling, to some extent, is focused on mediating conflict in a second-party format.

Culture

Fundamental to our broad and inclusive conceptualization of culture is the notion that each person has many cultures, just as they have many identities. Culture here is

Table 11.1 Assumptions About Conflict, Mediation, and Culture

Conflict

Microlevel conflict (interpersonal) can have macrolevel implications
Constructive or destructive
Necessary or unnecessary
Sometimes the result of wrong inferences rather than accurate facts
Can lead to innovation

Mediation

Aims at win-win outcomes
Mediators not necessarily neutral or unknown
Complex and dynamic
Fluid and adaptable
"Self"-mediation possible
Related to counseling

Culture

People have multiple cultures
Shared and learned
Includes norms, values, and structures (e.g., legal and political)
Includes "social system" variables (ethnographic, demographic, status, and affiliations)
Each person has unique set of identities
Identity is dynamic, not fixed
Provides guidelines for behavior
Is complex but not chaotic
Provides assumptions about others' behaviors

shared and *learned*. Culture includes norms, values, and structures (e.g., legal and political). This pool of "social system variables" might include (a) ethnographic variables, such as nationality, ethnicity, language, or religion, (b) demographic variables, such as age, gender, or place of residence, (c) status variables, such as social, educational, or economic, or (d) affiliation variables, such as formal affiliations to family and career, or informal affiliations to an idea or a value (Scott & Borodovsky, 1990). Note that cultures may be *shared* among a small group of people; the size of the group is not important, so long as it is salient to the individual.

Clearly, people have many sources of shared meaning, yet each person has a unique set of identities. This is to say, even though cultures have a strong effect in shaping each person's identities, there are numerous idiosyncratic variables that combine with culture to produce identity (Sue, Ivey, & Pedersen, 1996). No two people share the same static and unchanging culture or set of identities. Like cultures, identities are dynamic rather than fixed. Both develop and evolve over time and both shift according to contextual (e.g., social setting or relationship) and individual forces (e.g., mood or motivation, Markus & Nurius, 1986). To distinguish cultural and individual differences, one may ask, "Is this shared and learned?" Cultural differences grow from shared experiences, whereas individual differences can be traced to biological and genetic factors or the unique experiences of the individual. What is important in any given conflict is the *salience* of a given culture or identity.

Within any culture is a set of complex guidelines for behavior and the interpretation of events, but to these every individual contributes his or her own uniqueness. Furthermore, each culture is complex in itself, and with the myriad cultures available to any one individual, the complexity deepens. This may seem to be chaotic but, in fact, with all their complexity, cultures and identities are nonetheless systematic and internally consistent, though not without contradictions. Learning to deal with the many cultures and identities salient for ourselves and those around us is difficult but not impossible. Gaining awareness of assumptions that both grow from and underlie our own and others' cultures is the first of several steps that can lead to increased competence in intercultural mediation.

Intercultural Competence

Developing intercultural competence in mediating multicultural conflict depends first on making right assumptions about each culturally different circumstance, second on having accurate and comprehensive knowledge about the relevant factors in a given context, and third on being able to take the right action to bring about mutually beneficial effects (Sue, Bernier, Durran, Feinberg, Pedersen, Smith, & Vasquez-Nuttall, 1982). Each of these developmental stages depends on the successful satisfaction of each previous stage, with awareness of accurate assumptions becoming the foundation for competence (Pedersen, 1994; Sue, Arredondo, & McDavis, 1992).

Awareness

The first stage of awareness requires movement from being unaware to becoming aware of each person's identity as shaped by cultural influences. Culture teaches us who we are and in that way constructs the core of our identity. Culturally learned assumptions guide our behavior and therefore must be understood differently in each cultural context. Keeping in mind that culture is not simply demographic or ethnographic and that each individual has numerous cultures, it is useful to talk about some dimensions in which cultures vary. Inasmuch as research on national groups (e.g., Chinese Culture Connection, 1987; Hofstede, 1980) has revealed commonalities among large groups of individuals, we can use the dimensions of these commonalities to help us understand some widely shared assumptions. Remembering that these dimensions stem from *shared* experiences and often result in *shared* expectations, the dimensions can be used fruitfully to organize and make sense out of cultures that may initially seem strange and impenetrable. The danger of this is, of course, that one may forget the uniqueness of individuals or the importance of context in the salience of identities. Doing so results in stereotyping, which is quite contrary to our intentions. Nonetheless, we shall discuss some of these dimensions because they are a powerful tool in helping to recognize the variety of cultures and assumptions that are available to us and others.

Dimensions of Culture

Perhaps the broadest division of cultures is found in the contrast between Eastern and Western assumptions, recognizing that the West/East polarity is not, strictly speaking, a geographical concept. The basic intellectual and religious traditions of

Table 11.2 Selected Cultural Assumptions About Conflict

Western		*Rate Yourself*						*Non-Western*
Right a wrong	1	2	3	4	5	6	7	Maintain harmony
Mediator should be neutral	1	2	3	4	5	6	7	Mediator should be high-status person
Actions mediated	1	2	3	4	5	6	7	Relationships mediated
Informal	1	2	3	4	5	6	7	Formal
Simplify conflicts	1	2	3	4	5	6	7	Accepts complexity
Linear solutions	1	2	3	4	5	6	7	Non-linear, holistic solutions
Contractual trust	1	2	3	4	5	6	7	Interpersonal, intuitive trust
Short-term solutions	1	2	3	4	5	6	7	Long-term goals
Risk is acceptable	1	2	3	4	5	6	7	Risk less acceptable
Immediate solutions preferred	1	2	3	4	5	6	7	Deadlines irrelevant
Individual decisions	1	2	3	4	5	6	7	Decision by consensus
Written agreements preferred	1	2	3	4	5	6	7	Written and verbal agreements equal
Behaviors normal or abnormal	1	2	3	4	5	6	7	Context determines behavior judgments
Individuals basis of society	1	2	3	4	5	6	7	Groups basis of society
Circumscribed knowledge	1	2	3	4	5	6	7	Interrelated knowledge
Meaning from jargon	1	2	3	4	5	6	7	Meaning from context
Dependency is weakness	1	2	3	4	5	6	7	Dependency is essential
Interdependence secondary	1	2	3	4	5	6	7	Interdependence salient
Effects have a cause	1	2	3	4	5	6	7	Effects have many causes
Individual must fit system	1	2	3	4	5	6	7	Systems are more flexible
No sense of history	1	2	3	4	5	6	7	Strong sense of past
Culture is presumed	1	2	3	4	5	6	7	Culture is salient
Must make conflict explicit	1	2	3	4	5	6	7	Mediate (prevent) undeclared conflict
Individuals work out conflicts	1	2	3	4	5	6	7	Consensus solves conflicts
Private conflicts	1	2	3	4	5	6	7	Public conflicts
Reactive skills	1	2	3	4	5	6	7	Preventive skills
Ritual superfluous	1	2	3	4	5	6	7	Ritualized resolutions
Face-to-face resolutions	1	2	3	4	5	6	7	Intermediary resolutions
Beginning, middle, end to conflict	1	2	3	4	5	6	7	Conflict cycles
Emotions expressed clearly	1	2	3	4	5	6	7	Emotions implied subtly
Conflict is failure	1	2	3	4	5	6	7	Conflict is inevitable
Admitting fault important	1	2	3	4	5	6	7	Saving other's face acceptable
Apologies equal guilt	1	2	3	4	5	6	7	Apologies save face

Western and non-Western societies have organized their cultures differently, resulting in many divergent assumptions about the organization of self and society (Okabe, 1983), including many that are pertinent to the nature and appropriate management of conflict. We do not consider the terms Western or Eastern to be primarily geographic in nature; rather, they refer to the set of values and assumptions that generally characterize the intellectual and philosophical traditions associated with those areas. The wealthy, well-traveled, cosmopolitan Tokyoite may well be as "Western" as any New Yorker. At any rate, the assumptions of both East and West form an incomplete universe from which individuals draw. Some of these assumptions are juxtaposed in Table 11.2.

You may wish to rate yourself on each pair of assumptions to articulate your unique position. Remember that the labels Western and non-Western are not hard and fast, but merely exaggerated and polarized tendencies that are tempered by individual factors. The basic point is to become aware that there are alternative, and no less valid, cultural views and associated assumptions and guidelines to those that any one individual may hold. In going over the list, you may find yourself saying, "Well, it depends." You can take this as an indication that you hold both assumptions and one or the other may be salient depending on the context. A more fine-tuned yet still quite general examination of different cultures can use some basic dimensions that have emerged from research on values among national groups (e.g., Hofstede, 1980). We examine several of the most influential of these dimensions, recognizing that there are others not discussed here that may be important as well.

Individualism-Collectivism

Individualism-collectivism is, no doubt, the most widely used and researched cultural dimension. In the simplest terms, *individualism* means prioritizing individual goals over those of the group; *collectivism* means the opposite orientation (Hofstede, 1980; Triandis, 1990). Individualism emphasizes and idealizes individuality, uniqueness, and independence. Collectivism stresses the fundamental connectedness of humans by highlighting relationships, harmony of interaction, and the importance of conformity. Individualism has been associated with many northern and western regions of Europe, North America (especially the mainland United States), and Australia. Cultures in Asia, Africa, South America, and the Pacific Island region have been associated with collectivism.

Although research has shown that cultures can be said to emphasize one or another of these dimensions, we must note that individuals, as influenced by their many cultures, have been shown to hold *simultaneously* both independent (individualist) and interdependent (collectivist) images of self (Singelis, 1994b; Singelis & Sharkey, 1995; also see Markus & Kitayama, 1991). Pedersen and Ivey (1993) have organized one end of each Hofstede dimension into four synthetic cultures for training "culture-centered" counselors and interviewers. In addition, there is some evidence that the culture of women emphasizes collective values and, consequently, women are more interdependent than are men (Gilligan, 1982).

A number of studies have explored the relationship of individualism-collectivism to conflict management. Among the findings, collectivism is associated with equality in resource allocation (Leung & Bond, 1984) and strategies that maintain harmony between parties in a conflict, such as integrating (Lee & Rogan, 1991), obliging, avoiding, and compromising (Trubisky, Ting-Toomey, & Lin, 1991). Individualism has been associated with equity in resource distribution (Leung & Bond, 1984) and dominating styles of conflict management (Trubisky, Ting-Toomey, & Lin, 1991). In addition, individualism has been related to self-face maintenance, whereas collectivism is connected to other-face maintenance in conflict management (Ting-Toomey, et al., 1991).

Power Distance

Briefly, power distance is the degree to which the less powerful members of a culture expect and accept that power is distributed unequally (Hofstede, 1991). This dimension makes the relative statuses of self and other more salient and is often manifest in language structures that necessitate the use of different terms indicating relative status in a hierarchy. At the same time as these hierarchies are built on unequal power, there can be a great deal of interdependence within the hierarchy. In some regards, the organization of a social system around these hierarchies allows orderly and cooperative effort where individuals know and accept their place in the hierarchy and function accordingly, with resulting efficiency. At the national level, countries where a Romance language (e.g., Spanish and Portuguese) is spoken seem to be medium to high with regard to power distance, whereas in those countries whose people speak a Germanic language (e.g., German and English), inequality is less accepted (Hofstede, 1991).

Power distance is more or less salient in many of the cultures that shape individuals. For example, many work and educational cultures cannot function without some acceptance of inequality among the less powerful. And of course, social class is a major factor that must be considered with power distance.

Unfortunately, no studies that we know of have directly investigated the relationship of power distance to conflict or mediation. However, it might be hypothesized that the salience of status would be relevant when power distance is a strong cultural influence. Thus, members of high power-distance cultures might be expected to react quite differently in conflicts concerning superiors and subordinates. Furthermore, there may be less of a tendency for members of these cultures to express conflict toward their superiors, shifting the responsibility for managing conflict to the superior.

Masculinity-Femininity

Gender roles are important aspects of identity. At the cultural level, a distinction is made regarding the overlap or separation of values and traits according to sex. *Masculinity* refers to an emphasis on the separation of traditional sex roles. Men are supposed to be tough, assertive, and focused on material success; women are supposed to be modest, tender, and concerned with the quality of life. On the other hand, *femininity* indicates a culture where social roles overlap and *both* men and women are supposed to be tender, modest, and concerned with the quality of life (Hofstede, 1991). There are no clear geographic or regional trends that help predict which countries will be high on masculinity. Japan, Austria, and Venezuela scored highest on this dimension in Hofstede's survey (1980, 1991), whereas Yugoslavia, Costa Rica, and Sweden were among the most feminine countries.

Amid the many cultures an individual may have, the military would be quite masculine, hence its resistance to admitting gays and allowing women in combat roles. Femininity would certainly be more salient in the helping professions, such as social work and nursing, where men and women are allowed and expected to be nurturing, supportive, and concerned about the quality of life.

Again, not much research is available that relates directly to these constructs. A notable exception is Leung, Bond, Carment, Krishnan, and Liebrand (1990), who found that mediation was more preferred in feminist cultures than in masculine cultures due to its ability to bring harmony to the relationship of the conflicting parties. A reasonable belief is that feminine cultures would stress methods of conflict management that lead to growth and understanding, as opposed to leading to winners and losers.

High-Low Context

Using information theory, Hall (1976) developed a description of communication that explained the varying focus on code and context found in different communication styles. He identified two types of communication, high-context and low-context. High-context communication occurs when most of the information in a message is either in the physical context or internalized in the person, and very little is in the coded, explicit part of the message. Low-context communication occurs when the greatest amount of information is vested in the explicit communication code (Hall, 1976).

Through ethnographic observations, Hall noted that some cultures tend to use high-context communication more than others. He placed cultures on a continuum according to the communication style that predominated, with high-context and low-context at the poles. Japan, Korea, China, and Latin and African cultures tend to be high-context, whereas the United States, Australia, and most European cultures tend to be low-context. Notice that, to a great extent, these are the same countries where, respectively, collectivism and individualism are found. There is, in fact, a strong association between these two dimensions.

At a more micro level, intimate relationships, such as families and groups where there is a strong common understanding of shared information (e.g., religious cults), are high-context cultures. The ultimate in low-context communication is the interface between humans and computers, where the computer understands only explicit coded messages (this may or may not change as computers and their programs become more complex).

Because of the strong correlation between individualism-collectivism and high-low-context communication, it is difficult to clearly categorize research in which findings can be attributed to either dimension. Nonetheless, at least one study has specifically associated high-low-context cultures with conflict resolution styles (Chua & Gudykunst, 1987). This study's findings indicated that solution orientations were associated with low-context cultures, whereas nonconfrontational approaches were preferred in high-context cultures.

Applying Cultural Dimensions

At this point the reader may wish to return to the list of assumptions in Table 11.1 and go through them again. This time, try to identify which dimension is most relevant to each pair of assumptions. Certainly, most of the assumptions can be associated with several of the dimensions because the dimensions themselves are related. At least, high-context communication, collectivism, and power distance are strongly correlated at the cultural level (Hofstede, personal communication, September 1991). Nonetheless, trying to determine which dimension is most applicable will lead to a better understanding of how these dimensions lead systematically to assumptions that then guide individual behavior. At the same time, readers may also wish to think of their own cultures and identify how they may emphasize or make salient the dimensions and their associated assumptions. These exercises should lead the reader to an increased awareness of the many possible cultures and their complex influences on individuals. This awareness can allow one to separate fact from inference, thereby gaining knowledge in intercultural mediation.

Knowledge

The second stage of knowledge acquisition requires the collection of relevant facts and information leading to a more accurate comprehension of the complex cultural context. Becoming more knowledgeable leads to the understanding that everything you do and everything you do not do is meaningful. All action (or inaction) may be interpreted in terms of its political implications. Therefore, it is essential to gather specific information about a cultural group before attempting to work with that group. To work with people without knowing their cultures would be unethical. You also need to understand how those groups perceive you. What do they say about you when you are not around? How do they describe you to others? You need to be able to describe other groups so accurately that they will agree with your description. Finally, you need to relate your knowledge, facts, and information to the culturally learned assumptions from your first stage of developed awareness.

Without multicultural awareness, a person is likely to confuse fact and inference. Accurate knowledge requires us to separate fact from inference. A statement of fact concerns something that actually exists, occurs, or otherwise has an objective reality that can be proven by the testimony of an unbiased witness. A statement of inference is a conclusion that goes beyond the fact or event observed. We frequently assign expectations, attitudes, motives, or values to someone else that could probably not be verified by an objective witness. For example, if people do not look at me when I am talking, I might infer that they are not interested in what I am saying or do not like me. Statements of fact (a) are made after observation or experience, (b) are limited to what was observed, (c) attempt to achieve certainty, and (d) can become the basis for attaining agreements. For the preceding example, the only fact is that someone did not look at me. Statements of inference (a) can be made before, during, or after observation; (b) go beyond what we have actually observed; (c) are not limited to the particular situation; (d) represent probability rather than certainty; and (e) can easily result in an honest disagreement between persons.

An important issue to recognize is that behavior is not meaningful until it is understood in its cultural context. Behaviors are given meaning by their cultural context. In this way, similar behaviors may have different meanings, such as two persons not making direct eye contact: one out of respect and one out of disinterest. In the same mode, different behaviors may have the same meaning, such as showing respect by being very formal or by being very informal (Hofstede, 1991). To assess, interpret, or attempt to change behavior without regard for the cultural context of that behavior would be dangerous. Out of context, behavior has no fixed meaning. Our natural tendency, however, is to judge, interpret, or change behaviors in ways that each of us would consider meaningful for ourselves when that behavior is done by others, thinking that the behavior has the same meaning for others as it does for ourselves. This tendency is the *self-reference criterion,* and it leads to profound inaccuracy. Do not do unto others as you would have them do unto you unless you are sure that they want it done unto them.

Gathering accurate knowledge requires that you begin with a particular behavior that you have observed. Then, you attempt to understand the expectation behind that behavior, using an "If this . . . then that . . . ." relationship. If the person displayed that behavior, then he or she could expect something to happen. What was that expectation? A person might go to a lecture expecting to learn something, for example.

Then you identify the value behind the expectation, such as "learning." Finally, you seek to understand the source of that value within the different social system variables. Think of social system variables as the "culture-teachers" that have taught us our values, shaped our expectations, and determined our behaviors. Each behavior will have many different expectations and each expectation will be linked to many different values, just as each value will have been taught by many different "culture-teachers" among the social system variables. Using this sequence, you can understand a person's behavior in its cultural context.

Doing your homework is important. This requires gathering the salient facts and information about each participant's cultural context before attempting to mediate a conflict or even understanding a person's behavior. This can be done by making the right assumptions in the first stage of developing multicultural awareness and then by gathering the right information in the second stage of developing multicultural knowledge.

Skills

Skill is the accurate application of awareness and knowledge. Intercultural mediation requires widening one's repertoire of behaviors for a variety of cultural contexts. This is to say that, like assumptions and values, cultures shape the interpersonal skills of their members (Bhawuk & Brislin, 1992). Because no individual is accustomed to all of the available cultures, there is a range of skills beyond the normal set available to the average person. These skills are primarily communicative in nature. They involve sending and receiving both verbal and nonverbal messages in a way that is appropriate in a given intercultural conflict (see Singelis, 1994a). But in addition to being appropriate, to be successful, these messages must be understood by the other in the intended manner. The preceding sections dealt primarily with the reception or understanding of behaviors based on assumptions. Skills refers more to taking accurate, appropriate, and mutually effective action. Thus, we must learn to use new, often unfamiliar ways to communicate that match those of another's culture.

For example, people raised in an individualist culture have probably become skilled at expressing their emotions through both verbal and nonverbal means. This is a central task that is necessary to accomplish goals. These skills are taught in schools and often rewarded in individualist cultures (see Tobin, Wu, & Davidson, 1989). On the other hand, collectivists learn to control their emotions and express them in less direct, more subtle ways (Kitayama & Markus, 1994). The assumptions of a collectivist culture are based, in part, on maintaining a surface harmony; therefore strong, "self-focused" emotions that might disrupt that harmony must be controlled and perhaps expressed by subdued or subtle means. Thus, individualists mediating with collectivists must learn a new set of behaviors to express their emotions. Likewise, collectivists would be advised to develop more direct and expansive emotional expressions when in individualist contexts (see Triandis, Brislin, & Hui, 1988).

In addition to developing specific behaviors to fill out their repertoires, a sensitivity to context is necessary to understand others' messages and respond appropriately. This sensitivity is necessary because we cannot always be certain which of a person's many cultures is salient in a given interaction, and because the other person may be simultaneously adapting to our culture. Thus, there is skill involved in developing a range of behaviors and in acquiring the sensitivity to apply them appropriately in a given mediation. Remembering that these skills are based on the awareness and knowledge just described, perhaps the best way to develop skills is through contact with members of other cultures. There is a special set of circumstances necessary to allow contacts with members of other cultures to be fruitful in developing intercultural mediation skills.

Intercultural Contact

Manifesting multicultural skills does not always mean changing a person. These skills may also involve changing the environment. Amir (1969), in his research on the contact hypothesis, discovered that groups experiencing conflict who meet together under favorable conditions were likely to increase their harmony for working together. Groups who meet together under unfavorable conditions were likely to increase their disharmony still further. Finally, he discovered that most spontaneous contact between groups occurs under unfavorable conditions. Multicultural skills may involve creating the favorable conditions for cultural groups or persons to meet so that harmony can be increased.

Favorable conditions that reduce intergroup hostility include (a) equal-status contact between members of the two groups, (b) contact between representatives of the majority group and high-status minorities, (c) a social climate that promotes favorable contact, (d) intimate rather than casual contact, (e) pleasant and rewarding contact, and (f) interaction that is functionally important for both groups (see also Chapter 8, this volume). Unfavorable conditions that increase hostility include (a) contact that produces competition between the two groups, (b) contact that is unpleasant and involuntary, (c) contact resulting in one or both groups' lower prestige, (d) contact leading to frustration and scapegoating, and (e) contact where one or both sides' moral or ethical standards are violated. The Interpersonal Cultural Grid (Pedersen, 1993, 1994) provides an opportunity to recognize and organize conditions for productive intercultural contact, and a framework for applying the awareness, knowledge, and skills discussed previously.

Skill Applications

The Intercultural Grid for Mediating Conflict

Figure 11.1 provides an Interpersonal Cultural Grid to demonstrate how two culturally different people or groups might be brought together under favorable conditions. This is accomplished by separating behaviors from expectations and capturing the "common ground" of shared positive expectations without being distracted by behaviors that appear different or potentially hostile.

In Figure 11.1, you will note two dimensions of same and different behavior on one dimension matched to same and positive, or different and negative, expectation on the other dimension. This grid provides four cells. In the first cell, the behaviors between two culturally different persons or groups are similar and are matched to the same positive expectations. This cell involves a minimum of conflict and a maximum of harmony. The fourth cell matches different behaviors with different or negative expectations. This fourth cell involves a "war" situation where both individuals or groups have nearly given up coming to an agreement and are simply trying to hurt

BEHAVIOR

	Same	*Different*
Same and Positive	I High agreement High accuracy (ideal)	II High agreement Low accuracy (cross-cultural conflict)
Different or Negative	III Low agreement High accuracy (personal)	IV Low agreement Low accuracy (disengagement)

EXPECTATION

Figure 11.1. The Intercultural Grid

one another. The second cell provides a situation where the two people or groups share the same positive expectation but the behaviors by which they express that expectation are different. Unless both persons discover that they share the same positive expectation, they will judge the other negatively because of that person's behavior. This misunderstanding is common in intercultural conflicts.

Because one of the two parties is usually stronger than the other, the conflict is likely to move to cell three, where one of the two people will be forced to conform to the stronger party, but the expectation will then also move from a similar positive nature to a different or negative expectation. If cell two describes a cross-cultural situation, cell three describes personal conflict. By capturing conflict in the cross-cultural context of cell two, the two people are less likely to escalate the conflict to a personal level in cell three and ultimately a war situation in cell four. Having two people behaving differently from one another may be tolerable or even beneficial, as long as they share the same positive expectation for trust, respect, success, or safety. However, if that common ground of shared positive expectation is lost, then it does not matter whether the two persons behave similarly; harmony has no foundation.

Strategic skill suggests that specific and potentially conflicting behaviors be identified as early as possible in the relationship between two culturally different persons. The next step is to explore the degree of shared positive expectations between the two groups while attempting to construct a "platform" of common ground on which the two persons can agree and build their shared understanding. Once the common ground has been established, then the different and potentially hostile behaviors will become more acceptable and less threatening, because those behaviors express shared (common) positive expectations for the future.

Not recognizing shared positive expectations may lead to a negative chain of events. First, negative and presumably hostile behaviors lead one to hold negative and hostile expectations. The individuals will label each other *enemies* by judging each others' behaviors from their own cultural perspective rather than from the perspective of the other's culture. The next step will be for both parties to escalate the conflict as they respond to the other's perceived hostility. As the conflict escalates, neither partner will be aware of their original inaccuracy in misjudging the other person's behavior, and the opportunity for harmony will have been lost.

A positive chain of events involves acknowledging the different behaviors but then seeking any areas of positive shared expectation behind those different behaviors. An important step in this process is to look past any specific behavior and *assume* a positive shared expectation even when one does not *seem* to be indicated by the behavior. In this way, one sets the stage for the common ground of positive expectations, such as trust, that permits productive management of differences. Even if this assumption of positive expectations from the other is not initially warranted, it may serve as an expression of goodwill that will transform previously negative expectations into positive common ground. If this platform of common ground can be constructed and both parties can continue to identify shared positive expectations, then one or both partners may change their behavior without threat or loss of dignity. Furthermore, the different behaviors may now be tolerated or even celebrated as an enrichment of their multicultural harmony. Both parties will be led to accurately assess each other's behavior in a way that contributes toward harmony in the future. When individuals fail to accurately assess each other's behavior, the result is a spiral of conflict through the cells just described, and ultimately to disengagement.

The process of finding common ground, it should be noted, does not necessarily resolve a conflict—often a lot of hard work and compromises, concessions, or other techniques may be required. However, the process of working through a conflict is made possible by identifying common ground through the intercultural grid. Without it, intercultural conflicts will almost inevitably escalate unnecessarily.

Exercise for Skill Development

Hypothetical Examples

The advantage of hypothetical case examples is to bring the conflict of real-world situations into the classroom or lab in simulated form without the risks involved in real world conflict. Hypotheticals develop a "safe" setting for participant risk taking.

The following hypothetical situations were generated to demonstrate the opportunity for participants to mediate conflict in five different situations where the individuals in conflict are from extremely different cultural backgrounds. Participants should be asked to volunteer. They are given an opportunity to read the situation and both sides of the conflict. Then, they "take on" the roles of the individuals in the scenario and have a spontaneous conversation. Other participants observe the conversation for several minutes and then role play "mediators" attempting to help each pair-in-conflict to identify win-win outcomes based on the common ground of shared expectations. Following the mediation, each of the individuals who participated in the conflict should have an opportunity, "out of role," to discuss with the mediators what suggestions seemed to help and why.

Western–Non-Western

The situation is a conflict between a graduate student from a non-Western culture and that student's very Westernized academic advisor. On the surface, the problem seems to involve a disagreement about the student's dissertation topic. The deeper, perhaps hidden, problem is rooted in different assumptions.

Westernized Faculty Member. The student should select a topic that is important and makes a contribution to the literature. The professor feels that the student should take the initiative in finding a topic and feel strongly enough about the topic that he or she is willing to defend the choice with well-thought-out reasons. The topic should lead to a good job and publications as rewards for the student and the faculty. A good topic might involve the transfer of communication technology to emerging countries and the attendant development issues.

Non-Western Student. The student's concern is to please the faculty member and do what he or she wants, avoiding any direct confrontation or open disagreements. The student is particularly interested in the historical and religious traditions of her or his home culture, but expects the professor to recommend a topic for the dissertation. The student is also more concerned about returning home to her or his family, or bringing them here, than about the dissertation. These financial and family problems might mean dropping out of the university for 18 months.

High-Low Context

The situation is a conflict between a manager sent from the United States and her or his counterpart in a foreign country. They are negotiating a contract.

High-Context Host Culture Manager. The contract is like enlarging the "family" and adopting the employees of the new company. The discussion is very serious and emotional, with ideological issues figuring prominently. What are the long-range consequences? Will the new relationship contribute to harmony? How will all of the staff of both companies work together?

Low-Context Visiting Manager. There is lots of money to be made if both companies cooperate. The decision should be made in 48 hours so that work can begin before the competition hears about this. If this company does not decide soon, maybe a competing company abroad should be approached. Many jobs depend on success.

Individualism-Collectivism

The situation is a conflict between a child or young adult and his or her parents about the hypocrisy in society and the lack of honesty among adults, particularly in family relationships.

Individualized Child/Young Adult. What is best for me and my future? The new ways are good and the old ways are bad. Adults cannot be trusted because they say one thing and do another. They expect children to follow guidelines that they did not, or could not, meet in their childhood. Families cover over their problems and "pretend" a lot . . . at work, religion, leisure, professional life, and so forth. You have got to look out for yourself because nobody else will.

Collectivized Parent. Family harmony is not easy to achieve or protect, but it gives a permanence and stability to life beyond individual needs and wants. Sometimes it is important to pretend to protect harmony for the long-range benefit of the family. If you lose family, you have lost everything.

High-Low Power Distance

The situation involves conflict between a boss and an employee over managerial style. The boss uses, and prefers, a very authoritarian and domineering style, whereas the employee prefers a more open and participatory style. They are talking about a prospective 10% budget cut.

High Power-Distance Boss. I am the boss. Others need my strong and fair leadership and look to me to take control of things. If I fail, everyone fails. I can not delegate authority or responsibility without seeming weak. I will make the budget decisions by myself.

Low Power-Distance Employee. We need to work together to succeed. Openly sharing responsibility for decision making is the way to go. New blood will help. We need to discuss the budget implications with everybody who will be affected by the potential cut or else morale will suffer. We need to be less rigid and more flexible.

Masculine-Feminine

The situation is a conflict between two coworkers, one more masculine and one more feminine, who each want the same job. They like one another, but each feels better qualified for this particular job.

Masculine Worker. We need a game plan to win and a good coach to "put it to 'em where it hurts." This kind of hardball is not pretty, but it's necessary for the company and the workers. I've got what it takes to do the job and handle the consequences. An otherwise highly qualified woman would get eaten alive because—right or wrong—it's a male-dominated, sexist world out there.

Feminine Worker. You do not have to push people around to be successful. A more relationship-oriented perspective would be more satisfying and more successful for everybody. Making the situation more competitive will just make the decisions more political. I can make hard decisions also, but prefer to try every option before hurting people.

Conclusion

Intercultural conflict offers the opportunity for growth and development and has implications that reach far beyond the individuals involved. These are complex situations that require a variety of skills. Awareness of the cultural dimensions and associated assumptions that may be salient for ourselves and for others is the foundation of competence in mediating intercultural conflicts. With this awareness, it is possible to gain knowledge about the relevant facts and information that, in turn, leads to appropriate behaviors. The skills needed to enact appropriate and efficacious behaviors in intercultural conflicts can be gained through contact with members of other cultures, provided that contact is structured appropriately. The Intercultural Grid provides a method for individuals to see beyond differences in behavior and help find the common ground of similar positive expectations from which conflict can be successfully managed. Finally, the use of simulations is useful in developing all of the components of intercultural mediation competency.

References

Amir, Y. (1969). Contact hypothesis in ethnic relations. *Psychological Bulletin, 71,* 319-342.

Augsburger, D. W. (1992). *Conflict mediation across cultures: Pathways and patterns.* Louisville, KY: Westminster/John Knox.

Bhawuk, D. P. S., & Brislin, R. W. (1992). The measurement of intercultural sensitivity using the concepts of individualism and collectivism. *International Journal of Intercultural Relations, 16,* 413-436.

Chinese Culture Connection. (1987). Chinese values and the search for culture-free dimensions of culture. *Journal of Cross-Cultural Psychology, 18,* 143-164.

Chua, E., & Gudykunst, W. (1987). Conflict resolution style in low- and high-context cultures. *Communication Research Reports, 4,* 32-37.

Gilligan, C. (1982). *In a different voice: Psychological theory and women's development.* Cambridge, MA: Harvard University Press.

Hall, E. T. (1976). *Beyond culture.* New York: Anchor.

Hofstede, G. (1980). *Culture's consequences.* Beverly Hills, CA: Sage.

Hofstede, G. (1991). *Cultures and organizations: Software of the mind.* New York: McGraw-Hill.

Hofstede, G. (1991, September). Personal communication.

Jandt, F., & Pedersen, P. (1996). *Constructive conflict management in the Asia-Pacific region.* Thousand Oaks, CA: Sage.

Kitayama. S., & Markus, H. R. (Eds.). (1994). *Emotion and culture: Empirical studies of mutual influence.* Washington, DC: American Psychological Association.

Landry, E. M., Kolb, D. M., & Rubin, J. Z. (1991). *Curriculum for negotiation and conflict management.* Cambridge, MA: The Program on Negotiation at Harvard Law School.

Lee, H. O., & Rogan, R. G. (1991). A cross-cultural comparison of organizational conflict management behaviors. *International Journal of Conflict Management, 2,* 181-199.

Leung, K., & Bond, M. (1984). The impact of cultural collectivism on reward allocation. *Journal of Personality and Social Psychology, 47,* 793-804.

Leung, K., Bond, M. H., Carment, D. W., Krishnan, L., Liebrand, W. B. G. (1990). Effects of cultural femininity on preferences for methods of conflict processing: A cross-cultural study. *Journal of Experimental Social Psychology, 26,* 373-388.

Markus, H. R., & Kitayama, S. (1991). Culture and the self: Implications for cognition, emotion, and motivation. *Psychological Review, 98,* 224-253.

Markus, H., & Nurius, P. (1986). Possible selves. *American Psychologist, 41,* 954-969.

Okabe, R. (1983). Cultural assumptions of East and West: Japan and the United States. In W. Gudykunst (Ed.), *Intercultural communication theory: Current perspectives* (pp. 21-44). Beverly Hills, CA: Sage.

Pedersen, P. (1993). Mediating multicultural conflict by separating behaviors from expectations in a cultural grid. *International Journal of Intercultural Relations, 17,* 343-353.

Pedersen, P. B. (1994). *A handbook for developing multicultural awareness* (2nd ed.). Alexandria VA.: American Counseling.

Pedersen, P. & Ivey, A. (1993). *Culture-centered counseling and interviewing skills.* Westport, CT: Greenwood.

Rubin, J. Z. (1989). Some wise and mistaken assumptions about conflict and negotiation. *Journal of Social Issues, 45*(2), 195-209.

Scott, N. E. & Borodovsky, L. G. (1990). Effective use of cultural role taking. *Professional Psychology: Research and Practice, 21*(3) 167-170.

Singelis, T. M. (1994a). Nonverbal communication in intercultural interactions. In R. Brislin & T. Yoshida (Eds.), *Improving intercultural interactions: Modules for cross-cultural training programs* (pp. 268-294). Thousand Oaks, CA: Sage.

Singelis, T. M. (1994b). The measurement of independent and interdependent self-construals. *Personality and Social Psychology Bulletin, 20,* 580-591.

Singelis, T. M., & Sharkey, W. F. (1995). Culture, self-construal, and embarrassability. *Journal of Cross-Cultural Psychology, 26,* 622-644.

Sue, D. W., Arredondo, P., & McDavis, R. J. (1992). Multicultural competencies and standards: A call to the profession. *Journal of Counseling and Development, 70*(4), 477-486.

Sue, D. W., Bernier, J. B., Durran, M., Feinberg, L., Pedersen, P., Smith, E., & Vasquez-Nuttall, E. (1982). Position paper: Cross-cultural counseling competencies. *The Counseling Psychologist, 10,* 45-52.

Sue, D. W., Ivey, A, & Pedersen, P. B. (1996). *A theory of multicultural counseling and therapy.* Pacific Grove, CA: Brooks Cole.

Ting-Toomey, S., Gao, G., Trubisky, P., Yang, Z., Kim, H. S., Lin, S. L., & Nishida, T. (1991). Culture, face maintenance, and styles of handling interpersonal conflict: A study of five cultures. *International Journal of Conflict Management, 2,* 275-296.

Tobin, J., Wu, D., & Davidson, D. (1989). *Preschool in three cultures.* New Haven, CT: Yale University Press.

Triandis, H. C. (1990). Cross-cultural studies of individualism and collectivism. In J. Berman, (Ed.), *Nebraska symposium on motivation 1989* (pp. 41-133). Lincoln, NE: University of Nebraska Press.

Triandis, H. C., Brislin, R., & Hui, H. C. (1988). Cross-cultural training across the individualism-collectivism divide. *International Journal of Intercultural Relations, 12,* 269-289.

Trubisky, P., Ting-Toomey, S., & Lin, S. (1991). The influence of individualism-collectivism and self-monitoring on conflict styles. *International Journal of Intercultural Relations, 15,* 65-84.

Suggested Reading

Benesch, K. F., & Ponterotto, J. G. (1989). East and West: Transpersonal psychology and cross-cultural counseling. *Counseling and Values, 33,* 121-131.

Carnevale, P. J., & Pruitt, D. G. (1992). Negotiation and mediation. *Annual Review of Psychology, 43,* 532-582.

Cosier, R. A., Schwenk, C. R., & Dalton, D. R. (1992). Managerial decision making in Japan, the U.S., and Hong Kong. *The International Journal of Conflict Management, 3,* 151-169.

Duryea, M. L. (1992). *Conflict and culture A literature review and bibliography.* Victoria, British Columbia, Canada: University of Victoria Institute for Dispute Resolution.

Goldstein, A., & Segall, M. (Eds.). (1983). *Aggression in global perspective.* Elmsford, NY: Pergamon.

Janosik, R. J. (1987, October). Rethinking the culture-negotiation link. *Negotiation Journal,* 385-394.

Kim, Y. Y. (1988). *Communication and cross-cultural adaptation.* Clevedon, England: Multicultural Matters.

Krauss, E. S., Rohlen, T. P., & Steinhoff, P. G. (1984). Conflict: An approach to the study of Japan. In E. S. Krauss, T. P. Rohlen, & P. G. Steinhoff (Eds.), *Conflict in Japan* (pp. 3-15). Honolulu: University of Hawaii Press.

Lebra, T. S. (1984). Nonconfrontational strategies for management of interpersonal conflicts. In E. S. Krauss, T. P. Rohlen, & P. G. Steinhoff (Eds.), *Conflict in Japan* (pp. 41-60). Honolulu: University of Hawaii Press.

Leung, K., & Wu, P. G. (1990). Dispute processing. In R. W. Brislin (Ed.), *Applied cross-cultural psychology* (pp. 209-231). Newbury Park, CA: Sage.

Liberman, K. (1990). The collective character of disputes in aboriginal communities. *Sociolinguistics, 19*, 89-98.

Maruyama, M. (1992). *Context and complexity: Cultivating contextual understanding.* New York: Springer-Verlag.

Nader, L. B., Nader, M. K., & Broome, B. J. (1985). Culture and the management of conflict situations. In W. B. Gudykunst, L. P. Stewart, & S. Ting-Toomey (Eds.), *Communication, culture, and organizational processes* (pp. 87-113). Newbury Park, CA: Sage.

Pedersen, P. (1983). Asian theories of personality. In R. Corsini & A. Marsella (Eds.), *Contemporary theories of personality* (Rev. ed.) (pp. 537-582). Itasca, IL: Peacock.

Schneller, R. (1989). Intercultural and intrapersonal processes and factors of misunderstanding: Implications for multicultural training. *International Journal of Intercultural Relations, 13*, 465-484.

Sheikh, A., & Sheikh, K. S. (1989). *Eastern and Western approaches to healing: Ancient wisdom and modern knowledge.* New York: John Wiley.

Sunoo, J. J. (1990, October). Some guidelines for mediators of intercultural disputes. *Negotiation Journal*, 383-389.

Wall, J. A. (1990). Mediation in the People's Republic of China. In M. A. Rahim (Ed.), *Theory and research in conflict management* (pp. 109-119). New York: Praeger.

12

Empathy in Cross-Cultural Communication

Colleen Mullavey-O'Byrne

> You never truly understand a person until you consider things from his point of view
> . . . until you climb into his skin and walk around in it.
>
> Harper Lee, *To Kill a Mockingbird* (1960, p. 60).

Empathy can be described as the ability to put oneself in another's place, to know others' experiences from their perspective, and to communicate this understanding to them in a way that is meaningful, while at the same time recognizing that the source of one's experience lies in the other. In this module, participants explore the concept of empathy from a cross-cultural perspective and develop skills in using empathy to enhance understanding, communication, and relationship building in situations where people have different cultural backgrounds. Although examples are drawn primarily from health delivery and educational contexts, the content and skill-development exercises are relevant to other cross-cultural settings, such as international business and the tourist industry.

Contents

Introductory Exercises

The terms *empathy, empathic understanding, empathic communication, accurate empathy, generalized empathy, relational empathy,* and *cultural empathy* are frequently used in the literature. Alternate ways of using these terms to introduce a cross-cultural empathy training session are provided in the two exercises that follow.

Exercise 1

This exercise provides an opportunity for members of your training group to explore and share the various meanings ascribed to these terms. The exercise serves to clarify ideas about the concept of empathy and to engage members in an exercise that involves turn-taking, observing, attending, and responding—skills associated with communicating empathic understanding.

For the exercise to be most effective, use the following guidelines to complete each of the three steps.

Step 1. Form groups of three to work on this part of the exercise. In each group of three, establish who will be speaker, listener, and monitor for the first round of the exercise.

Speakers must select one of the terms and to explain their understanding of that term to the listeners. Speakers need to focus on making sure that the listeners grasp their understanding of the term, that is, the meaning it has for them. Speakers should provide listeners with feedback about the accuracy of their (the listeners') response.

Listeners must give the speaker their full attention, attempt to follow the speakers' efforts to explain the meaning of the term as they see it, and temporarily suspend their own understanding of the term to attend to the speakers' understanding of it. Listeners will need to clarify and summarize to the speakers their understanding of what the speakers said, and modify this in response to the speakers' feedback.

Monitors must ensure that the guidelines are followed and give the participants feedback at the end of the turn. Participants should rotate roles until all three have taken a turn in each role.

Step 2. The group's next task is to discuss the feelings each experienced during the exercise. One might begin by talking about how it felt to have people give their full attention to them when they were the speaker, whether they were aware at any time that their attention had shifted away from them and, if so, how they knew this was happening and how it felt. Follow this discussion with an exploration of the experience of being a listener, how it felt to give another person one's full attention, and the highlights and the low points of that experience.

Step 3. The last task in the small group is to identify what was learned from the experience.

Exercise 2 (alternate exercise)

This exercise provides an alternate way of exploring the same terms. The exercise commences with discussion and exchange of ideas, and then builds on this by introducing an action component in role-play techniques. Role play has been used extensively in empathy training. The application of role play in intercultural training is discussed in Mullavey-O'Byrne (1994).

As with the previous exercise, participants will need to complete each step for the exercise to be most effective.

Step 1. Join with a small number of participants and discuss each one's understanding of each of the terms given at the beginning of the chapter. One might begin by attempting to develop definitions for each of the terms that are acceptable to the group. When this has been done, ask the following questions:

- What are the core elements of empathy identified in the definitions?
- What other elements contribute to differences in the definitions?
- In what ways do the definitions that have developed for the last four terms contribute to the understanding of empathy?

Step 2. Work with other members of the small group to devise ways to illustrate similarities and differences in the definitions that have been developed. Consider using role-play techniques or nonverbal techniques such as mime or mirroring to do this. Share some of the examples with members of the larger group. An interesting and useful exercise can be for members of the group to guess which definitions are being illustrated in the examples presented.

Step 3. Share individual experiences of, and feelings about, the activity in Step 2.

Case Study and Suggestions for Discussion

The internationalization of the student body in institutions of higher education throughout the Western world has drawn attention to issues associated with providing learning environments, instructional methods, and support systems that are appropriate and relevant to a student body characterized by cultural and linguistic diversity. Cultural and linguistic differences take on additional meaning when international students are involved in programs of study in which fieldwork or clinical placements in the host country are an essential component of their overall course requirement. The case study that follows draws on a real situation that crosses education, supervision, and rehabilitation. The case study provides an opportunity for educators, academics, and health professionals, among others, to explore the cultural interface at an interpersonal communication level and to explore the potential for cross-cultural empathy.

The "Failing" International Student

Background to the Incident

Chen Wong, a trained nurse, is an international student. She was awarded a scholarship from the Chinese government to come to Australia to undertake a graduate clinical specialty course. Part of the course includes 6 weeks of supervised clinical training in a teaching hospital. The incident occurred toward the end of Chen's first week on the rehabilitation ward.

Mary Jane Smithers is the student nurse supervisor on the rehabilitation ward. She is committed to providing Chen with quality supervision but is a little anxious because Chen is her first international student.

The Incident

(From the nursing unit manager's perspective). In the weekly report provided by the nursing unit manager to the student nurse supervisor, Chen received an excellent report for clinical skills and efficiency, but a very poor report for "interpersonal competency." The report stated, ". . . this student is likely to fail her clinical placement because of her very poor communication skills and her lack of care toward her patients." A particular incident was cited to illustrate the nature of the problem. The incident involved an elderly man in a wheelchair whom Chen was instructed to collect from the landing near the lift and return as quickly as possible to his bed. After Chen had returned him to the ward, the patient complained to the nursing unit manager that Chen had been rude and inconsiderate; she had not spoken to him to inform him where she was taking him, but had simply pulled him backwards into the lift. When the patient protested, he reported that Chen had simply replied, "It is time for you to go back to bed." The patient asked why and insisted that he wanted someone else to wheel the chair. Chen did not take notice of his protests but continued on her way and returned him to his bedside.

The Incident From the Student's Perspective

At the first of their weekly supervisory meetings, Chen is very surprised when Mary Jane informs her that there is a problem with her clinical work—that she does not relate properly to her patients. She cannot see how this can be, as she is very efficient and careful in carrying out nursing procedures. She always finishes her duties on or before time and believes this is because she does not waste time on unnecessary talk. When she is required to touch her patients, she does so with respect and concern for their comfort and safety. When Mary Jane questions her about the incident with the patient in the wheelchair, Chen is very puzzled; she simply cannot understand how there could be a problem in what she did. Chen says that she was asked to take the patient back to the ward as quickly as possible. She believes that she acted promptly and appropriately and managed to get the patient back to his bed just in time. She was surprised and embarrassed by the way the patient had behaved toward her but believed that she maintained a professional approach to the situation.

Chen remained quiet after her supervisor had spoken to her, although she was feeling quite distressed. Her supervisor expected more discussion, some explanation, or some indication that Chen understood the problem as she did, but it was not forthcoming.

On reflection, Chen decided that the problem must be that she does not speak English well enough and that her patients do not understand her because of her accent. She had no trouble communicating with either patients or staff when she was nursing in China. "Yes," she thinks, "It is my very bad English. The patients do not understand what I say to them. I think it is the problem. It can be fixed if I speak Australian English better. I will ask my supervisor where I can take lessons." (based on Fitzgerald & Mullavey-O'Byrne, 1995).

Discussion Questions

The questions that follow are designed to focus on issues associated with empathy in the case study.

1. Is cultural empathy an issue in this case study? If so, in what way, and for whom?
2. Are personal or cultural values an issue? If so, how, and for whom?
3. Is the communication of empathic understanding an issue? If so, what is the issue? What other issues do you see?
4. Would you expect things to be different, and if so, how, if
   a. the patient and the student, Chen, shared the same cultural and linguistic backgrounds?
   b. the supervisor had some knowledge of Chinese culture?
   c. Chen Wong had an understanding of Australian culture and the delivery of health care within that system?
5. Do you think Chen's decision, that her poor Australian English language skills are the problem, is correct? If so, is this the only problem? What other problems do you see in the situation?

Skill Concepts

Evidence to support the concept that human beings have the ability to understand the feelings, ideas, and experiences of another person from that person's perspective is widely documented in the literature (Lewis & Brookes-Gunn, 1979; Hoffman, 1978). This type of understanding involves cognitive and affective responses and comes about through a process of "psychological feeling into" or "putting oneself in the other's place" (Clyne, 1974, p. 262). The term used to describe this concept is *empathy*.

The scope and complexity of empathy are reflected in the descriptors that have been adopted to qualify the concept, and in the use of the term *empathy* to qualify other concepts, for example, *empathic understanding* and *empathic communication*. A brief discussion of terms most frequently used in the literature follows.

Empathy and Related Terms

Empathic understanding refers to the kind of understanding that derives from experiencing another's feelings and experiences "as if" one were that other, while at the same time recognizing that the source of one's experience lies in the other.

Empathic communication is used to describe the transmission of empathic understanding to another in a meaningful way. The mode of communication may be verbal, nonverbal, or involve a combination of both.

Accurate empathy is a term that is frequently used in the literature concerned with counseling and helping relationships. The term is used to describe an empathic response that reflects or closely approximates the content and feelings contained in an interpersonal communication (Egan, 1982; Carkhuff, 1969).

Generalized empathy is used to describe the ability to extend empathic understanding beyond the immediate "one to one" situation to groups, communities, cultural groups, and humankind in general. Generalized empathy may require knowledge of others beyond one's immediate associates and environment. However, such knowledge is not necessarily associated with generalized empathy.

Relational empathy is a term used primarily by Barrett-Lennard (1993; 1976) to describe interpersonal empathy in a reciprocal relationship. The term encompasses empathic turn-taking and the potential that, over time, participants in a relationship will develop a relational system that permits "looking through your eyes at me with you." This ability has also been referred to as *meta-empathy* (Barrett-Lennard, 1993, p. 10).

Cultural empathy refers to the individual's ability to understand others within the framework of their cultural backgrounds and the facility to communicate that understanding to them in a meaningful way. *Intercultural empathy* is used to describe empathy between members of different cultural groups, whereas the term *cross-cultural empathy* encompasses differences in empathy, usually empathic communication, across cultural groups.

Empathy Across Cultural Groups

Cross-cultural research suggests that empathy may be a basic human characteristic related to social adaptation (Borke, 1973) that acts as a bridge between the internal events of people and permits them to verify each other's feelings and thoughts (Lewis & Brookes-Gunn, 1979). However, the communication of empathic understanding is modified by cultural values, beliefs, norms, guidelines for interpersonal behavior, and culturally accepted patterns of communication (Dahl, 1989; Roe, 1977; Grove, 1976). Cross-cultural differences in communication styles, language, the meanings ascribed to nonverbal communications, interpersonal space requirements, the interpretations placed on verbal messages, and the possibility that shared meaning may be limited across cultural boundaries, all contribute to the challenges inherent in attempting to communicate empathic understanding across cultures and linguistic groups. Irrespective of the areas of potential difficulty that have been identified, empathy is counted among the list of conditions identified with intercultural communication competency (Ruben, 1976).

The communication skills required for effective intercultural interactions do not appear to differ significantly from those required for interacting effectively within a cultural group. What is different is the way these skills are emphasized and used in different situations, the degree of flexibility associated with their use, and the different meanings attached to them in different situations (Dahl, 1989).

Definitions of Empathy and Domains of Inquiry Into Empathy

There is no single definition of empathy that meets with general agreement in the literature. This is not surprising, because the concept is multifaceted and complex. However, definitions and research tend to focus on three main areas: empathic ability (intrapersonal attributes and abilities), interpersonal or relational empathy (empathy communication skills), and the empathy process (elements and phases in an empathic response). A theme that cuts across these domains and is strongly represented in the literature concerned with communication competencies for both intercultural and intracultural interactions is the need for training in interpersonal communication skills (Egan, 1982; Lynam 1992; Mullavey-O'Byrne, 1987).

Lynam (1992) emphasized the need for training to include opportunities for participants to explore and recognize their own belief systems, develop an appreciation of the client's perspective, develop communication skills, and develop skills in identifying cultural bias in the manner in which certain programs, for example in health care, are organized and operationalized. Other recommendations for training in effective intercultural interactions include training in different communication styles; accumulating knowledge relevant to understanding differences in cultural values and norms, gender roles, courtesy behaviors, and political structures; problem-solving skills; attending and responding skills; dealing with ambiguity, frustration, and stress; and elementary training in language skills.

Empathic Ability: Intrapersonal Attributes and Abilities

Definitions of empathy that are concerned with empathic ability focus on intrapersonal attributes, such as perception, attitudes, cognition, affect, and feelings. They usually recognize or imply that there are internal processes associated with an empathic response (Hoffman, 1978; Hogan, 1969; Parke & Asher, 1983). The foundations of an empathic response are based on

- a genuine desire to understand others from their perspective and to communicate this understanding to them in a way that is meaningful to both parties;
- an ability to tune into one's personal feelings and responses and distinguish them from those belonging to the other;
- an ability to perceive and understand how events, structures, organizations, and relational factors in the environment affect individuals;
- an ability to perceive and understand others' experiences and feelings from their frame of reference;
- recognition that the source of one's experiences and feelings lies in the other and not in the self; and,
- translating these perceptions and insights into verbal and nonverbal symbols of communication.

The extracts that follow provide examples of definitions that focus on empathic ability or the intrapersonal dimensions of empathy. Empathy has been defined as

. . . the intellectual or imaginative apprehension of another's condition or state of mind without experiencing that person's feelings. (Hogan, 1969, p. 308)

. . . the arousal of affect in the observer that is not a reaction to his own situation but a vicarious response to another person's situation. (Hoffman, 1978, p. 227)

. . . an experiencing of the consciousness behind another's outward communication, but with the continuous awareness that this consciousness is originating and proceeding in the other. (Barrett-Lennard, 1976, p. 174)

. . . a construct involving complex interactions between cognitive and affective components which vary according to age, the nature of the emotion and situational factors. (Parke & Asher, 1983, p. 472)

These definitions support a view that intrapersonal empathic ability may be viewed as a component of the personality structure—an individual personality trait.

To the extent that a person possesses qualities that are identified with empathy, that person may be described as being "more" or "less" empathic. However, a person who has a high level of empathic ability does not necessarily and consistently behave empathically toward others. This may be due to personal reasons, attitudes toward the other, inadequate interpersonal communication skills, or contextual factors, such as cultural differences.

The ability to empathize is central to the acquisition of social knowledge and is a key element in learning to recognize similarities and differences between self and others (Lewis & Brookes-Gunn, 1979). Although it is generally accepted that human beings have the ability to empathize, research suggests that individuals have different levels of empathic ability. Contextual factors also appear to influence the accuracy of an individual's empathic understanding of the other.

Empathic understanding is essentially an intrapersonal experience that may or may not be expressed. For empathic understanding to be conveyed to another, the initial intrapersonal experience of empathic understanding must be translated into nonverbal and verbal symbols and communicated to another person. Verification of the level and accuracy of the empathy communicated occurs when the other feels understood from their perspective.

Interpersonal Empathy and Relational Empathy: Empathic Communication

Interpersonal empathy is both subtle and multidimensional and largely dependent on intrapersonal attributes, attitudes, and abilities; communication skills; situational or contextual factors; and cultural influences. Intrapersonal attributes, attitudes, and abilities are preconditions for empathic communication and have been addressed briefly in an earlier section of this chapter.

Communication Skills

The ability to communicate relatively accurate empathic understanding is recognized as an important factor in effective interpersonal relating across a wide range of situations, including helping relationships in counseling, health, education, and welfare. The professional literature also strongly supports the need for helpers to receive training in empathy and other core interpersonal helping skills (Alroy & Ber, 1982; Sanson-Fisher & Poole, 1978).

Communication skills associated with interpersonal empathy include the ability to be fully present in attending to the other's verbal and nonverbal messages; listening on all levels, and communicating respect, genuine regard, and interest; communicating an understanding of the other's experiences and feelings from the other's frame of reference; and the use of a style of communication and language that is attuned to the other person and is meaningful to them and their life situation.

Situational and Contextual Factors

Situational factors have an effect on empathy and the way empathic understanding may or may not be communicated, and it is recognized that some situations are not conducive to the communication of empathy. In a study reported by Stotland, et al

(1978), student nurses experienced conflict between their sympathetic feelings and desire to help their terminally ill patients and the discomfort associated with their empathic responses to these same patients. The discomfort they experienced on seeing the condition of their patients caused many to find excuses to withdraw or frequently absent themselves from direct contact situations where empathic communication could have been important to the nursing process.

The conflict reported in this study may well be explained by another closely related concept, *emotional contagion.* Emotional contagion refers to experiencing another person's feelings or experiences in an "as if" sense, but without recognition that the feelings or experiences are located in the other person. Although there remains some disagreement in the literature about the precise nature of an empathic response, it is generally agreed that affect and cognition are both necessary conditions of empathic understanding.

Interpersonal environments that encourage openmindeness, nonjudgmental, and noncritical attitudes toward others and that emphasize the value of patience, tolerance and courtesy facilitate the development of empathic understanding. Organizations that hold genuineness, respect, and positive regard for others as core organizational values, and that strive to minimize structural and procedural discrepancies and inconsistencies, create organizational environments that are conducive to the communication of empathic understanding.

Cultural Influences

Intrapersonal attributes and abilities, interpersonal communication skills, and situational factors relevant to communicating empathic understanding are also influenced by cultural values, norms, beliefs, and guidelines for interpersonal behavior and relationships. Cultural differences in any one of these factors can cause verbal and nonverbal messages to be misinterpreted and result in total lack of or inadequate understanding of the underlying feelings, thoughts, and experiences of the other. Similarly, cultural differences in verbal and nonverbal communication behaviors can cause an empathic response to be misinterpreted and the intent of the response to be misunderstood. Clearly, a broad framework or schema is required that can be used to explain the effect of cultural differences on core conditions associated with effective communication in intercultural interactions. Together, the dimensions of low-high context communication (Gudykunst & Ting-Toomey, 1988; Hall, 1976) and individualism-collectivism (Brislin, 1994; Gudykunst & Ting-Toomey, 1988; Hofstede, 1980) provide a useful framework for understanding the nature of these differences when they occur, and possible reasons for the effect such differences have on interpersonal communications. They also provide useful guidelines for exploring potential strategies to overcome culturally based issues that can create barriers to effective cross-cultural communication.

The Empathy Process: Elements and Phases in an Empathic Response

The intrapersonal attributes and abilities identified with empathic ability and the communication skills essential to relational empathy are seen as critical elements in the empathy process. Barrett-Lennard (1993) suggests that the process involves three distinguishable and overlapping phases: reception and resonance on the part of one person to the feelings or experience of the other person "as if" they were that person; verbal and nonverbal communication of this responsive awareness to the other person; and an awareness on the part of the other person that they are "being understood." Although these phases are distinguishable, they are not clear cut, nor do they necessarily occur in a step-by-step sequence.

Much of what has been written about empathic communication comes from the counseling and helping professions and is primarily concerned with helper communication of empathic understanding to a client—a "one-way street." Outside the formal helping relationship—in relationships between friends, colleagues, and partners, for example—the empathy process is more likely to involve reciprocal turn-taking. In communication events that involve reciprocal relationships, the roles of "empathizer" and "empathee" move back and forth between partners. (Barrett-Lennard, 1993). Combined with knowledge about culture concepts (for example, the various dimensions on which cultural groups may vary), this process-oriented relational model of empathy provides a theoretical basis for developing additional strategies to use in training to enhance intercultural competency in culturally diverse training groups.

Core Conditions Associated With Intercultural Empathy

Within the literature, a number of core conditions have been linked to the communication of empathic understanding in intercultural contexts. As indicated earlier in this module, these are very similar to the conditions associated with communicating empathic understanding within a cultural group. Included among the conditions associated with effective communication across cultures are observational skills and the ability to react appropriately, sensitively, and with a reasonable level of accuracy to cross-cultural stimuli; the capacity to project a genuine interest in others; acceptance of others; perceptual acuity; openmindedness; a nonjudgmental and noncritical attitude coupled with the ability to suspend judgment; the ability to discriminate and select appropriate strategies; flexibility to try different strategies as required and persistence to overcome setbacks; and an interest in and knowledge of different cultural systems, with the accompanying ability to use that knowledge in intercultural communications (Dahl, 1989; Hammer, Gudykunst, & Wiseman, 1978; Hannigan, 1990; Ruben, 1976).

Cultural Factors That Influence Empathy: Cultural Variability

Research suggests that it is possible to differentiate between cultures on a number of broad dimensions. These dimensions of variability provide a theoretical framework for understanding issues associated with intercultural communication of empathic understanding.

Values

Cultural values, "the constructs, groupings, and orientations by which people decide what is normative, preferred, or obligatory of members of their society," are one of the forces that serve to integrate a society (Cushner & Brislin, 1996, p. 319). They provide a framework to guide such things as decision making and judgments about what is good and what is not good, what is desirable and what is not, and what is worthwhile and what is not. Cultural values derive from and reflect a society's attempts to deal with the major issues that are seen to confront all societies, including the innate nature of human beings, the relationship of humans to nature and to possible higher-order beings, and humans' orientation to time, to activity, and to other human beings. Individuals must deal with concrete representations of these abstractions in their daily routines and relationships with others. Cultural values underpin and guide the decision-making and priority-setting actions of the group so that it will better deal with life's tasks and relationships. Cultural values also contribute to the assumptions people make about how others will and ought to respond and behave. When the expectations that flow from these assumptions are disconfirmed, responses and actions may be misinterpreted and interfere with the empathy process necessary to support effective interpersonal communication. Issues may also arise in interpersonal relationships when value orientations differ.

The flow of empathic understanding in interpersonal communication is easier to achieve when the parties involved share similar values. Shared knowledge makes it easier to see the world from the other's perspective. However, even when people share similar cultural values, individual differences in personal values still pose a challenge to the communication of empathic understanding. A clue to dealing with this issue appears to be linked to the ability to appreciate that values are relative, not absolute.

The ability to accept that one's values are relative and to understand and accept others within the framework of their own value system is a prerequisite for effective empathic communication within and across cultural groups. Walter (1978) identified the ability of the counselor to recognize, accept, and relate to others as a total person within the framework of their cultural identity as a critical factor in counseling international students.

Individualism-Collectivism

This dimension is concerned with the extent to which the good of the individual or the good of the group is more valued in a society (see also chapter 3 in this volume). From this flow beliefs and norms that influence such things as relationships and guidelines for interpersonal communication. In societies that tend toward individualism, the goals of individuals are valued more highly than the goals of the group; group goals are downplayed and individuals are rewarded for behaving independently, making their own plans, and working toward achievement of personal goals (Brislin, 1994). The good of the wider group is seen to be achieved through the pursuit and achievement of individual goals. Friendships are developed on the basis of liking and common interests.

In societies that have a collectivist orientation, the good of the group is the primary focus, and emphasis is placed on loyalty to the group. The needs of the group are considered more important than those of the individual and interdependence and reciprocity in accordance with the accepted norms is an expected behavior among members of the ingroup. Kinship ties may take precedence over expertise in matters of appointments and promotions (Brislin, 1994; Hofstede, 1980), and friendships are based on family ties and early childhood relationships.

Low-High Context Communication

Hall (1976) suggested that all cultures have a predominant style of communication and that it is possible to differentiate between cultures on the basis of the degree to which the communication style that dominates is low- or high-context (see also Chapter 11 in this volume). A high-context communication is one in which the greater part of the message is conveyed through the physical content or internalized within the message-giver; that is, a great deal of the message is conveyed nonverbally and often indirectly. The recipient of the message is expected to take contextual material into account when interpreting the message and formulating a response. This style of communication has been linked to societies in which collectivist values are predominant and ingroup-outgroup norms influence the nature of interpersonal contact. In high-context cultures, uncertainty is likely to be increased if one is not able to empathize with strangers or those who are not members of one's ingroup (Kreps & Kunimoto, 1994). The importance placed on the nonverbal mode and contextual factors in collectivist, high-context cultures has implications for the choice of culturally appropriate strategies for communicating empathy in intercultural interactions. Limited evidence to support the use of nonverbal communication strategies in cross-cultural helping situations is present in the literature. Rothenberger (1990) described the use of body language to replace verbal communication in transcultural nursing situations, and Sandhu (1991) reported that neurolinguistic mirroring of movement enhanced intercultural communication of empathy in counseling situations involving adolescents.

In societies that are primarily individualistic in their orientation, low-context communication appears to be the predominant style of communication. The message is embedded in and conveyed through the verbal content of a communication. Although less emphasis is placed on the nonverbal mode, it is normally expected that the two modes (verbal and nonverbal) work together to send a consistent message.

In low-context cultures, emphasis is placed on the verbal mode in communicating empathic understanding and in training programs to enhance empathy communication skills. This inevitably leads to a consideration of language and the cultural differences associated with sound, structure, and meaning in different language groups.

Each language has its particular inventory of sounds, often referred to as a particular type of accent. The way words and sentences are structured differs across linguistic groups. This is sometimes evident in the way second-language speakers transfer structural elements from their first language to their second language while still using the vocabulary of the second language.

Language is also a conduit for conveying meaning. Concepts that are meaningful and significant to one group may be less significant, difficult to identify, or absent from the vocabulary of another group. The extent to which the empathic message communicated to the empathee has meaning is a critical measure of empathic understanding irrespective of cultural orientation. The challenge is to find out what is meaningful to the other person and then to identify culturally appropriate ways of communicating empathic understanding to them.

In situations where the language barrier is able to be bridged (for example, one or both parties have some level of proficiency in one's first language, or an interpreter service is available) metaphor and imagery can be powerful means of communicating empathy (Barrett-Lennard, 1993; Rodwell & Blankebaker, 1992). The effective use of metaphor and imagery requires some understanding of cultural metaphors and their meaning in different linguistic communities, and the perceptual skills to identify when and to whom it would be appropriate to use such a communication strategy.

The potential for disruption to occur to the empathy process in social communication between people who have different cultural backgrounds, value orientations, and communication styles is abundantly evident. Yet the process involved in empathic understanding is a powerful strategy for reducing uncertainty in interpersonal encounters. Empathic understanding has also been linked to empowering clients in therapeutic encounters in cross-cultural social work (Pinderhughes, 1979).

The ability to appreciate the relativity of values, including one's own, an interest in learning about cultural differences, and the ability to accept the cultural identity of others, provide the basic building blocks on which to develop communication skills to use empathic understanding effectively in intercultural interactions.

Integrating Exercise

The Faculty Working Party

This exercise affords participants an opportunity to explore the effect of situational and contextual factors and interpersonal environments on empathic understanding and communication.

The faculty of health established an International Student Center to provide support for the increasing numbers of international and local students enrolling in its professional education programs for whom English is a second language. Members of the senior academic staff have formed a working party to discuss and explore solutions to problems that still appear to be present, irrespective of the excellent support services provided by well-qualified staff at the center. Comments from specific members of the working party illustrate some of the issues that are causing concern.

Lois (Senior academic, coordinator of the first-year biological sciences program). "I am convinced that the international students are not making best use of the center. They attend the presemester orientation program and that's all. After that they keep bothering busy academic staff to help them with what are basic English language problems, like understanding what they are required to do in an assignment. I don't mind helping students, but there has to be a cut-off point."

Ken (academic, coordinator of the physiotherapy course). "I must say, I agree with Lois. I can even give you a concrete example. This student from China came to see me about difficulties he was having in the cardiopulmonary course. I tried to help him at first; then, when it became obvious that I wasn't getting through to him and that the problem was that he didn't understand English well enough, I referred him to the center. I even organized the appointment for him while he was sitting in my office. Can you believe it, after all the trouble I had gone to to help him, he didn't even keep the appointment! He was pretty casual about it when I confronted him later. All he could say was that he was sorry he did not keep the appointment, he was unable to attend at that time, but thought he might attend at some time soon. I was not impressed!"

Marion (director of the International Student Center). "This is not typical of our international student group. However, there are a number of students who do not keep their initial appointments. Once they do attend, we tend not to lose them. The difficulty in some cases seems to be attending that first appointment. Perhaps we need to run a training program for academic staff to help them deal more effectively with international students."

Alan (professor and head of the School of Health Informatics). "Are you seriously suggesting that busy academic staff should take time out to learn to talk to students from non-English speaking backgrounds? Frankly, I wouldn't be willing to let my staff attend such a program. The role of the academic staff member is to teach and supervise research students. When students have difficulties outside academic content, our role is to refer them to the experts. None of us are qualified to help these students with cultural and language problems. We would do them a disservice if we were to attempt to do so. The faculty invested good money in a center with staff who are employed to provide that service. They should be sorting this problem out—not us!"

Group Task

1. Divide into groups of 3 to 5. Each small group will take on the role of an external consulting group that has been called in by the dean to help the working party resolve the situation. (Some members of the working party have let it be known that they are not very happy about the consultants being called in.) In your small group, identify what you see as the main problems and the underlying issues.

2. Identify what further information you will need to help you in your task and how you propose to gather that information.

3. Develop a preliminary strategy for your first meeting with the working party. Based on the written information you have to date, develop a broad plan to address the issues at the root of the problem. What are the critical factors you must take into account to gain initial acceptance for your plan and, later, the procedures you may want to have set in place to ensure the plan will be carried through?

4. On reflection, was intercultural empathy an important issue in this situation? If so, in what way? What other issues did you identify?

Independent Exercise

Reflective Exercise

This exercise is not a test of your empathy skills, but simply a set of statements to help you reflect on some factors associated with cross-cultural empathy and the way you use empathy in your daily life. As you reflect on each statement, you might find it useful to think about situations you have been involved in that support your response. If you find your response is, "It depends," ask yourself a further question, "It depends on what?"

When I think about my relationships with others, I would say that

1. I have a genuine interest in others and an ability to communicate this to them.

   always   frequently   sometimes   it depends

2. I am able to sense another's thoughts, feelings, experiences, and needs, and to communicate a reasonably accurate and complete reflection of them to the other person.

    always   frequently   sometimes   it depends

3. I am able to sense another's thoughts, feelings, experiences, and needs, but have difficulty communicating my understanding to them.

    always   frequently   sometimes   it depends

4. I am sensitive to the needs of those who have norms, values, and beliefs that are different from those I hold.

    always   frequently   sometimes   it depends

5. I am comfortable with my interactions in cross-cultural encounters and receive positive feedback from people from different cultural groups.

    always   frequently   sometimes   it depends

6. I am comfortable with ambiguous situations.

    always   frequency   sometimes   it depends

7. I believe there are basic guidelines for living and relating to others that all people should follow.

    always   frequently   sometimes   it depends

References

Alroy, G., & Ber, R. (1982). Doctor-patient relationship and the medical student: The use of trigger films. *Journal of Medical Education, 57*, 334-336.

Barrett-Lennard, G. T. (1976). Empathy in human relationships: Significance, nature and measurement. *Australian Psychologist, 11*(2), 173-184.

Barrett-Lennard, G. T. (1993). The phases and focus of empathy. *British Journal of Medical Psychology, 66*, 3-14

Borke, H. (1973). The development of empathy in Chinese and American children between three and six years of age: A cross-cultural study. *Developmental Psychology, 9*(1), 102-108.

Brislin, R. W. (1994). Working co-operatively with people from different cultures. In R. Brislin & T. Yoshida (Eds.), *Improving intercultural interactions: modules for cross-cultural training programs* (pp. 17-33). Thousand Oaks, CA: Sage.

Cushner, K., & Brislin, R. (1996). *Intercultural interactions: A practical guide* (2nd ed.). Thousand Oaks, CA: Sage.

Carkhuff, R. R. (1969). *Helping and human relations: A primer for lay and professional helpers.* (Vol. 1.). New York: Holt, Rinehart & Winston.

Clyne, M. B. (1974). How personal is personal care in general practice? *Journal of The Royal College of General Practitioners, 24*, 264.

Dahl, C. I. (1989). Some problems of cross-cultural psychotherapy with refugees seeking treatment. *American Journal of Psychoanalysis, 49*, 19-32.

Egan, G. (1982). *The skilled helper: Models, skills and methods for effective helping* (2nd ed.). Monterey, CA: Brooks Cole.

Fitzgerald, M. H., & Mullavey-O'Byrne, C. (1995). Critical incident reflection. Visions for the future. New South Wales Association of Occupational Therapists 8th Annual State Conference, Gosford, NSW, Australia.

Gudykunst, W. B., & Ting-Toomey, S. T. (1988). *Culture and interpersonal communication.* Newbury Park, CA: Sage.

Grove, C. L. (1976, February). Non-verbal behaviour, cross-cultural contact, and the urban classroom teacher. *Equal Opportunity Review,* 1-6.

Hall, E. (1976). *The hidden dimension.* New York: Doubleday.

Hammer, M. R., Gudykunst, W. B., & Wiseman, R. L. (1978). Dimensions of intercultural effectiveness: an exploratory study. *International Journal of Intercultural Relations, 2,* 382-393.

Hannigan, T. P. (1990). Traits, attitudes and skills that are related to intercultural effectiveness and their implications for cross-cultural training: A review of the literature. *International Journal of Intercultural Relations, 14,* 89-32.

Hofstede, G. (1980). *Culture's consequences.* Beverly Hills, CA: Sage.

Hoffman, M. L. (1978). Towards a theory of empathic arousal and effect. In M. Lewis & L. Rosenblum (Eds.), *The development of affect* (pp. 227-256). New York: Plenum.

Hogan, R. (1969). Development of an empathy scale. *Journal of Counselling and Clinical Psychology, 33,* 307-316.

Kreps, G. L., & Kunimoto, E. N. (1994). *Effective communication in multicultural health care settings.* Thousand Oaks, CA: Sage.

Lee, H. (1960). *To kill a mockingbird.* Philadelphia, PA: J. B. Lippincott.

Lewis, M., & Brooks-Gunn, J. (1979). *Social cognition and the acquisition of self.* New York: Plenum.

Lynam, M. J. (1992). Towards the goal of providing culturally sensitive care: Principles upon which to build nursing curricula. *Journal of Advanced Nursing, 17,* 149-157.

Mullavey-O'Byrne, C. (1987). *A study of empathy training with occupational therapy students.* Unpublished master's honors thesis, Macquarie University, Sydney, Australia.

Mullavey-O'Byrne, C. (1994). Intercultural interactions in welfare work. Improving intercultural interactions: Modules for cross-cultural training programs. In R. Brislin & T. Yoshida (Eds.), *Improving intercultural interactions: Modules for cross-cultural training programs* (pp. 197-220). Thousand Oaks, CA: Sage.

Parke, R. D., & Asher, S. R. (1983). Social and personality development. *Annual Review of Psychology, 34,* 472-473.

Pinderhughes, E. B. (1979). Teaching empathy in cross-cultural social work. *Social work, 24*(4), 312-316.

Rodwell, M. K., & Blankebaker, A. (1992). Strategies for developing cross-cultural sensitivity: Wounding as metaphor. *Journal of Social Work Education, 28*(2), 153-165.

Roe, K. V. (1977). A study of empathy in young Greek and U.S. children. *Journal of Cross Cultural Psychology, 8*(4), 493-502.

Rothenberger, R. L. (1990). Transcultural nursing: Overcoming obstacles to effective communication. *AORN Journal, 51*(5), 1349-1363.

Ruben, B. (1976). Assessing communication competence for intercultural adaptation. *Group and Organisation Studies, 1,* 334-354.

Sandhu, D. (1991, March). Cross-cultural counseling and neurolinguistic mirroring: An exploration of empathy, trustworthiness and positive interaction with Native American adolescents. Presentation at the Annual Meeting of the American Association for Counseling and Development, Baltimore.

Sanson-Fisher, R. W., & Poole, A. D. (1978). Training medical students to empathise. *The Medical Journal of Australia, 1,* 473-476.

Stotland, E., Mathews, K. E., Sherman, S. E., Hansson, R. O., & Richardson, B. E. (1978). *Empathy, fantasy and helping.* Beverly Hills, CA: Sage.

Walter, J. H. (1978, July). Counselling appropriateness: An exploration from a cross-cultural perspective. Presentation at the Speech Communication Association Summer Conference on Intercultural Communication, Tampa, FL.

Name Index

Subject Index

About the Contributors

Roya Ayman is Director of the Industrial and Organizational Program in the Psychology Department at the Illinois Institute of Technology in Chicago. Born in Iran and a native speaker of Persian, she received her PhD in social, organizational, and cross-cultural psychology from the University of Utah. She has published in the areas of global leadership and the role of gender and culture in leadership perception, work teams, and women managers. She is coeditor of the book *Leadership Theory and Research: Perspectives and Directions* (1993). She has worked as a consultant for, and offered training programs to, such major organizations as Arthur Anderson and Company, the Federal Emergency Management Agency, Motorola, and General Motors. She has also taught and consulted in Guangzhou and Beijing, China; Weinacht, Switzerland; Tehran, Iran; and Monterrey, Mexico.

Dharm P. S. Bhawuk is Assistant Professor in the College of Business Administration, University of Hawaii. He received his PhD from the University of Illinois. Soon after receiving his first degree in engineering, he was head of training at Royal Kathmandu Airlines, Nepal. He has consulted with the Peace Corps and the United Nations and is author of many articles in scholarly publications in the field of cross-cultural training.

Richard Brislin is Professor of Management and Industrial Relations in the College of Business at the University of Hawaii at Manoa, and formally with the East-West Center, Honolulu, Hawaii. He is author of several books that have been used in a variety of cross-cultural courses: *Cross-cultural Research Methods* (1973); *Cross-cultural Encounters: Face to Face Interaction* (1981); *Intercultural Interactions: A Practical Guide* (1986; 2nd ed., 1996); *Understanding Cultures' Influence on Behavior* (1993); and *Intercultural Communication Training: An Introduction* (1994). Since 1975, he has organized a wide variety of workshops at the East-West Center for researchers, college professors, practitioners, and cross-cultural trainers. He was a G. Stanley Hall Lecturer for the American Psychological Association in 1988. He is coeditor of *Improving Intercultural Interactions: Modules for Cross-Cultural Training Program, Vol. 1* (1994).

Kenneth Cushner is Associate Dean for Student Life and Intercultural Affairs and Associate Professor of Education at Kent State University, Kent, Ohio. He is author of several books and articles in the field of intercultural education and training, including *Intercultural Interactions: A Practical Guide* (1986; 2nd ed., 1996) and *Human Diversity in Education: An Integrative Approach* (1992; 2nd ed., 1996). A former East-West Center Scholar, he is a frequent contributor to the professional development of educators through writing, workshop presentations, and travel program development. He has developed and led intercultural programs on six continents.

Jan Fried is the program coordinator and instructor for the American Sign Language/Interpreter Education Program at Kapi'olani Community College and is affiliated with the Center for Interpretation and Translation at the University of Hawaii. She works with cross-cultural and intercultural communication issues on a regular basis as an ASL/English interpreter in private practice. She completed her master's degree in teaching interpretation at Western Maryland College, the only program of its kind in the United States. She is interested in how interactions are negotiated between deaf and hearing people and in promoting the idea that effective interpreters are educated to be thoroughly bicultural in addition to bilingual.

Ann-Marie Horvath is an East-West Center Degree Fellow with the Program on Education and Training, pursuing a PhD in clinical psychology with special emphasis in cross-cultural and intercultural mental health. A member of a military family, her intercultural experiences began at an early age through involvement with members of the international military community. Her current research projects include a study on the conceptualization of the "self" across cultures and an analysis of multicultural group therapy techniques. She is coauthor of the chapter on cross-cultural training and education for the forthcoming *Handbook of Cross-Cultural Psychology*.

S. Suzan Jane received her BA in psychology from the University of Wisconsin and a MA in international relations from the United States International University at San Diego. She is currently a doctoral candidate in political science at the University of Hawaii at Manoa. She writes, consults, and instructs women and minorities in the skills and tactics necessary for breaking through the glass ceiling in academic institutions and business corporations. Currently, Suzan resides in Honolulu and is conducting dissertation research on women and minorities—facilitators and inhibitors in career advancement in a comparative study of civil service workers in California and Hawaii.

Izumi Matsumoto is a program coordinator and instructor for the Japanese business, language, and culture division of the Office of Community Services at Kapi'olani Community College (KCC), Honolulu. She holds an MA in English as